Toward Well-Oiled Relations?

The Nottingham China Policy Institute series

The Nottingham China Policy Institute series brings together cutting-edge scholarship, policy relevance and accessibility. It includes works on the economics, society, culture, politics, international relations, national security and history of the Chinese mainland, Taiwan, and Hong Kong in the twentieth- and twenty-first centuries. Books in this series are written in an accessible style, although they are based on meticulous research. They put forward exciting ideas and research findings that specialist academics need to take note of while policy-makers and opinion leaders will find inspiring. They represent innovative multidisciplinary scholarship at its best in the study of contemporary China.

Titles include:

David Kerr (*editor*)
CHINA'S MANY DREAMS
Comparative Perspectives on China's Search for National Rejuvenation

Shujie Yao and Pan Wang (*editors*)
CHINA'S OUTWARD FOREIGN DIRECT INVESTMENTS AND IMPACT ON THE WORLD ECONOMY

Andreas Fulda (*editor*)
CIVIL SOCIETY CONTRIBUTIONS TO POLICY INNOVATION IN THE PR CHINA

Shujie Yao and Maria Jesus Herrerias (*editors*)
ENERGY SECURITY AND SUSTAINABLE ECONOMIC GROWTH IN CHINA

Jing Zhang
FOREIGN DIRECT INVESTMENT, GOVERNANCE, AND THE ENVIRONMENT IN CHINA
Regional Dimensions

Steve Tsang (*editor*)
THE VITALITY OF TAIWAN
Politics, Economics, Society and Culture

Niv Horesh (*editor*)
TOWARD WELL-OILED RELATIONS?
China's Presence in the Middle East Following the Arab Spring

The Nottingham China Policy Institute series
Series Standing Order ISBN 978–0–230–36922–1

You can receive future titles in this series as they are published by placing a standing order. Please contact your bookseller or, in case of difficulty, write to us at the address below with your name and address, the title of the series and the ISBN quoted above.

Customer Services Department, Macmillan Distribution Ltd, Houndmills, Basingstoke, Hampshire RG21 6XS, England.

Toward Well-Oiled Relations?

China's Presence in the Middle East Following the Arab Spring

Edited by

Niv Horesh
Professor (Chair) of the Modern History of China and Director of the China Policy Institute at the University of Nottingham, UK

First published 2016 by
PALGRAVE MACMILLAN

Palgrave Macmillan in the UK is an imprint of Macmillan Publishers Limited,
registered in England, company number 785998, of Houndmills, Basingstoke,
Hampshire RG21 6XS.

Palgrave Macmillan in the US is a division of St Martin's Press LLC,
175 Fifth Avenue, New York, NY 10010.

Palgrave Macmillan is the global academic imprint of the above companies
and has companies and representatives throughout the world.

Palgrave® and Macmillan® are registered trademarks in the United States,
the United Kingdom, Europe and other countries.

ISBN: 978–1–137–53978–6

This book is printed on paper suitable for recycling and made from fully
managed and sustained forest sources. Logging, pulping and manufacturing
processes are expected to conform to the environmental regulations of the
country of origin.

A catalogue record for this book is available from the British Library.

Library of Congress Cataloging-in-Publication Data

    Toward well-oiled relations? : China's presence in the Middle East following
the Arab Spring / [edited by] Niv Horesh.
        pages cm. — (The Nottingham China Policy Institute series)
        ISBN 978–1–137–53978–6
    1. China – Foreign relations – Middle East. 2. Middle East – Foreign
relations – China. 3. China – Foreign economic relations – Middle East.
    4. Middle East – Foreign economic relations – China. I. Horesh, Niv, editor.

DS740.5.M53T69 2016
327.51056—dc23   2015025775

Contents

v

List of Figures

List of Tables

Notes on Contributors

Gawdat Bahgat is Professor of National Security Affairs at the National Defense University's Near East South Asia Centre for Strategic Study. He is an Egyptian-born specialist in Middle Eastern policy, covering Egypt, Iran, and the Gulf region. His areas of research include energy security, proliferation of weapons of mass destruction, counter-terrorism, the Arab-Israeli conflict, North Africa, and American foreign policy in the Middle East. Bahgat's career combines academia with practicing national security, and he has served as an advisor to several governments and oil companies. He is the author of eight books, including *Energy Security* (2011), *International Political Economy* (2010), *Proliferation of Nuclear Weapons in the Middle East* (2007), *Israel and the Persian Gulf* (2006), and *American Oil Diplomacy* (2003).

Robert R. Bianchi is a political scientist and international lawyer with special interests in China and the Islamic world. He earned his doctorate and law degrees from the University of Chicago. He has taught at the University of Chicago, The University of Pennsylvania, The American University in Cairo, Nanjing University, Qatar University, and The National University of Singapore. His books include *Islamic Globalization: Pilgrimage, Capitalism, Democracy, and Diplomacy, Guests of God: Pilgrimage and Politics in the Islamic World, Unruly Corporatism: Associational Life in Twentieth-Century Egypt,* and *Interest Groups and Political Development in Turkey.* Currently he is writing a book about China's deepening relations with the Islamic world and their impact on the changing balance of power in Afro-Eurasia and beyond.

Manochehr Dorraj is Professor of Political Science at Texas Christian University and teaches courses in international and comparative politics. He has written extensively on the politics of the Middle East and North Africa, regional foreign policies and international affairs. His latest book, a co-edited volume, is titled *China's Energy Relations with the Developing World.* He has also published numerous scholarly articles and book chapters on China–Middle East energy relations and China–Iran relations. He has been an invited speaker to universities and think tanks throughout the United States, Europe, and the Middle East. He has also given numerous interviews to international, national, and local media on Middle Eastern affairs and their global impact.

Yasser M. Gadallah is Professor of Economics and is the Director of the Chinese-Egyptian Research Center, Helwan University (HU) in Cairo, Egypt. He completed a BA in International Economics from Helwan University and received a licentiate of law from Cairo University. He holds an MA and PhD in International Economics (intellectual property: patents). Previously, he was deputy director of the Foreign Trade Center, HU (2003–2005), Associate Professor of Economics (2008–2013), director of the Quality Assurance Unit (2006–2007), consultant of strategic planning at the Ministry of Higher Education, Egypt (2006–2012); consultant of intellectual property economics at the Information Decision Support Cabinet (2008–2010), League of Arab States (2010–2012). He has authored more than 15 papers on economics, the labor market, higher education, and intellectual property. He has participated in different research projects funded by the World Bank, the Organization of Economic Cooperation Development, the League of Arab States, and the European Training Foundation.

John W. Garver is a professor at the Sam Nunn School of International Affairs at the Georgia Institute of Technology. He is a member of the editorial boards of the journals *China Quarterly, Journal of Contemporary China,* and the *Journal of American-East Asian Relations,* and a member of the National Committee on US–China Relations. He is the author of 11 books and over 100 articles dealing with China's foreign relations. He holds a PhD in Political Science from the University of Colorado. He specializes in Asian international relations and China's foreign relations.

Niv Horesh is Professor of the Modern History of China and Director of the China Policy Institute in the School of Contemporary Chinese Studies at the University of Nottingham. He completed his PhD in Asian Studies at the Australian National University and has worked at the University of Western Sydney, Australia. His researches include the economic history of China, China in world history, the socio-economic history of Shanghai, and eighteenth- and nineteenth-centuries depictions of East Asia.

Christina Lin is a fellow at the Center for Transatlantic Relations at the Paul H. Nitze School of Advanced International Studies (SAIS), Johns Hopkins University, where she focuses on China's increasing footprint in the Mediterranean basin and on ways that China, NATO, and US allies can cooperate to resolve regional security issues. She is a former visiting fellow at the Washington Institute for Near East Policy and was selected as a 2011 National Security Fellow at the Foundation for Defense of Democracies. She has extensive US government experience, having served at the Office of the Secretary of Defense, the National Security Council, the Department of State, the Export-Import Bank of the United States, and the federally funded Institute for Defense Analyses. She holds a PhD and an MSc from the London School of Economics, an MA from the Johns Hopkins University School of Advanced International Studies, and a BA from the University of California, Irvine.

Neil Quilliam is senior research fellow at Chatham House, where he currently runs a two-year Foreign & Commonwealth Office (FCO)-funded project, Future Trends in the Gulf. He served as Senior MENA Energy Adviser at the Foreign & Commonwealth Office (FCO) between 2009 and 2014. Prior to working with the UK government, Quilliam led Control Risks' Middle East and North Africa practice and advised governments and multinationals, including IOCs, on political risk. He played a key role in helping a number of multinationals negotiate a return to the Middle East region following a series of evacuations during the early 2000s. He holds a PhD in International Relations from Durham University and wrote his thesis on Syria and the New World Order. He has authored several books on Syria and contributed many chapters in edited volumes on Jordan, Saudi Arabia, Iraq, Gulf Co-operation Council states, and serves on the Advisory Committee to Chatham House's GCC Energy Intensity project.

Mohammed Shareef is a fellow of the Royal Asiatic Society (London). He has worked for the United Nations and is Lecturer in Politics and International Relations of the Middle East at the University of Exeter in the United Kingdom and Lecturer in International Relations at the University of Sulaimani in Iraqi Kurdistan. Shareef holds a PhD in International Relations at the University of Durham and has an MSc in International Relations from the University of Bristol. He is a founding member and member of the board of directors of the London Kurdish Institute. His research interests include US foreign policy in the Middle East. He is the author of *The United States, Iraq and the Kurds: Shock, Awe and Aftermath* (2014).

Yitzhak Shichor is Professor Emeritus of Political Science and Asian Studies at the University of Haifa and the Michael William Lipson Chair Professor Emeritus at the Hebrew University of Jerusalem. A former dean of students at the Hebrew University and head of the Tel-Hai Academic College, his main research interests include China's Middle East policy;

international energy relations; Chinese defense conversion; labor export; East Asian democratization processes; Sino–Uyghur relations and the Uyghur Diaspora.

Michael Singh is a managing director of the Washington Institute for Near East Policy, a nonpartisan think tank. He was formerly senior director for Near East and North African Affairs at the White House (2007–2008) and also served as special assistant to Secretaries of State Colin Powell and Condoleezza Rice. He co-chaired Governor Mitt Romney's state department transition team in 2012, and served as a Middle East advisor to the Romney presidential campaign. He has served as an adjunct fellow at the Belfer Center at Harvard's Kennedy School of Government and as an economics instructor at Harvard University, and is a senior advisor to Callaway Capital Management, an emerging markets investment firm. His writings have appeared in *The Washington Post*, *The New York Times*, *The Wall Street Journal*, *International Security*, and elsewhere, and he has appeared as a commentator on CNN, NBC, BBC, and Fox News.

Zan Tao is Associate Professor of Turkish Studies, History Department, and Deputy Director of the Center for Global Modernization Studies at Peking University. He completed his PhD in History at Peking University in 2007. He has been a visiting scholar at Middle East Technical University (2005–2006), Center of Afro-Oriental Studies in Brazil (2008), Bogazici University (2008), and Indiana University-Bloomington (2012–2013). He also worked at Tibetan University (2010–2011).

Ruike Xu has completed his PhD in the School of Politics and International Relations at the University of Nottingham. He holds an MA from Shandong University, China. His research focuses mainly on Anglo–American relations, Israeli–American relations, Alliance theories and China's foreign policy.

Introduction

Niv Horesh

What is at stake?

Over the last few years, China has definitively surpassed the United States as the world's leading energy consumer and net importer of oil. Thus, China's relations with the Middle East appear poised to become an ever more important issue with global implications, as the latter region possesses the world's largest crude oil reserves.[1] In this pioneering volume, we attempt to clarify for lay readers several closely related topics that are critical to understanding the relevance of China's rise to the aspirations of various Middle Eastern nations, how Chinese energy needs are changing, and the ways in which a more economically powerful China might seek to reconfigure its ties with various Middle Eastern stakeholders.

No single formula exists from which to extrapolate the nature of China's future relations with the Middle East exist. China's presence in the region is tripartite in orientation rather than bilateral; its policy is still strategically grounded in the American-policed security and institutional architecture. The US is the de facto arbiter of Chinese overtures to, for example, major oil producer Saudi Arabia, even if Chinese and US rhetoric remains ostensibly at loggerheads over the Iranian nuclear programme.

Neither can the current People's Republic of China (PRC) leadership under Xi Jinping be portrayed as actively seeking to undermine American hegemony in the region, even if its emerging global leadership narrative is bolder than was the case under Hu Jintao. To the contrary, as China becomes more reliant on Middle Eastern oil and the American security architecture that permits free navigation across the Hormuz Straits, there is a strong Sino-American convergence of interests in the Middle

East that might actually *alleviate* Pacific tensions between the US and China in the future.

These findings may temper alarmists' view about a supposedly inevitable global military confrontation between China and America. Harvard Law School's Noah Feldman has, for example, asserted that China and the United States are on the verge of *not* a Cold War but of a "Cool War," in which a "classic struggle for power is unfolding at the same time as economic cooperation is becoming deeper and more fundamental...." Feldman further alluded to a "resource race" that might pit China against the US through proxy wars across the Middle East, particularly in regard to Iran's ambitions to become a regional hegemon.[2]

The Arab Spring has gravely alarmed policy makers in Beijing not just because of concerns over oil supplies, but also because of the spread of social media as a means to challenge the established order. On the other hand, there are no signs yet that the so-called China Dream/ China Model is inspiring serious economic or political reform across the Middle East, even if admiration for China's economic achievements does exist.[3] As the Obama administration's enthusiasm for Arab-Spring– like – often Islamist-led – democratisation wanes, so do Chinese geopolitical concerns. In the words of eminent Middle East expert, Anoush Ehteshami, who was one of the first to observe the region's tilt eastwards two decades ago, China is poised to play a much bigger role around the Gulf than Japan or Korea ever did. Yet China's supplanting of the US as the world's leading superpower or even as the Middle East's security arbiter is far from certain; until the 1990s, Japan had been mooted as an Asian powerhouse that was about to take over from the US. However, Japanese power and ambition never transcended the economic realm.[4]

Policy rationale and specific themes

Xi Jinping's taking of the helm of the Chinese Communist Party (CCP) and of China has arguably put to rest Deng Xiaoping's long-running hide-and-bide policy. In other words, China is seeking to project soft power in parts of the world where it had hitherto been operating more quietly. The academic literature on Chinese soft power is growing rapidly, yet little to date has been published on the degree to which China's newly acquired economic cachet and soft-power projections are actually shifting popular perceptions in the developing world.

While the US has arguably become more self-reliant in terms of energy production over the last two years and is supposedly considering divesting itself from the Middle East following two controversial wars,

China is ostensibly ramping up its presence there. CCP media hints that if a US redeployment to East Asia (Pivot to Asia) is concretized, China will seek to more visibly edge the US out of the Middle East. Xi's much touted recent initiative One Road, One Belt that is themed on the ancient Silk Road may in fact be designed to that end. But most of the contributors to this volume contend that these are rhetorical maneuvers that will have little bearing on the strategic bonds that will continue to unite China and the US for the foreseeable future.

In the opening chapter, Professor Yitzhak Shichor broadly suggests that Middle Eastern perceptions of China can be divided into three periods. In the first period, from the 1950s to the 1970s, regional governments, intellectuals, and the media perceived China as a marginal player of inconsequent value – political, economic and military. Even revolutionary organizations and national liberation movements (not to mention governments) tended to keep away from China and were suspicious of any of Beijing's actions that undermined the status quo. Instead, they preferred to associate with the Soviet Union or the United States. Mao's style of revolution, while attractive to some, was ultimately rejected. As China was beginning its post-Mao reform in the 1980s and 1990s, the uncertainty about China's success and progress was reflected not only inside China but also abroad, including in the Middle East. It is only since the beginning of the 21st century, and especially in the second decade, that China's rise has appeared irreversible and its global role unchallenged.

Middle Eastern perceptions of China now reflect a number of contradictory attitudes. For one, China has gained respect and admiration for achieving fast economic growth through market-friendly reforms but without relinquishing authoritarianism. Nevertheless, concern about China's economic and cultural expansion does exist particularly in Islamist circles. And, finally, there are now expectations that Beijing – given its perceived power – will play a more proactive role, not just in terms of trade benefits but most importantly in concrete deeds and politics in safeguarding and promoting the Middle East, e.g. by helping the Palestinian cause.

Our contributors survey in detail which regional actors are engaging with Chinese partners and how different regional actors are responding to that engagement. Given the different motivations that specific groups have, what do they have to gain from joining or rejecting China's engagement? Does China's engagement reduce or exacerbate existing cleavages? Do China's engagements elsewhere in the world suggest what outcomes might emerge in the Middle East in terms of both public discourse and geo-strategy?

In addition, this volume explores the degree of Sino-Russian coordination on the one hand and the oft-perceived rivalry between the US and China on the other. How do these perceptions sway public opinion across the Middle East? Is there much substance to China's rhetorical backing of Vladmir Putin's stance on Syrian President Assad, when it has so much at stake concerning its nascent special relationship with Saudi Arabia? How does China's treatment of its Uyghur minority in Xinjiang province affect its image across the Islamic world? While our contributors do not always provide uniform answers to these more nuanced issues as compared with the bigger picture framing Sino-American parleys in the Middle East, we hope that their viewpoints will help readers better grasp the complexity and significance of China's growing presence across the region.

Notes

1. http://www.iea.org/publications/freepublications/publication/
   KeyWorld2014.pdf
2. Noah Feldman, *Cool War: The Future of Global Competition* (New York: Random House, 213), pp. xii; 106–108.
3. http://www.ictsd.org/downloads/2013/04/china-in-the-eyes-of-the-saudi-media.pdf; See also Emma Murphy, (2009). "Learning the Right Lessons from Beijing: A Model for the Arab World?". In Springborg, Robert ed. *Development Models in Muslim Contexts: Chinese, 'Islamic' and Neo-liberal Alternatives.* Edinburgh: Edinburgh University Press. 85–114.
4. Anoush Ehteshami (2015), "Middle East-East Asia Relations: Between Geopolitics and Globalization" in ibidem et al ed. *The Emerging Middle-East East Asia Nexus*, pp. 8–31. London: Routlege.

1

Sino-American Crosscurrents in the Middle East: Perceptions and Realities

Yitzhak Shichor

Introduction

With few exceptions, all recent analyses and commentaries that link the US and China to the Middle East share similar conclusions, pointing to two main inter-related phenomena reflecting one fundamental assumption: that the US and China are engaged in a competition (or even rivalry) in the Middle East. Many seem to believe that the US is losing ground in the region because of its crippled commitment to its allies, its policy of "rebalancing" or "pivoting" to the Asia-Pacific region, and its expected withdrawal from Iraq and Afghanistan. Also, the US has allegedly become more self-reliant in terms of oil production and no longer needs Middle Eastern oil. Consequently, the conventional wisdom argues that the US is planning to gradually divest itself from the region. According to these views, Beijing will fill the vacuum created by the US withdrawal; indeed, it already seems to be ramping up its presence there. Reportedly, CCP media often hinted that if US redeployment in East Asia is implemented, China will seek to more visibly corner the US in the Middle East. Is Beijing interested in or capable of doing it? This chapter tries to challenge these conclusions and to offer alternative ones.

To a great extent, these conclusions originated in the Cold War era when Beijing regarded the US (and also later the Soviet Union) as its main adversary in the Middle East. Indeed, much of China's Middle East (mostly rhetorical) offensive up to the late 1960s had been directed against the US. The first part of this chapter concentrates on the legacies of Sino-US relations in the Middle East. The second part shows how legacies of the past are still affecting Sino-American relations in the Middle East. To a certain extent this is true, though not everywhere, not all the time and not in all spheres. The third and final part of the chapter looks at perceptions of Sino-American animosity and rivalry in the Middle East and suggests why they should be modified. It deals with the large degree of convergence of Beijing's and Washington's policies and behavior in the Middle East, which is contrary to conventional wisdom. Still, convergence by no means implies collaboration. Finally, I try to suggest ways to overcome the divergence between China and the US in the Middle East and to facilitate greater cooperation between the two.

Legacies

Mao's China regarded the US presence in the Middle East as a link in a ring that encircled China and as a base for denying Chinese access into the region. There was little Beijing could have done to diminish US influence in the Middle East, let alone drive it away. Mao's China was a marginal player in the Middle East, at best, and by no means a challenge to the US.[1] This asymmetry has gradually modified since the 1980s as the PRC acquired more political, economic, and military capabilities. By the early 1990s China had established diplomatic relations with all Middle Eastern countries and had launched new activities including arms sales, increased trade, labor export, construction projects and, later on, loans and investments.[2]

Initially, most of these activities hardly affected US interests in the Middle East. In fact, the 1980s were the best period in Sino-US relations and their effects were also felt by other countries with interests in the Middle East. For example, to neutralize an expected negative Soviet response to its own military transactions with China, Washington tacitly approved (if not initiated) Israeli arms sales to the PRC.[3] Beijing's unprecedented intrusion into the Middle Eastern arms markets was by and large tolerated by Washington. Chinese arms supplies to Iran and Iraq, engaged in brutal fighting throughout the 1980s, had failed to raise US alarm until 1987, when US tankers were hit by Iran's Chinese-made Silkworm missiles.[4] It was only then that Washington began leaning on the two sides to end the hostilities leading to the termination of the war in 1988. In hindsight, 1988 may have signaled the beginning of a turnabout in Sino-US collaboration in the Middle East and the end of the honeymoon phase. It happened in Saudi Arabia.

Revealed in March 1988, Beijing's sale of DF-3 IRBMs to Saudi Arabia apparently came as a surprise to Washington. This deal, the first of its kind, had been facilitated following a US refusal to provide advanced weapon systems to Saudi Arabia, which pushed it toward China. This pattern was repeated later (e.g., in the case of Turkey). While Washington must have been aware of the Sino-Saudi negotiations, supposedly conducted in secret, it had the power to block the deal, but did not. While in retrospect the missile deal proved to be of no more than symbolic value, it had paved the ground for the establishment of Saudi-Chinese diplomatic relations and, even more important, it indicated China's growing role in the Middle East and the erosion of US assets in the region[5] – long before becoming an international issue by the end of the first decade of the 21st century. Indeed, by the end of the 1980s, Beijing had already begun to tread on US toes in the Middle East, and elsewhere.[6]

Sino-US friction, which had nothing to do with the Middle East, was an outcome of the Tiananmen massacre and the Soviet collapse. Washington's disillusionment about China's alleged free-market "democratic" orientation and fundamental upholding of hard-core CCP authoritarianism has been underlined by the Soviet disintegration. Beijing now lost its value as a US partner against Moscow since Sino-Russian relations have been improving quickly and substantially, primarily in military terms and on global issues including the Middle East. As the Moscow challenge diminished, Washington began to consider Beijing as the new "threat." Although the subsequent deterioration in Sino-US relations had little to do with the Middle East, it still determined US-China relations in this region; and Sino-Israeli relations were immediately affected.

Tolerated if not welcomed throughout the 1980s, Israeli military transfers to China had begun to attract US fire since the early 1990s. Accused of transferring US military technologies to China, Israel was forced to cancel some deals, to pay Beijing a hefty compensation to establish a new Department of Defense Export Control in its Ministry of Defense, and to enact laws regarding arms export supervision. In 2005 Washington forced Israel to stop upgrading Israeli-made Harpy UAVs, sold to Beijing in the mid-1990s, and to return them to China. Firm US opposition also made it difficult for Israeli security companies to offer their services at the Beijing 2008 Olympic Games. In late 2013 the director of the newly created Department of Defense Export Control in Israel's Ministry of Defense had to resign after apologizing to the US because a sensitive military component sold to a European company ended up in China.[7] Washington's close monitoring of Israel's arms sales to China – whether direct or indirect – indicates clearly that its concern about China was growing.

Yet China's higher profile in the world, and in the Middle East, is not unconnected to US policies. Beijing has been able to increase its role mainly because of the withdrawal of the US and other Western governments from the Greater Middle East. Quick to seize the opportunity, China stepped in, occasionally by invitation, to fill the vacuum. This scenario occurred in Sudan, an Arab League member, which has become China's first solid base in Africa. China also expanded its interests in Libya and Iraq, becoming the dominant player in their energy sector. Likewise, Washington's refusal to sell missiles to Turkey opened the door for the Chinese, whose FD-2000 air defense system was commissioned by Ankara in a deal worth US $4 billion, though not yet final at the time of writing.[8] Washington continues to fight hard to abort the deal.[9] Although China's military transactions with Turkey are still marginal, and by no means threaten US predominance, they are nevertheless significant as Turkey is a NATO member.[10] For the first time since its admission to NATO, Turkey appears to have a choice: China.

Needless to say, China has become a major economic player in the Middle East, increasingly at the expense of the US.[11] In Saudi Arabia, a close US ally, China is becoming the top trading partner – overtaking the US and Japan, something inconceivable twenty years ago. Late in 2009, China's oil imports from Saudi Arabia had for the first time surpassed those of the US, thus turning Saudi Arabia into China's leading oil supplier.[12] In May 2010, Saudi Arabia's state oil company Aramco (Arabian-American Oil Company, partly controlled – until 1980 – by several US oil companies) held its board of directors meeting – for the first time ever – in Shanghai. Symbolically, if not (yet) practically, it reflected America's decline and China's rise.

Thus, despite a Sino-US "honeymoon" in the Middle East that lasted through the 1980s and that offers a precedent for future collaboration and partnership, the fundamental Sino-US legacy demonstrates mutual hostility, competition, and rivalry until the early 1970s and once again from the early 1990s on. It is this legacy of friction that shapes common perceptions of US-China relations today, in the Middle East and elsewhere.

Perceptions

Most interpretations of Sino-US relations in the Middle East reflect their perceived and inherited mutual hostility. Beijing, a relative newcomer in the Middle East and a rising global power, is perceived as trying to encroach on US assets and win friends by blocking or diluting Washington's attempts to impose sanctions on "axis of evil" countries such as Sudan, Iran, and Syria. Moreover, upholding their "non-intervention" policy, the Chinese are perceived as trying to avoid becoming actively involved in Middle Eastern affairs not only in the region but also in the UN and the Security Council votes, where they initially tended to abstain or even to be absent. Regarded as a declining superpower, the US has criticized Beijing's behavior of supporting "rogue" regimes that abuse human rights, oppose democracy, and nurture terrorism and expect Beijing to become a "responsible stakeholder". At the same time, the Chinese fail to hide their concern about Washington's alleged relocation to East Asia.

This alleged US forthcoming withdrawal from the Middle East is based on a number of signals. Conventional wisdom argues that its new "rebalancing" and "pivoting" policy will lead the US to turn to the Asia-Pacific region, at the expense of the Middle East. Apparently linked to the belief that China has become the main threat to the US, and following the planned US evacuation of Iraq and Afghanistan, American troops and military bases would shift from the Middle East to the Asia-Pacific region, leaving the Middle East less protected. There are also hints that Washington has become fed up with the Middle East conflicts, primarily with the Israeli-Palestinian one, and may try to retire from its attempts to bring the parties together. However, the most important reason commonly given for the alleged US withdrawal from the Middle East is the so-called "shale oil revolution." According to this argument, the US is not only going to become self-sufficient in oil but an oil and gas exporter that would overtake the world's leading oil and gas exporters. Under these circumstances, the US would no longer need the Middle East to provide its energy needs and, consequently, could give up its presence (primarily military), which had supposedly been built to ensure energy supply.[13]

Many of those scholars and journalists who uphold the "US withdrawal from the Middle East theory" also expect, or anticipate, China to replace the US as the new hegemon in the Middle East. This perception appears to be shared by some in the region, including Turkey and definitely Iran (see note 27 below). According to public opinion polls, Middle Eastern respondents are more favorable to China than to the US (with the notable exception of Israel, see Table 1.1). The Middle East was the only region in the world where favorable attitudes toward China (49%) were higher than toward the US (30%, less than half of all other

Table 1.1 Favorable Middle Eastern attitudes toward China and the US, 2007–2014 (%)

Country	2007 US	2007 PRC	2008 US	2008 PRC	2009 US	2009 PRC	2010 US	2010 PRC	2011 US	2011 PRC	2012 US	2012 PRC	2013 US	2013 PRC	2014 US	2014 PRC
Egypt	21	65	22	59	27	52	17	52	20	57	19	52	16	45	10	46
Jordan	20	46	19	44	25	50	21	53	13	44	12	47	14	40	12	35
Israel	78	45	–	–	71	56	–	–	72	49	–	–	83	38	84	49
Lebanon	47	46	51	50	55	53	52	56	49	59	48	59	47	56	41	53
Palestine	13	46	–	–	15	43	–	–	18	62	–	–	16	47	30	61
Tunisia	–	–	–	–	–	–	–	–	–	–	45	69	42	63	42	64
Turkey	9	25	12	24	14	16	17	20	10	18	15	22	21	27	19	21

Adapted from: Pew Research Center, *America's Global Image Remains More Positive than China's* (18 July, 2013), 10, 24; idem., *Global Opposition to U.S. Surveillance and Drones, but Limited Harm to America's Image* (14 July 2014), 8, 14, 26.

regions). Likewise, Middle Eastern confidence in US President Obama – the lowest in the world – has consistently declined between 2009 and 2014 (again, with the exception of Israel).[14] With few exceptions, Middle Eastern respondents consider China as a partner rather than the US and consider the US an enemy, rather than China (see Table 1.2).

Although thus far Beijing has been reluctant to engage more actively in Middle Eastern affairs, there have been expectations not only among the Middle Eastern countries but also among Chinese intellectuals that China should play a greater role in this region.[15]

Realities

Despite the perception of mutual hostility between the US and China in the Middle East, there is a relatively high convergence between their attitudes, policies, and behavior on a variety of Middle Eastern issues.[16] Not all of Beijing's Middle Eastern policies have been aimed at the US or motivated by anti-American considerations, at least not directly. One example is China's policy on sanctions. For many years Beijing has categorically rejected *in principle* the imposition of sanctions even by the United Nations let alone by other governments. In its view, sanctions not only represent oppressive superpower politics but also harm ordinary people more than governments, cause injustice, and generate resentment – not to mention that they are often ineffective. Beijing's rejection of sanctions also reflects its own experience, especially during the 1950s and 1960s, when the Western embargo coupled

Table 1.2 Middle Eastern perceptions of the US and China as partner or enemy, 2013 (%)

Country	Partner		Enemy		Neither	
	US	PRC	US	PRC	US	PRC
Egypt	19	28	26	18	43	46
Jordan	15	48	29	13	54	34
Israel	90	15	1	13	7	67
Lebanon	38	36	46	18	15	44
Palestine	4	26	76	12	15	51
Tunisia	34	51	31	9	23	27
Turkey	14	16	49	36	24	30

Adapted from: Pew Research Center, *America's Global Image Remains More Positive than China's* (18 July 2013), 12, 26.

with the Soviet withdrawal crippled China's economy and military development.

Yet, by the early 1990s the Chinese had realized they could no longer escape addressing the issue of sanctions. This realization emerged following Saddam Hussein's invasion of Kuwait, an obvious case of aggression, unprovoked and unjustified. The Chinese made a distinction between the ultimate sanction, the use of force, which they could by no means approve, and other kinds, which they could. Consequently, and *along with the US*, Beijing voted *for* all 11 UN Security Council resolutions that imposed sanctions on Iraq, including Resolution 661 (economic and military sanctions); 665 (a naval blockade); and 670 (an air blockade).[17] While China abstained on most UN Security Council resolutions imposing a variety of sanctions on Sudan, it nonetheless *joined the US* in voting for resolutions such as 2035 (17 February 2012), which imposed sanctions on individuals and entities blamed for "impeding peace in Sudan"; and 2046 (2 May 2012) that *threatened* to use sanctions against Sudan and South Sudan.[18]

China also voted *for* a number of UN Security Council Resolutions, imposing a variety of sanctions against Iran. These included Resolution 1696 (31 July 2006), which prohibited the transfer of any materials for Iran's nuclear and ballistic missile programs; 1737 (23 December 2006), which imposed additional sanctions against Tehran for failing to stop its uranium enrichment program; 1747 (27 March 2007), which agreed to tighten the sanctions imposed on Iran in connection with its nuclear program, impose a ban on arms sales, and intensify the freeze on assets already in place; and Resolution 1929, which imposed further sanctions on Iran for failing to comply with earlier Security Council resolutions concerning Iran's nuclear program. Beijing also endorsed sanctions imposed on Libya (Resolution 1970, 26 February 2011), although it abstained on most other relevant UN Security Council resolutions. In all these votes Beijing could have blocked the US-inspired resolutions by casting a veto, but it did not do so.[19]

In the more than 44 years since its admission to the UN, Beijing used its veto power eight times, and only three times on Middle Eastern issues. All of China's vetoes on Middle East resolutions were made together with Russia, and all were related to Syria (4 October 2011; 4 February 2012; and 19 July 2012). These were China's only vetoes on a Middle Eastern question.[20] China's veto on Syria was a reaction to the so-called Libyan "deception" when China (and Russia) agreed to withhold their veto power after having been notified that the UN Security Council's "no flight zone" resolution was aimed at preventing Qadhafi from using his

Air Force against civilians. Only later did Beijing (and Moscow) learn that the real intention had been to remove him. China's Syria veto, therefore, was meant not only to block the UN Security Council-sponsored intervention in Syria but – and much more dangerous – a unilateral intervention *outside* the UN Security Council that could have triggered a Middle Eastern war with far reaching consequences to all parties concerned, including China. It was also a loud and clear Chinese message to the US to stop interfering in the internal affairs of other countries.

Beijing's Syria veto, however, was an exception. Contrary to the conventional wisdom, the Chinese not only actively participated in the UN Security Council votes (rather than abstained) but also sided with the US on most of them. Since China's admission to the UN in October 1971, the UN Security Council adopted over 500 resolutions on various aspects of the greater Middle East (also covering Iran, Turkey, Cyprus, Sudan, and North Africa). Of these, China voted *for* some 430 resolutions (84%) along with the US; abstained on 26 (only 5%) and did not participate in 56 votes (11%), for the *last* time on 23 November 1981, some ten years after its admission. In this respect, at least, China has definitely complied with the US demand to increase its involvement in international affairs and to become a "responsible stakeholder."

While public opinion polls show that Middle Eastern respondents do favor China more than the US, when asked "how much does China consider your country's interests" most of them replied "not too much or not at all." This response does not mean that the US is regarded as more considerate of Middle Eastern interests (see Table 1.3). Except for Israel (and perhaps Lebanon) there is no dramatic difference between China and the US commitment to Middle Eastern interests. China has no real advantage in this respect over the US, at least not according to the polls reported in Table 1.3.

There is no official indication that China wants to replace the US in the Middle East. Yet this is not to say that China is totally absent from the region in a political sense. Contrary to conventional wisdom, Beijing has been playing a significant, even crucial, role in the Middle East. Through its votes on the UN Security Council resolutions, Beijing facilitated not just the imposition of sanctions but also the 1991 US-orchestrated offensive against Iraq. However, China's political contribution to settling Middle Eastern problems has been done on a case-by-case basis. China prefers the US to continue to be tied to the region, far away from East Asia. But will the US continue to maintain its presence in the Middle East? According to the common perception it will not, yet reality may be different.

Table 1.3   China and US consideration of Middle Eastern interests, 2013 (%)

Country	Not Too Much or Not at All		A Great Deal or a Fair Amount	
	China	United States	China	United States
Israel	79	31	16	69
Jordan	71	76	25	19
Turkey	68	75	18	18
Palestine	67	81	19	16
Egypt	66	83	25	16
Tunisia	59	66	27	24
Lebanon	52	73	45	26

Adapted from: Pew Research Center, *America's Global Image Remains More Positive than China's* (18 July 2013), 13, 31.

Often cited as the main reason for its alleged forthcoming withdrawal from the Middle East, US self-sufficiency in oil is not only doubtful but also partly irrelevant. Shale oil, based on new technologies (also known as "tight oil"), is more expensive to produce, ecologically controversial, and may add only 15% to the US oil supply. In the meantime, US population growth is expected to increase oil demand despite more efficient use. Therefore, notwithstanding the so-called "shale oil revolution," the US will have to continue importing oil for a long time to come.[21] Closer to the consumers, oil from Canada and Mexico is perhaps easier to ship, but could hardly compete in the long run with the abundance of Persian Gulf oil. In fact, in January 2014 the share of Persian Gulf oil in US total oil imports was still 23.6% (*increasing* from 21.2% in August 2013), over twice the amount of oil the US imported from Mexico. Unlikely to eliminate, nor even substantially reduce, US imports of Persian Gulf oil, US tight oil production is expected to peak very quickly by 2020 and then gradually decline. In 2012, the share of tight oil in US oil consumption was 12%; by 2040 (with over 60 million more people) it is expected to reach no more than 17%. Consequently, conventional oil imports, which constituted 40% of the US consumption in 2012, are anticipated to decline in 2040, but only to 32% – still nearly one third of consumption.[22] Canada, which in 2012 provided 29% of imported US oil, is unlikely to substantially increase oil exports to the US by 2040. In other words, the US will have to continue relying on Persian Gulf oil for decades to come.

It should be underlined that even if Persian Gulf oil would no longer be needed to satisfy US consumption, it would still be imported in order to export oil products. Whereas crude oil exports are still banned in the US (since the 1970s), there is no ban on the exports of oil products. Over the last decade, US oil refineries have been utilized at around 86% of their capacity (87.2% in January 2014), and US refiners are planning to add at least 400,000 barrels of oil-refining capacity a day to existing facilities by 2018.[23] To feed this refining overcapacity, which will be used to export petroleum products, the US will have to rely on external sources of crude supply, primarily from the Persian Gulf. Because Persian Gulf oil is much cheaper to produce than domestic tight oil, it is, therefore, more profitable – even if shipping costs are taken into account.

This argument brings us to the final one: contrary to conventional wisdom, the US is likely to stay in the Middle East, but oil is not the only reason. What other country or power has the will or capability to push the US out of the region? China does not have the power or will to do so. And, the US will remain in the Middle East primarily because US "rebalancing" or "pivoting" to the Asia-Pacific region may fail, and not necessarily due to Beijing's opposition (as evidenced in its recent militancy at sea and in the air.)[24] More likely, "rebalancing" may prove difficult to accomplish given the US defense budget cuts,[25] the economic downturn, and public opinion reservations (in the US and East Asia). In fact, the US Central Command (which includes the Greater Middle East) requires 60% of the US defense budget. Whatever the increase in allocation to the Asia-Pacific region, it would still be lower than that allocated to the Middle East. As long as Middle East unrest remains a major challenge to the US, the shift to East Asia appears less likely.[26]

Conclusion

Recently, a number of commentaries pointed to China's growing role in the Middle East.[27] While true in economic terms, any real growth in political influence remains unlikely. Beijing is hardly as familiar with Middle Eastern affairs compared with other powers. Another reason China does not want to become entangled in the region's conflicts is that their involvement would be likely to lessen the US burden, making their move to Asia-Pacific more plausible. As long as China is encircled by the US military presence in Asia, they have no incentive to collaborate with the US in the Middle East, let alone to replace it. In fact, given its core interests, Beijing prefers that the US not only maintain its deployment in the Middle East (rather than in the Asia-Pacific region), but also to incur as many penalties as possible. A US withdrawal from East Asia – rather than from West Asia – may herald a new era in Sino-US relations worldwide, including the Middle East.[28]

Notes

1. For Sino-Middle Eastern relations in Mao's time, see: Yitzhak Shichor, *The Middle East in China's Foreign Policy 1949–1977* (London and New York: Cambridge University Press, 1979). Reprinted 1981, digitally printed version 2008.
2. Yitzhak Shichor, "China's Economic Relations with the Middle East: New Dimensions," *China Report*, Vol. 34, Nos. 3&4 (1998), 419–439. See also: *idem*, "Competence and Incompetence: The Political Economy of China's Relations with the Middle East," *Asian Perspective*, Vol. 30, No. 4 (2006), 39–67. On China's arms sales to the Middle East, see: Yitzhak Shichor, "Unfolded Arms: Beijing's Recent Military Sales Offensive," *The Pacific Review*, Vol. I, No. 3 (October 1988), 320–330; and *idem*, "Israel's Military Transfers to China and Taiwan," *Survival*, Vol. 40, No. 1 (Spring 1998), 68–91.
3. On US-China military relations, see: US Department of State, "Technology Transfers and Military Sales to China," Top Secret Memorandum (February 26, 1980), declassified November 19, 1990 (Carter Library). US concern is evident in declassified documents. See: CIA National Foreign Assessment Center, "Prospects of US Sales of Defense-Related Equipment to China," Secret Memorandum (12 May, 1981), declassified and sanitized.
4. On China and the Iran-Iraq War, see: Yitzhak Shichor, "The Year of the Silkworms: China's Arms Transactions, 1987," in: Richard H. Yang (Ed.), *SCPS Yearbook on PLA Affairs 1987* (Kaohsiung: Sun Yat-sen Center for Policy Studies, National Sun Yat-sen University, 1988), 153–168.
5. See: Yitzhak Shichor, *A Multiple Hit: China's Missiles Sale to Saudi Arabia*, SCPS Papers, No. 5 (Kaohsiung: Sun Yat-sen Center for Policy Studies, National Sun Yat-sen University, 1991); idem, *East Wind Over Arabia: Origins and Implications of the Sino-Saudi Missile Deal*, China Research Monographs No. 35 (Center for Chinese Studies, Institute of East Asian Studies, University of California, Berkeley, 1989).
6. Reports in 2013 said that Saudi Arabia deployed Chinese-made missiles "targeting Iran and Israel" and in late April China's DF-3 missiles were displayed for the first time in a military parade. See: "Saudi Arabia Said to Target Iran, Israel with Chinese Missiles," *The Times of Israel*, 12 July 2013; Saudi Missiles Parade a Signal to Iran, Israeli Defense Expert Tells 'Post'," *The Jerusalem Post*, 1 May 2014. In fact, the missiles target the US more than anything else.
7. *Ma'ariv*, 22 December 2013. See also: Ran Dagoni, "Harpy UAV Compromise with US: No Upgrades for China," *Globes*, 25 May 2005. See also: Yitzhak Shichor, "The U.S. Factor in Israel's Military Relations with China," *China Brief* (Washington: The Jamestown Foundation), Vol. V, Issue 12 (24 May 2005), 7–9, and "Forced Landing: Sino-Israeli Security Relations in the Early 2000s," in: K. Santhanam and Srikanth Kondapalli (Eds.), *Asian Security and China 2000–2010* (Delhi: Shipra, 2004), 387–399.
8. "Chinese Firm Wins Big Turkish Air-Defense Deal," *Defense News*, 26 September 2013; "Concerns Mount Over Turk-China Defense System," *Defense News*, 29 September 2013; Tuba Eldem, "Turkey's Difficult Choice: A Co-Produces Defense System with China?" *Eurasia Daily*, Vol. 10, Issue 191, the Jamestown Foundation (25 October 2013).

9. On US efforts, see: http://www.israeldefense.co.il/?CategoryID=760&ArticleI
   D=6742 (31 July 2014).
10. More details in: Yitzhak Shichor, "China and Turkey in the Post-Cold War
    World: Great Expectations," in: Bruce Gilley and Andrew O'Neil (Eds.), *Middle
    Powers and the Rise of China* (Georgetown University Press, 2014), 192–212.
11. In 2014, the following countries' trade with China was higher than with the
    US: Saudi Arabia, the United Arab Emirates, Iran, Turkey, Iraq, Oman, Qatar
    and Egypt. Source: IMF.
12. *Global Times*, 19 December 2010; "China Taps More Saudi Crude than US,"
    Financial Times, 21 February 2010; "China Exceeds US in Saudi Oil Export,"
    New York Times, 10 March 2010. See also: Yitzhak Shichor, "Sweet and Sour:
    Sino-Saudi Crude Collaboration and US Crippled Hegemony," in: David
    Zweig and Yufan Hao (Eds.), *Sino-US Energy Triangles: Resource Diplomacy
    under Hegemony* (London and New York: Routledge, 2015), pp. 75–91.
13. "Fracking Pushes U.S. Oil Production to Highest in 20 Years," Bloomberg,
    9 January 2013; "Analysis: Awash in Oil, U.S. Reshapes Mideast Role 40
    Years after OPEC Embargo," Reuters, 17 October 2013; "Saudi America," *The
    Economist*, 15 February 2014; "US to Become Self-Sufficient in Oil Production
    in 23 Years," *Middle East Monitor*, 9 April 2014.
14. Pew Research Center, *America's Global Image Remains More Positive than China's*
    (18 July 2013), 6, 19, 21; *Global Opposition to U.S. Surveillance and Drones, but
    Limited Harm to America's Image* (14 July 2014), 18. See also: Richard Wike,
    Bruce Stokes and Jacob Poushter, *Global Publics Back U.S. on Fighting ISIS,
    but Are Critical of Post-9/11 Torture: Asian Nations Mostly Support TPP, Defense
    Pivot – but Also Value Economic Ties with China*, Pew Research Center, June 23,
    2015, pp. 8, 24, 26, 28, 29, 31, 32.
15. Wang Jisi, "'Marching Westwards': The Rebalancing of China's Geostrategy,"
    International and Strategic Studies Report, No. 73 (Center for International and
    Strategic Studies, Peking University, 7 October 2012); Wang Yizhou, "'Creative
    Involvement': A New Direction in Chinese Diplomacy," in: Mark Leonard
    (Ed.), *China 3.0* (London: European Council on Foreign Relations, November
    2012), 106–111. See also: Zhou Shixin, "Zhongguo dui zhongdong bianju de
    jianshexing jieru" [Strategic Thinking on China's Constructive Involvement
    in the Middle East Turmoil], *Alabo shijie yanjiu* [Arab World Studies], No. 2
    (March 2013), 40–52.
16. Zhang Jiadong, "Zhong Mei zai zhongdong de gongtong liyi yu fenqi"
    [Common Interests and Differences of China and the US in the Middle East],
    Alabo Shijie Yanjiu [Arab World Studies], No. 2 (March 2007), 50–59.
17. Richard Clutterbuck, *International Crisis and Conflict* (New York: St. Martin's
    Press, 1993), pp. 186–187.
18. See also: James Reilly, "China's Unilateral Sanctions," *The Washington
    Quarterly*, Vol. 35, No. 4 (Fall 2012), pp. 121–133.
19. For more on China's "non-intervention" policy, see: Yitzhak Shichor,
    "Fundamentally Unacceptable yet Occasionally Unavoidable: China's
    Options on External Intervention in the Middle East," *China Report*, Vol. 49,
    No. 1 (2013), 25–41.
20. Draft Resolutions S/2011/612; S/2012/77; S/2012/538: http://www.un.org/
    depts/dhl/resguide/scat_veto_En.shtml.

21. "US Still Needs to Import 50 Percent of Its Crude Oil Requirements Despite Increasing Shale Oil Production," *Crude Oil Peak*, 13 December 2012. See also: "The Myth That the US Will Soon Become and Oil Exporter," *Our Finite World*, 16 April 2012.
22. All data from: US Energy Information Administration, *Annual Energy Outlook 2014 Early Release Overview* (Release Date: 16 December 2013), 13.
23. *Wall Street Journal*, 3 March 2014.
24. Ely Ratner, "Rebalancing to Asia with an Insecure China," *The Washington Quarterly*, Vol. 36, No. 2 (Spring 2013), 21–38.
25. *New York Times*, 24, 26 February 2014. See also: "Obama's Asia Rebalancing Turns into a Big Foreign Policy Headache," *The Guardian Weekly*, 28 January 2014.
26. David C. Gompert and Phillip C. Saunders, *The Paradox of Power: Sino-American Strategic Restraint in an Age of Vulnerability* (Washington: Center for the Study of Chinese Military Affairs, Institute for National Strategic Studies, National Defense University, 2011), 25–26.
27. For example: "Beijing Eyes Broader Role in Middle East," *South China Morning Post*, 10 January 2014; Zachary Keck, "China Wants to Join Middle East Peace Quartet," *The Diplomat*, 15 January 2014; Muhammad Zulfikar Rakhmat, "Why China Could Be Effective in the Middle East," *The Diplomat*, February 20, 2014; Abbas Varij Kazemi and Xiangming Chen, "China and the Middle East: More Than Oil," *The European Financial Review*, 21 February 2014; Andy Polk, "China: A Major Power in the Middle East?" *War on the Rocks*, 5 March 2014; Paul Rivlin, "Will China Replace the U.S. in the Middle East?" *Iqtisadi: Middle East Economy*, Vol. 4, No. 3 (25 March 2014).
28. Yitzhak Shichor, "*Quid pro Quo*: US-China Middle East Relations in an East Asian Perspective," U.S.-China-Israel Trilateral Conference: Challenges and Opportunities in the Middle East, Washington, DC, The Brookings Institute, February 12–13, 2014, unpublished paper.

2
An Alternative Partner to the West? China's Growing Relations with Turkey

Zan Tao

The relationship between Turkey and China has rarely been a point of focus for international observers in the early 21st century. However, the number of symposia, forums, panels, articles, columns, think tanks, and researchers focusing on Sino-Turkish relations has been increasing. The change is mostly due to the impressive rise of both Turkey and China as powers on both regional and global levels. Today, Turkey is the 16th largest economy and China the second largest, and they are beginning to pay attention to each other.

This chapter begins with background on the relationship between Turkey and China. In the second section, two key issues affecting the current Turkish-Sino relationship – the imbalance of trade and the Uyghur issue – are discussed. Finally, the position of China in Turkey's international strategy is assessed.

The Turkish-Sino relationship in the 20th century

After the establishment of the Turkish Republic in 1923, an official relationship emerged between Kemalist Turkey and Nationalist (Kuomintang) China. In the early 20th century, Turkey was a model for Chinese reformists, revolutionaries, and even early Communists.[1] After the end of the Chinese civil war in 1949, the diplomatic relationship between Turkey and the Kuomintang's Taiwan continued until the early 1970s.[2]

At the height of the Cold War, Turkey, an ally of the United States, actively participated in the Korean War. From a Sino-Turkish perspective, this event led to mutual negative perceptions.[3] The governing elites of Turkey maintained a staunch anti-Communist position, whereas the

19

Chinese government, especially in the high Communism period of the 1960s, publicly declared support for the development of anti-American movements in Turkey. The mouthpiece of the Chinese Communist Party, *People's Daily*, also gave its support to Turkish leftists in one of its editorials.[4]

The establishment of an official, diplomatic relationship between the Turkish Republic and the People's Republic of China occurred only in 1971,[5] with the US rapprochement with China as its backdrop. Since then, bilateral relations between Ankara and Beijing have improved, with reciprocal visits of high-level statesmen, lower-level members of parliaments, and delegations from ministries and other state agencies. In addition, numerous agreements on the economy, tourism, cultural exchange, and military cooperation have been signed.[6]

However, from 1971 to the late 1990s, the relationship between Turkey and China remained superficial. Not until the beginning of this century did Sino-Turkish relations "began to enjoy the most brilliant period in their history."[7] Chinese Prime Minister Wen Jiabao's visit to Turkey in October 2010 lifted the bilateral relationship to a strategic cooperative level.[8] In 2012, with Chinese Vice President Xi Jinping's visit to Turkey in February and Turkish Prime Minister Recep Tayipp Erdogan's visit to China in April, the relationship between the two nations entered a "honeymoon" phase.[9]

Key issues concerning the Turkish-Sino relationship

Economic relations

The speed of trade development between Turkey and China is indicated in Table 2.1. Turkish exports to China amounted to $1.43 billion in 2008, and Turkey's imports from China were $15.6 billion in the same year.[10] In 2010, foreign trade volume between Turkey and China rose 36%, amounting to $20 billion. In 2011 and 2012, Turkish-Chinese two-way trade totaled $24.1 billion.[11]

However, the lopsided amount of trade and business between the two sides has made the Turkish government uneasy. Ender Öncü, the commercial counselor at the Turkish Embassy in Beijing, stated that Turkey should seek to diversify goods exported to China.[12]

Future competition between Turkey and China will likely involve their similar production structures.[13] A report on China produced by a Turkish research center (Etüd-Araştırma Servisi) shows that problems between Turkey and China will involve competition between the countries' textile sectors.[14]

Table 2.1   Turkish-Sino trade (US$ million)

Year	Exports to China	Imports from China	Total Volume	Balance
2000	96.010	1,344.731	1,440.741	–1,248.721
2001	199.373	925.620	1,124.993	–726.247
2002	268.229	1,368.317	1,636.546	–1,100.088
2003	504.626	2,610.298	3,114.924	–2,105.672
2004	391.585	4,476.077	4,867.662	–4,084.492
2005	549.764	6,885.400	7,435.164	–6,335.636
2006	693.038	9,669.110	10,362.148	–8,976.072
2007	1,039.523	13,234.092	14,273.615	–12,194.569
2008	1,437.204	15,658.210	17,095.414	–14,221.006
2009	1,600.296	12,676.537	14,276.833	–11,076.241
2010	2,269.175	17,180.806	19,449.981	–14,911.631
2011	2,466.316	21693.336	24159.652	–19227.020
2012	2,833.255	21295.242	24128.497	–18461.987

Note: The data are from the Turkish Institute of Statistics (TÜİK).

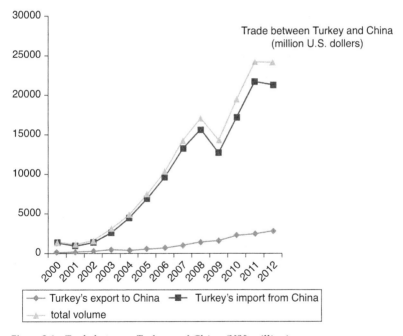

Figure 2.1   Trade between Turkey and China (US$ million)
Source: The chart is prepared according to data from the Turkish Institute of Statistics.

The uyghur issue

The Uyghur issue is the most sensitive topic between Turkey and China, especially on the Chinese side. Turkey used to serve as a shelter for the Uyghur exiles and activists from the Xinjiang autonomous region in northwest China, and Turkey sympathized with the Uyghur people's resistance to the Communist government. However, with the development of stronger bilateral relations, the Turkish government, in its attempt to improve relations with China, has aimed to restrain the activities of the Uyghurs who have migrated to Turkish territory. Following the visit of Turkish President Süleyman Demirel to China in 1995, the Turkish government issued a confidential circular, signed by Prime Minister Mesut Yılmaz, which noted that the Chinese government was uneasy about the activities of Turkish associations established by citizens of Uyghur origin and forbade any minister or civil servant from participating in their meetings.[15]

Staunch sympathizers for Uyghurs in Turkey are against this policy transformation, and they adopted an economic argument as well as a political one. For them, China is an economic giant that is only using Turkey as a springboard (*sıçrama tahtası*) to relay Chinese products to the European Union. They also argue that the principle that a country should not interfere in the domestic affairs of an ally country is an "illogical excuse."[16]

An example that demonstrates the sensitivity between Turkey and China in regard to the Uyghur issue is the 2009 riots in Urumqi, the capital of Xinjiang, in which more than 200 people were killed (referred to in China as "the July 5th incident"). In the aftermath of the riots, a deputy from Turkey's ruling Justice and Development Party (AKP) resigned from the Turkey-China Interparliamentary Friendship Group. In addition, Turkey's industry and trade minister called on Turks to boycott Chinese goods to protest the continuing ethnic violence. After demonstrations in Ankara and Istanbul, Prime Minister Erdogan said, "These incidents in China are as if they are genocide. We ask the Chinese government not to remain a spectator to these incidents."[17]

Erdogan's remarks aroused widespread rage among Chinese people, particularly Chinese youth, who voiced their disapproval on the Internet,[18] and China demanded that Erdogan retract his accusation. Later, a phone conversation between China and Turkey's respective foreign ministers reaffirmed the importance of Turkish-Chinese relations, and Turkish Foreign Minister Ahmet Davutoğlu said that Turkey did not intend "to interfere with the domestic affairs of China."[19] In

November 2010, Davutoğlu toured China for six days and met with his counterpart, Yang Jiechi. Among the joint initiatives the foreign ministers created was a Turkish industrial zone in Xinjiang and a pledge to jointly crack down on separatism and terrorism, including anti-China separatist activities in Turkey.

In Yitzhak Shicor's study on the Uyghur issue as it relates to Turkey and China, he explores the key historical events that relate to the current dispute.[20] Shicor's assertion that the Uyghurs "in no way represent an existential threat" to China is problematic. There is no doubt that the Chinese government views anything endangering the regime's stability, such as ethnic conflicts and national separatism, as a threat. Xinjiang has been defined as part of the core interests of China.[21] In fact, "the July 5th incident" and other small-scale terrorist attacks have put Xinjiang at the forefront of China's "stability maintenance" (*wei wen*) movement.

Turkey's concession to Chinese pressure on the Uyghur issue may be an indication of its understanding of how sensitive the issue is to China. But this should not be read as meaning that Turkey will completely share China's standpoint on the Uyghur/Xinjiang issue, since Turkish public opinion on their "fellowmen" of "Eastern Turkistan" would always pressure the politicians to do something. In terms of ethnic issues, Turkey has similar concerns, such as Kurdish terrorism and separatism and the Northern Cyprus problem. It is hard for Turkey to maintain a double standard on similar issues.[22]

Conclusion: China is on the map of Turkey's foreign strategy

China represents a great opportunity for Turkey's economy

Turkey has undergone a transformation from a security-oriented state to a trading state.[23] Sinan Ulgen defines a trading state as one that emphasizes the role of economic interdependence in its foreign policy, in contrast to states that rely on military capabilities and hard power.[24] Since the end of the Cold War, by pursuing the status of a "central country," Turkey's position as a "frontier country" for the West has diminished.[25] Turkey's adoption of an export-oriented growth strategy, its increasing trade and investment volume, and the rise of "Anatolian tigers" (the small- and mid-sized, yet dynamic enterprises of the trading cities of inner Anatolia) have led to the emergence of a trading state.

Bearing in mind Turkey's large increase in trading volume and its trade deficit with China, it is understandable that it regards the rise of China as an opportunity. In 2007, Turkey's ambassador to China, Oktay Özüye, quoted in a Chinese magazine, said: "In Turkey, both politicians and businessmen regard the rise of China as a chance instead of a threat. So, we are actively working hard to look after chances of cooperation with our Chinese partners."[26]

China is Turkey's potential strategic partner

The multidimensional nature of foreign diplomacy is a prominent feature characterizing Turkey's recent international strategy. Mostly due to security concerns, and also partly due to its ideological orientation, Turkey used to be a Western-oriented nation, often ignoring other nations, especially those in the East. However, in the late 1980s under Ocal, a tendency to pursue a more balanced strategy emerged. During the AKP's time in power, this orientation has only intensified. Writes Ulgen, "Ankara's lessened preoccupation with issues of survival and territorial integrity has thus significantly reduced the West's leverage over Ankara's policy choices."[27] Some in the West also claim that Turkey is drifting away.[28] The Turkey's government stand on this drift is that Turkey is conducting its foreign policy "autonomously." As Davutoğlu said, "We do not receive instructions from any other powers, nor are we part of the others' grand schemes."[29]

Turkey is attaching more importance to the Middle East and the Far East as its diplomacy effort become more multidimensional. In this respect, what concerns China the most is Turkey's entry into Central Asia and the possibility of military cooperation with China.

As a member of NATO, Turkey used to receive military equipment and technology from the West. But Turkey is increasingly dissatisfied with the stringent arms policies of the United States. As a result, Turkey wants to share technology with China, especially missiles.[30] In September 2013, news outlets reported, "U.S.-Sanctioned Chinese Firm Wins Turkey Missile Defense System Tender." The same source noted that the Chinese firm would co-produce (with the United States) $4 billion in long-range air and missile defense systems and that Turkey had rejected bids from Russian, American, and Europeans firms.[31] This news upset some Western policy makers, whose opinion was that Turkey was "sending a message to the West by choosing China for [its] defense system."[32]

In addition, Turkey became a "dialogue partner" of the Shanghai Cooperation Organization (SCO) in 2012. While Turkey offers the SCO its position as a bridge to the West and its cooperation with China in the field of counterterrorism, it is hard to explain what actual gain Turkey receives from the SCO, especially considering that it is "still an organization very much in search of a mission." Turkey's wooing of SCO as a "dialogue partner" could be read as "a step with unclear practical consequences but substantial symbolic import," which means "courting the non-Western world, where there is increasing unhappiness with the US/Europe-dominated world order and which sees in the SCO at least an attempt at countering that."[33]

However, Turkey's pursuit of a balanced strategy does not mean that it will leave the West for the East even though, historically, when Turkey feels frustrated with the West, it turns to the East. For instance, in the 1970s, the relationship between Turkey and the West deteriorated due to the Cyprus crisis. With Turkey's 1974 military intervention in Cyprus, "the U.S. Congress implemented an arms embargo on Turkey in 1975, and Ankara sought to develop its relations with its Arab neighbors, the socialist countries, and the non-aligned countries." [34] Since the AKP took office in 2002, the idea that "the West is losing Turkey" has been heard.[35] This claim was illustrated through four prominent events: Turkey's refusing the US request for use of its military base in 2003, the impasse between Turkey and Israel due to the Marmara flotilla event, Turkey's advocating of "zero problems with neighbors," and the stalemate of Turkey's EU process. However, when troubles in the East become irresolvable, Turkey turns to the West. The Cold War and the current crisis in Syria are examples, with Turkey again firmly in the Western camp. Since the onset of the Arab Spring of 2011, especially the deteriorating situation in Syria, Turkey has adjusted its gesture towards the West. The Syrian crisis posed a threat that Turkey cannot confront by itself. Facing the prospects of a weak and divided state next door, "the United States will be an indispensable ally helping the Turks to cope. Ankara now wants to work closely with Washington in order to shield itself from the instability of the Syrian War."

Turkey's proxy war against Iran in Syria is also a driving force behind Ankara's rapprochement with Washington.[36] With President Obama's help,, Turkey and Israel restored their relationship in 2015.[37] During this process, by finally accepting NATO's missile umbrella, Turkey reaffirmed its stance in the Western camp.[38] While Turkey was hosting the NATO radar system, Iran felt threatened and announced it would make Turkey its first target if Iran were attacked.[39] Thus, it could be argued that Turkey remains a country anchored in the Western camp, although it has been pursuing a more multidirectional foreign strategy. In this vein, China is just a potential partner for Turkey, but in a limited strategic sense. Though Turkey and China will continue to increase their relations, Turkey is not likely to pursue China at the expense of its ties with other countries.

Turkey's capacity for influence lies in soft power

Turkey's capacity for influence lies mainly in its soft power. As E. Fuat Keyman has argued, although Turkey has no power in regard to pursuing regime change in the Middle East, "[it] is a country with a seriously strong capacity to achieve regional and global transformation through soft power for good and democratic government of society, for economic development, and for making a contribution to the development of civil society." He further notes that this capacity is found in Turkey's fields of state-building, nation-building, and economic development.[40]

Indeed, Turkey's comprehensive influence in Central Asia has been established mainly through soft power. Historical links of ethnicity, language, culture, and religion are present between the two areas. Turkey's potential influence in China in this aspect is the attraction of Chinese Muslims to it, mainly Uyghurs and intellectuals. In spite of Turkey's claim that it has given up pan-Turkism from the time of Kemal Ataturk or the "unity of the Turkic World" of the AKP era,[41] its attraction among Uyghur people is becoming more pronounced.

The recent close cooperation between Turkey and China in the field of Islamic education[42] is another way that Turkey's soft power in China is evident. In fact, China is not comfortable with the more extreme teachings of Islam, whether from Pakistan, Afghanistan, or Saudi Arabia, and "sees the Turkish version of mystic, inner-oriented, and peaceful Islamic teachings as a bulwark against extremism." [43]

The rapid increase of bilateral trade volume between Turkey and China; a closer relationship in the areas of military, culture, and tourism; and Turkey's acceptance as a "dialogue partner" in the Shanghai Cooperation Organization, do not necessarily lead to the establishment of a substantial strategic relationship, although leaders of both countries have spoken of "strategic partnership" since 2010. Both China and Turkey share the reasons for a strategic relationship being unlikely. It should be noted that this chapter evaluates the Turkish-Sino relationship only from the perspective of Turkey. As argued in the previous section, Turkey's turning to the east is not a strategic shift, but rather a way of keeping a balance between the West and the East. The West brings Turkey institutions, security, markets, and technology. For Turkey, the importance of China is mainly economic, especially considering that China has become the third biggest trade partner with Turkey in the last decade, after Russia and Germany. But the huge trade deficit on the Turkish side should not be forgotten. And the Uyghur issue will be very hard, if not impossible, to be removed from the Turkish-Sino relationship. Based on these considerations, it is safe to argue that for Turkey, China is just a potential partner but not the alternative partner to the West.

Notes

The author would like to express his deep gratitude to Mimi Kirk, Research Director of the Middle East Institute, not only for her help in editing this essay, but also for many provocative questions that pushed me to think deeply. The author also wants to use this opportunity to acknowledge the support of the "Program for Junior Scholars" (2013–2016) of Beijing Municipal Commission of Education."An Alternative Partner to the West? Turkey's Growing Relations with China" by Zan Tao was originally published by The Middle East Institute through its Middle East Asia Project (MAP) on October 25, 2013: http://www. mei.edu/content/alternative-partner-west-turkey%E2%80%99s-growing-relations-china.

1. Dong Zhenghua, "Chinese Views of Atatürk and Modern Turkey," *Uluslararası Konferans: Atatürk Ve Modern Türkiye*, Ankara Üniversitesi Siyasal Bilgiler Fakültesi, ed. (Ankara: Ankara Üniversitesi Basımevi, 1999), 669–675.
2. Selçuk Çolakoğlu and Arzu Güler, "Turkey and Taiwan: The Relationship Seeking Its Ground," *USAK Policy Brief*, No. 2, August 2011.
3. Çağdaş Üngör, "Perceptions of China in the Turkish Korean War Narratives," *Turkish Studies* 7, 3 (September 2006): 405–420.
4. *People's Daily*, 5 May 1960.
5. On August 4, 1971, with a signed protocol between Turkey's ambassador in Paris, Hasan Esat Işık, and his Chinese counterpart, Huang Chen, the diplomatic relationship between Turkey and China was established. At the time, the first Nihat Erim government was in office and the Turkish minister of foreign affairs was Osman Olcay. *Türkiye-Çinİlişkilerinin 40 Yılı (1971–2011)*, http://www.sde.org.tr/userfiles/file/Rapor-_TUrkiye-Cin_iliskilerinin_40_ Yili_(1971–2011)___042012-son.pdf, p. 7.
6. *Ülke Raporu: Çin Halk Cumhuriyeti* (ÜRÇHC), Etüd-Araştırma Servisi, 2006, 24–26.
7. Selçuk Çolakoğlu, "Turkey's East Asian Policy: From Security Concerns to Trade Partnerships," *Perceptions* 17, 4 (Winter 2012): 146.
8. "China, Turkey to Establish Strategic Cooperative Relationship," *China Daily*, 8 October 2010, http://www.chinadaily.com.cn/china/2010–10/08/ content_11386689.htm.
9. Zan Tao, "Zhong guo wai jiao ban tu zhong de tu er qi (Turkey on the Map of China's Foreign Affairs)," *Dong Fang Zao Bao (Oriental Morning)*, 10 April 2012.
10. "Turkey-China Trade Relations Weaken as Crisis Hits," *Today's Zaman*, 19 March 2009.
11. Data are from the Turkish Institute of Statistics (TÜİK).
12. "Turkey-China Trade Relations Weaken as Crisis Hits." *Today's Zaman*, 19 March 2009

13. According to the Global Trade Negotiations homepage, "Turkey Summary" (2004), Turkey's principal exports are textiles and clothing, followed by agricultural products, iron, steel, and machinery.
14. *Ülke Raporu: Çin Halk Cumhuriyeti* (ÜRÇHC); *Turkish Daily News*, 24 May 2008.
15. "Başbakanlık'tan gizli Doğu Türkistan genelgesi," *Hürrieyt*, 4 Şubat 1999.
16. Nuraniye Hidayet Ekrem, "Türk-Çin İlişkilerinin Gelişmesi," *Uzak Doğu-Pasifik Araştırmaları Masası*, 22 August 2006, http://savunmavestrateji.blogcu.com/turk-cin-iliskilerinin-gelismesi/481827; see also Necip Hablemitoğlu, "Türkiye-Çin İlişkilerinde Gözardı Edilen Bir Boyut: Hükümet-Çin-Doğu Türkistan," *Yeni Hayat Dergisi*, No., 57, http://www.guncelmeydan.com/pano/turkiye-cin-iliskileri-dr-necip-hablemitoglu-t22615.html
17. "Mass rally in Turkey to support China's Uyghur," *Presstv*, 13 July, 2009, http://edition.presstv.ir/detail/100544.html
18. "网民批土耳其总理:做暴力犯罪分子帮凶没好下场！(Netizens Delivered a Broadside to Turkish Prime Minister: Those Who Stand by Criminals of Violence Will Come to no Good End) http://opinion.people.com.cn/GB/9675952.html;   http://news.xinhuanet.com/comments/2009–07/17/content_12635113.htm; http://tieba.baidu.com/p/2375147675
19. "Turkish Foreign Minister Davutoğlu Talks to his Chinese Counterpart on the Phone," *Anadolu Agency*, 12 July 2009, http://www.aa.com.tr/en/news/38872-turkish-foreign-minister-davutoglu-talks-to-his-chinese-counterpart-on-the-phone
20. For examples, Ottoman Sultans' support to Yaqub Beg in late nineteenth century, Uyghur presence and activism in Turkey, military cooperation between Turkey and China, etc. Yitzhak Shicor, "Ethno-Diplomacy: The Uyghur Hitch in Sino-Turkish Relations," *Policy Studies* 53 (2009).
21. Wu Xinbo, *China and the United States: Core Interests, Common Interests and Partnership*, Special Report 277 of the United States Institute of Peace, June 2011.
22. Mehmet Ali Birandonce warned those who support Xinjiang that China might exploit the Kurdish issue as a kind of revenge. "China's Kurdish Policy is Changing," *Turkish Daily News*, 28 February 2006.
23. Çolakoğlu, "Turkey's East Asian Policy: From Security Concerns to Trade Partnerships."
24. Sinan Ulgen, "A Place in the Sun or Fifteen Minutes of Fame? Understanding Turkey's New Foreign Policy," Carnegie Papers, Carnegie Europe, Carnegie Endowment for International Peace, No. 1, December 2010, 9–11.
25. According to Davutoğlu, Turkey is a "central country" both geographically and conceptually sense. Turkey's geography gives it a specific central country status. "Just as geography, history, too, may come to constitute a country as a central country." "Turkey occupies a center of attraction in its region." Ahmet Davutoğlu, "Turkey's Foreign Policy Vision: An Assessment of 2007," *Insight Turkey* 10, 1 (2008).
26. Oktay Özüye, "To Be a Good Role of Bridge between West and East: An Interview with Turkey's Ambassador to China," *Business Weekly*, 26 October 2007.
27. Sinan Ulgen, "A Place in the Sun or Fifteen Minutes of Fame? Understanding Turkey's New Foreign Policy."
28. E. Fuat Keyman, "Rethinking Turkish Foreign Policy," *Turkish Weekly*, 27 May 2013.

29. Ahmet Davutoğlu, "Principles of Turkish Foreign Policy and Regional Political Structuring," *Turkey Policy Brief Series*, International Policy and Leadership Institute, Third Edition, 2012, 4.
30. Nuraniye Hidayet Ekrem, "Türk-Çin İlişkilerinin Gelişmesi," *Uzak Doğu-Pasifik Araştırmaları Masası*, 22 August 2006, http://savunmavestrateji.blogcu.com/turk-cin-iliskilerinin-gelismesi/481827.
31. "U.S.-Sanctioned Chinese Firm Wins Turkey Missile Defense System Tender," *Reuters*, 26 September 2013.
32. *Sunday's Zaman*, 28 September 2013.
33. Joshua Kucera, "Turkey Makes It Official With SCO," 28 April, 2013, http://www.eurasianet.org/node/66896
34. Selçuk Çolakoğlu, "Turkey's East Asian Policy: From Security Concerns to Trade Partnerships," *Perceptions* 17, 4 (Winter 2012): 134.
35. Soner Çağaptay, "The AKP's Hamas Policy,"*Hurriyet Daily News*, 29 June, 2010.
36. Soner Cagaptay, "Syrian Crisis Leading towards Open Turkey-Iran Conflict,"26 May, 2013, http://washin.st/1cMHv5A
37. Suzan Fraser, "Gaza Flotilla Victims' Compensation Discussed By Israel And Turkey,"22 April, 2013, http://www.huffingtonpost.com/2013/04/22/gaza-flotilla-victim-compensation-israel-turkey_n_3131297.html
38. Thom Shanker, "U.S. Hails Deal With Turkey on Missile Shield," *New York Times*, 15 September, 2011 "NATO Deployment of Patriot Missiles to Turkey," http://aco.nato.int/nato-deployment-of-patriot-missiles-to-turkey.aspx; "NATO support to Turkey : Background and timeline,"http://www.nato.int/cps/en/SID-E6526D70-39BD4AD0/natolive/topics_92555.htm?
39. "İran'dan Türkiye'ye Füze Kalkanı Tehdidi," *Milliyet*, 10 October, 2011.
40. E. Fuat Keyman, "Rethinking Turkish Foreign Policy," *Turkish Weekly*, 27 May 2013.
41. Mehmet Ozkan, "Turkey's 'New' Engagements in Africa and Asia: Scope, Content and Implications," *Perceptions* 16, 3 (Autumn 2011): 125.
42. It was reported that a protocol of cooperation on religious education was signed between Turkey's Presidency of Religious Affairs (Diyanet İşleri Başkanlığı) and Islamic Association of China (中国伊斯兰教协会) in 2011. The same source said that every year a certain number of Chinese Muslim students would be sent to Turkey for further religious education either in Imam Hatip schools or in theology faculties. Duygu Bektaş, "Çin'den İmam hatiplere öğrenci," *İhlas Haber Ajansı*, 17 Feb., 2011,http://www.iha.com.tr/egitim/cin-den-imam-hatiplere-ogrenci/160687; Abdullah Bozkurt, "China Seeks Further Engagement from Turkey in Xinjiang Region," *Today's Zaman*, 1 April 2012.
43. Abdullah Bozkurt, "China Seeks Further Engagement from Turkey in Xinjiang Region," *Today's Zaman*, 1 April 2012.

3

A New Eurasian Embrace: Turkey Pivots East While China Marches West

Christina Lin

Introduction

In 2002, Turkish General Tuncer Kilinc, Secretary General of the National Security Council (MGK)–Turkey's top decision-making body, called for Turkey to seek alternatives to the European Union (EU) and North Atlantic Treaty Organization (NATO) and turn toward its old regional foes, Iran and Russia instead.[1] Speaking at the conference, "How to Establish a Peace Belt Around Turkey," held by the Military Academies Command, General Kilinc expressed frustrations at the EU's policies towards Turkey and urged Ankara to start looking eastward for new allies.[2] Although the notion was not taken seriously in the mainstream, "Eurasianism" as a geopolitical discourse caught on with some Turkish intellectuals. In 2004, Istanbul University convened a symposium entitled, "Turkish-Russian-Chinese and Iranian relationships on the Eurasian axis."[3] A decade later, AK Party leader Recep Tayyip Erdogan is seriously considering abandoning the bid for EU membership to join the China-led and Russian- supported Shanghai Cooperation Organization (SCO).[4] On 26 September 2013, Turkey shocked its NATO allies when it chose a US-sanctioned Chinese firm to co-produce a US$3.4 billion long-range air and missile defense system.[5] Turkey, with its increasingly Eurasian geopolitical trajectory, seems to be at a crossroads of choosing whether to remain anchored in the West, or fundamentally shift its axis eastward toward Eurasia.

This chapter examines this emerging trend in the Eurasia region. It focuses on the growing Sino-Turkey relationship and places it within the broader context of increasing Eurasian integration via the "New Silk

Road."[6] It highlights drivers for Turkey's eastward shift away from Europe and toward Eurasia as well as drivers for China's westward march. It also examines the role of Xinjiang as a platform for Sino-Turkey cooperation across Eurasia and concludes with implications of Sino-Turkey ties for transatlantic security.

Turkey's Eurasian orientation

Eurasianism (*Avrasyacilik* in Turkish) stands for a political, economic, and cultural alliance with non-western Eurasian countries, such as Russia, Iran, the Turkic countries in Central Asia, as well as Pakistan, India, and China.[7] Russian author Aleksandr Dugin in his work *Foundations of Geopolitics* (1997) first discussed Russian Eurasianism creating a "supra-national Empire" in which ethnic Russians will occupy a "privileged position." A "grand alliance" of Russia and Turania should divide impe-rial spoils with "the Islamic Empire in the South" composed of the Caucasus, Central Asia, Mongolia, Iranian Empire, Armenia.[8] After the demise of the Soviet Union, Turks discovered their kinship with this geography and kindled a wave of pan-Turkish sentiment. Turkey's presi-dent at the time, Suleyman Demirel, spoke often of a "Turkish World from the Adriatic Sea to the Great Wall of China," referring to almost all territories of Turkic states in the Caucasus and Central Asia, as well as the former Ottoman territories in the Balkans and possibly the Arabian Peninsula.[9] In the face of the stalled EU accession process, both the Turkish citizens and the Turkish government are rediscovering Eurasia and turning towards the east for alternatives.

According to Ihsan Dagi of Ankara's Middle East Technical University, the Turkish people and economy are drifting away from the EU, and "this process is almost irreversible."[10] There has been a structural transforma-tion in Turkey's engagement with the EU, as the flow of EU investment funds has been decreasing in recent years accompanied by a declining share of EU countries involved in trade with Turkey . In 2003, more than 55% of Turkey's trade was with EU countries; in 2014 it had shrunk to 40%.[11]

Likewise, Professor Hasan Unal, a prominent political scientist at Ankara's Bilkent University, expressed similar Euroskepticism that Turkey would ever obtain EU membership. "Why should the EU allow a Muslim country to become its largest and most powerful member, and in so doing move its borders to countries like Iran and Iraq? The EU will never admit Turkey."[12] In this vein, others also argue for Turkey to shift away from Europe and relinquish NATO membership. A week before General Kilinc was detained in 2009 in relation to the Ergenekon coup plot case, he spoke at a panel together with Sule Perincek, wife of Dogu Perincek, the leader of the nationalist-leftist Workers party held in prison as a suspect in the Ergenekon case. There, Kilinc publicly restated that Turkey should leave NATO, which, according to Cengiz Candar from the *Yeni Safak* newspaper, reflects a sentiment that prevails at the higher ranks of the Turkish Armed Forces.[13]

In the aftermath of the EU's Eurozone crisis and defense austerity measures, some mid-level ranks of the Turkish military are also adopting the Eurasian sentiment. A Turkish naval officer has referred European armies to "bonsai armies" and explained that Turkey is looking eastward because "China is on the way of great power."[14] Bonsai is a Japanese miniature tree the size of a potted plant. In November 2011, Christian Molling of the Berlin-based Stiftung Wissenschaft und Politick (SWP) wrote an article assessing how defense budget cuts will produce European bonsai armies over the next five years, with ever shrinking armies and diminishing capabilities. "In Germany, France, and Great Britain there will be miniature versions of armies...these tiny armies will hardly offer serious military power anymore."[15]

These European "bonsai armies" thus will not be able to support Turkey's defense policy of becoming a stronger security actor. In 1998, under the leadership of then Chief of the Turkish General Staff (TGS), General Huseyin Kivrikoglu, Turkey released a Defense White Paper that represented a major shift in Turkish national security strategy, by articulating a Forward Defense concept to pre-emptively solve problems and stabilize neighbors before they could impact Turkey.[16] His successor General Hilmi Ozkok was also committed to maintaining the basic tenets of the 1998 White Paper, but in 2003 when Turkey and the US fell out over the Iraq invasion and the US was able to conduct a "decapitation" strike without using Turkey's territory, it signaled to the Turks that they were no longer essential to American security.[17] US attempts to change Turkish foreign and defense policies have resulted in the creation of ill will in Turkey, and moved forward the notion of Turkey to become an independent security actor.

To this end, Turkey needs to develop a dominant regional military capability with an autonomous military production system capable of supporting unilateral security actions. Ankara is thus looking to Eurasian countries to help develop an internal production system that can free Turkey from the restrictions of western and NATO arms suppliers. For example, in 2013 Japan and Turkey sought a joint development and production of an engine for the Altay, a planned indigenous Turkish tank. Turkey's traditional engine supplier had been MTU of Germany, which has been reluctant to share critical engine technology.[18] Similarly, co-production and technology transfer sweeteners propelled Turkey to select the Chinese missile defense system over those of its NATO allies. Given Turkey's aspiration to be a rising regional power and its growing rift in foreign policy with its European allies, it seems Turkey is increasingly identifying itself as a Eurasian country.

Eurasian identity

According to Professor Selcuk Colakoglu at the Ankara-based International Strategic Research Organization (USAK), in the 1990s Turkey began to identify itself as a Eurasian country. In a recent USAK report, "Turkish Perceptions of China's Rise," Colakoglu observed that the emergence of Turkic Republics in the Caucasus and in Central Asia after the demise of the Soviet Union had a strong effect on this shift.[19] Leftist nationalist groups in Turkey who believe Turkey should not only turn to the East politically, but also develop defensive cooperation with Russia and China to oppose the Western world reinforce this view.[20]

According to Dogu Perincek, founding chairman of the Worker's Party (*Isci Partisi*), Turkey is in danger of being divided by a US mandate tied to the EU's door. Some factions in Turkey think the EU scheme is to lure Turkey with promises of membership into making concessions over the Kurds, Cyprus, and territorial disputes with Greece in the Aegean. Thus the goals are to free Turkey from the US mandate and ensure national integrity by befriending China and Russia. Perincek sees the Shanghai Cooperation Organization (SCO), which includes Turkic Central Asian republics, as a Turkic-Russian-Chinese alliance where Turkey belongs, and that Turkic republics can only be united in a Eurasian alliance.[21] A large cross-section of Turkish society and polity, which includes the business sector and the AKP government, joined the leftist-nationalist group's pro-China and Eurasian orientation. This trend signaled a fundamental eastward shift rather than a movement something endogenously driven by the AKP government. As the second largest economy in the world, China offers immense opportunities to Turkish businessmen, and AKP sees China as a political balancer against NATO and the EU.[22] To that end, Turkey joined SCO as a Dialogue Partner in 2012 with a view towards eventual membership.[23]

SCO holds additional attraction in that Russia and Iran – Turkey's top energy suppliers – are also key players in this Eurasian grouping. As with China, Russia is an UN Security Council member, and Turkey is taking advantage of the recent rapprochement between Iran and the West. In

February 2014, Turkey signed a preferential trade deal with Iran to reach $30 billion in 2015. Ankara also expects to increase energy imports from Iran, now that sanctions are easing, and it is seeking to improve ties after earlier disagreements with that country over Syria.[24]

Eurasian military integration

Following Perincek's notion of uniting Turkic republics in Eurasia, on 30 January 2013 Turkey, Azerbaijan, Kyrgyzstan, and Mongolia agreed to create a joint armed force of Turkic-language countries, which they named TAKM using the initials of the four founding members.[25] The official name is "Eurasian Law Enforcement Organization of Military Status," with the goal to foster cooperation between Central Asian Turkish republics and prepare a fertile ground for common defense.[26] It is based in Ankara with an open door policy for other Central Asian republics, and Kazakhstan, Uzbekistan, Afghanistan, and Georgia have expressed interest in joining TAKM.[27]

TAKM is modeled on the Association of European and Mediterranean Gendarmeries and Law Enforcement Forces with Military Status (FIEP), which Turkey joined in 1998. The symbol of TAKM is a horse, an important cultural symbol of its members' nomadic past.

TAKM's leading power is Turkey, which is playing an important role in the military build-up of both the member states and aspiring members. Post-Soviet countries intending to join TAKM have been given preferences to Turkish-made military products, weapons, communication devices, military vehicles, and optical systems.[28] Currently Turkey is implementing joint programs in military and military industry spheres with Azerbaijan, Kyrgyzstan, Kazakhstan, and Turkmenistan. Many of these countries are also NATO Partnership for Peace (PfP) countries, so NATO member Turkey can apply NATO standards for interoperability.

Eurasian economic integration

Turkey is also advancing Eurasian integration on the economic front via the Economic Cooperation Organization (ECO).

Based in Tehran, ECO was founded in 1985 by Turkey, Iran, and Pakistan to build a free-trade zone of non-Arab Muslim nations; it was expanded in 1992 to include the five Turkic central Asian republics and Azerbaijan as well as Afghanistan. Because many ECO and SCO members overlap, there has been joint cooperation in a series of transport infrastructure projects.

China is establishing its own Islamic corridor with ECO transport projects to link China's Xinjiang with Iran via Afghanistan and Central

Asia. In October 2011, ECO established a rail link from the Iran port of Bandar Abbas to Almaty in Kazakhstan that connects with China, and is now planning a China-Afghan (Kashgar-Herat) railway to link China with its growing investments in Afghanistan's extractive industries. This link will enable China to have a stronghold in Afghanistan post-NATO in 2015 Additionally, this link to Iran would US and EU energy sanctions over Iran's nuclear program and facilitate continued trade with Iran and the Middle East.

In 2012, the ECO Istanbul-Tehran-Islamabad train was constructed to boost trade among member states in Central Asia.[29] This rail line will be part of the longer trans-Eurasian corridor connecting Beijing to London across Eurasia. Eventually, a train that departing from London would pass through the Marmaray and follow the Baku-Tbilisi-Kars railway (linking Azerbaijan, Georgia, and Turkey) along the Caspian Sea to reach Beijing. Marmaray, Turkey's first undersea tunnel in Istanbul (underneath the Bosphorus strait) that connects Europe and Asia, was inaugurated on 29 October 2013.[30] Completion of the Baku-Tbilisi-Kars railway is scheduled for 2014 and will enter into service in 2015.[31]

During the seventh representatives meeting of the Turkish-Eurasia Business Council diplomatic mission on 4 February 2010 in Ankara, Turkey's Foreign Minister Ahmet Davutoglu stated that "Eurasia is a transit area of great importance between the people's republic of China, India, south Asia, and Europe. This region is one of the major points which help develop world politics and economy."[32] Sinan Ogan, founder and director of the Center of International Relations and Strategic Analysis, agreed that, with the revival of the Silk Road, Turkey would act as an interconnector linking the east and the west.[33] Thus, it is on this new Silk Road, that Turkey is pivoting East and China is marching west.

China's march west across Eurasia

In a 2010 article in *Beijing Xiandai Guoji Guanxi* [Beijing Contemporary International Relations] published by State Council's Chinese Institute of Contemporary International Relations (CICIR), the deputy director of the PLA's National Defense University, Tang Yongsheng, wrote an article expounding China's Westward Strategy.[34] He argues that China, with its vast land and rising strength, is not only a Pacific nation but also a nation in the Eurasia heartland. As such, Tang stated that China would now place importance on this westward strategy while maintaining vigilance on managing the Asia-Pacific area, in a two-pronged approach

coordinating and strengthening its eastern seaward and western land-
ward strategies.

Tang observed that recent developments have made Europe and
Asia geographically closer than ever via economic and technological integration, "and the penetration of different modes of thinking
have caused *all geographic barriers to become surmountable.*" According
to Tang, China wants to advance European, Russian and Chinese relations across the Eurasia continent, because the "tendency of geographical center of Europe to move eastward and the geographical center
of the entire Eurasian continent to move inward, have shortened the
distance between China and EU."[35] Tang proposed that the SCO could
be China's vehicle to enhance regional cooperation, especially in transport corridors, as well as to conduct oil diplomacy in the Middle East,
the Caspian Sea, and Central Asia. Xinjiang is to be the centerpiece of
the westward Silk Road strategy, especially in building transport corridors across Eurasia. Wang Mengshu, a member of Chinese Academy of
Engineering and professor at Jiaotong University, corroborated this Iron
Silk Railway view: "China's overseas high-speed rail projects serve two
purposes. First, we need to develop the western regions. Secondly, we
need natural resources."[36]

As such, China is engaged in frenzied constructions of rail links, highways, and energy pipelines westwards across Eurasia. Indeed, today
high-speed rail, gas and oil pipelines, highways and fiber optic cables
(information superhighways) have replaced camel caravans on the Silk
Road. Rather than trading silk and porcelain and collecting tributes such
as pearls and spices, China is trading in rail technology, Huawei telecommunications technology, automobiles, and in return collecting tributes
of equities in infrastructure projects such as seaports, airports, railways,
roads, oil and gas fields, strategic minerals, and mines.

Energy security and Xinjiang linkage

Energy security primarily drives China's "March West" strategy.
Domestically, the Chinese Communist Party's legitimacy and regime
survival rests on continued access to energy to fuel China's economic
growth, while hedging against US naval interdiction of energy supplies
over potential conflicts across the Taiwan straits, East China Sea, or South
China Sea. This is the "Malacca Dilemma" whereby 80% of China's oil
imports pass through the choke point of the Strait of Malacca, and China
is worried about the security of its energy supply line.

Beijing is also concerned about the territorial integrity of Xinjiang.
This region is one-sixth the size of China, three times the size of France,

borders eight countries. It is also a site of strategic mineral resources, and a key geographic bridge for China's overland pipelines and transport corridors for its energy supplies from Central Asia, the Caspian Sea, and potentially, Iran, Iraq, and Afghanistan. In short, Xinjiang is key to China's hedging strategy of having an overland energy supply line in the event the US Navy cuts off its maritime supply line over conflicts in the Western Pacific. Uyghur separatists in Xinjiang who want to establish an independent "East Turkestan" thus directly threaten China's energy security, and Beijing will try to garner support from the Muslim world for the "One China Policy."

The 2009 Xinjiang uprising underscored how much Xinjiang's stability hinges on support from the global Muslim community. When Turkey's Prime Minister Erdogan labeled China's crackdown on Turkic Uyghurs as "near genocide," this further fueled Beijing's concerns that the global Muslim community may increasingly support the Uyghur separatist cause to the detriment of Chinese interests. As such, since 2009, China has beefed up its domestic security, with its internal security budget *surpassing* the defense budget every year since then,[37] while internationally it is proactive in courting the Muslim world to garner support for China's policies. It particular, China is seeking Turkey's cooperation on Xinjiang with a series of bilateral trade and investment agreements dating from 2010, including a Turkish industrial zone for Turkish companies to operate.[38] According to Professor Selcuk Colakoglu at USAK, the Chinese ambassador in Ankara is also very proactive in ensuring Turkey does not encourage the Uyghur separatist term East Turkestan when referring to Xinjiang, given there are about 30,000 to 50,000 Uyghurs living as diasporas in Turkey who support the term East Turkestan.[39]

The geostrategic significance of Xinjiang is illustrated in Figure 3.1. The city of Kashgar in Xinjiang, two thirds the distance between Beijing and the Persian Gulf lies within China, with only one third of the distance left between Kashgar and the Strait of Hormuz. Thus China is building pipelines from Xinjiang to the energy-rich Caspian Sea region and Persian Gulf to diversify its energy supply routes.

Syrian terrorism and Xinjiang linkage

China's interest in counter-terrorism includes preventing internationalization of the Uyghur separatist cause, which is increasingly tied to China's support of Assad in Syria.

Syria is what some Chinese scholars call a new Afghanistan, a witch's brew of international jihadist groups exporting terrorism. In Syria, China faces a new threat: the internationalization of the Uyghurs' separatist

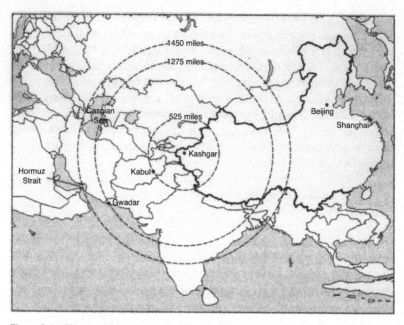

Figure 3.1   The world from Kashgar

Source: Kent E. Calder, *The New Continentalism: Energy and Twenty-First Century Eurasian Geopolitics* (New Haven, CT: Yale University Press, 2012), 157. Reproduced with permission.

cause forming in the crucible of the Syrian war. The first signs of linkage between localized separatist movements with the global terrorist network appeared in 2011.

    Chinese authorities noticed that in the July 2011 Xinjiang bombings, the Uyghur separatists planted a Salafist flag (black with Arabic writings) rather than their usual East Turkestan flag (blue with star and crescent similar to Turkey's flag). Uyghurs also began proclaiming aspirations to join the Middle East jihadi movement, stoking China's fears that Uyghurs would garner global jihadist support from Al-Qaeda and its affiliates such as Al Qaeda in the Islamic Maghreb (AQIM). The AQIM group attacked Chinese workers and infrastructure projects in Algeria in 2009.

    Some Chinese Uyghurs from Xinjiang as well as those residing in Turkey have gone to Syria to join jihadi fighters, with the goal of returning to Xinjiang to launch attacks. China's concern centers around the possibility of that Chinese Uyghurs would link up with international jihadist groups, giving rise to the radicalization of China's 20 million Muslims.

In a December 2013 *Global Times* article, the Chinese Communist Party's mouth piece, an article ran that outlined how the Uyghur terrorist group ETIM is collaborating with Al-Qaeda and its affiliates, naming the Pakistani Taliban, the Afghan Taliban, Islamic Jihad Union, Islamic Movement of Uzbekistan, Islamic Emirate of the Caucasus,. and the Al-Nusra Front in Syria.[40]

Adding to this fear is the increasing home-grown radicalization of Islam across Central Asia, which undermines the stability that China has hitherto enjoyed with the region's secular dictators. Beijing worries that if Assad falls and is replaced by an Islamist regime, it will export extremism and quickly spread to the Muslim republics in Central Asia, destabilizing China's backyard. Xinjiang already faces attacks by jihadists launched from the Federally Administered Tribal Area (FATA) in Pakistan, and Beijing does not want to see the opening of new fronts from Central Asian Republics.

Finally, the territorial integrity of Muslim Xinjiang itself is a core interest for Beijing. One key aspect of Xinjiang that is sorely neglected in press coverage regarding terrorism is China's nuclear arsenal. Xinjiang hosts China's nuclear test site Lop Nur and elements of the Second Artillery Corps ("2nd Arty"), China's strategic missile force. Some of the Second Artillery's vaunted tunnels – the so-called "underground great wall" for hiding missiles and nuclear warheads – also surround Urumqi, the capital of Xinjiang and site of the July 2009 riots that killed 200 people and injured almost 2,000 others. Persistent unrest on a national scale has left at least China's Xinjiang-based nuclear warheads vulnerable, similar to the unrest during the Cultural Revolution.[41] Should such instability occur again – probably on a scale even more substantial than that seen in 1989 – these weapons might become vulnerable to seizure by Uyghur militant groups. As such, any instability of Xinjiang and potential access by jihadists to China's nuclear arsenal is a red flag for Beijing.

Transatlantic implications of Sino-Turkey Eurasianism

Beijing and Ankara thus find mutual interests in lunching Xinjiang as a "Friendship Bridge" for cooperation across the Eurasian Silk Road. "Uyghurs are playing the role of a friendship bridge between China and us. The role will make a contribution to carrying our relations to much higher levels," said former Turkish president Abdullah Gul while visiting Xinjiang in 2009.[42] Likewise, during an October 2010 visit to Xinjiang, Foreign Minister Ahmet Davutoglu also stressed that better relations between Turkey and China will help Turkey increase its contribution to Turkic Muslim Uyghurs living in the province.

Moreover, since the Central Asian republics declared independence when the Soviet Union collapsed, China also feared that Xinjiang would follow suit and declare independence from China. For many years, the Turkic Uyghurs in Xinjiang also enjoyed protection and sympathetic support of their separatist movement in Turkey. As such, China is now seeking Turkey's cooperation and reciprocity in respecting Xinjiang as China's territory in exchange for supporting Turkey's stance on the Kurds in Turkey. To that end, the SCO is an effective vehicle through which both could cooperate and expand their influence in Central Asia. As Dogu Perincek has observed, friendship between Turkey, China, and Russia benefits their Turkic inhabitants, and Uyghurs and others would thrive as equal and free citizens of their countries in the Greater Eurasia Union. This union consists of the Turkic-Russian-Chinese Alliance, made up of Turkic states such as Azerbaijan, Turkmenistan, Kazakhstan, and Kyrgyzstan.[43] As such it appears Sino-Turkey relations are poised to expand.

By contrast, the year 2014 seemed to be a pivotal year that punctuated Turkey's orientation away from the EU. After months of increasingly authoritarian rule by Erdogan, a *New York Times* article observed that the portal of the EU club was closing on Turkey. German politician Andreas Scheuer and EU Commissioner for Enlargement Stefan Fule both express concern over Turkey's ban on social media and its tilt away from European values.[44] Turkish and Western media equally criticize Erdogan's increasing autocratic rule – e.g., his clamp down on judges, prosecutors, the media, and banning social media – as moving away from democratic principles.[45]

Other scholars have observed that Erdogan got what he needed out of the EU process. Hugh Pope of the International Crisis Group argues that Erdogan's initial pro-EU posture brought foreign capital to Turkey to fuel economic growth that underpinned his political popularity, and EU membership conditions further allowed his government to sideline the military. However, in Pope's view, after Erdogan consolidated his power, he no longer wanted more of the EU because this meant a dilution of his own power.[46]

Thus Erdogan's Turkey is shifting towards the SCO, where upholding democracy and civil liberties are not conditions for membership. This shift culminated in 2013 when Turkey defied NATO allied concerns to pursue a missile defense deal with a Chinese firm that had been sanctioned by the US for WMD proliferation.

Security driver for Eurasian shift – China missile defense deal

As mentioned, in September 2013 Turkey shocked its NATO allies when it chose a US-sanctioned Chinese firm, CPMIEC, to co-produce a US$3.4 billion long-range air and missile defense system. Despite NATO's repeated warnings that such a system would compromise NATO intelligence and therefore not be interoperable with its early warning assets, Erdogan chose to make the deal.

Professor Serhat Guvenc from Kadir Has University in Istanbul observed that Turkey's selection of the Chinese firm for NATO missile defense would not go through, unless AKP decides it wants to fundamentally shift its axis away from the West.[47] Turkey can have parts, systems, and hardware from other countries such as China, Japan, South Korea, etc. as standalones, but missile defense has always been the "flagship of interoperability" within NATO, Guvenc noted. Insistence on the Chinese system would send a strong political signal to Western allies of Turkey's shift, and Guvenc dismisses its rationale for technology transfer and price as mere excuses for AKP's orientation.[48]

Given Turkey's frustrations with NATO allies over Syria and Egypt, and the rift in its relationship with the US over the Gezi park protests in 2013 and increasing authoritarian policies of Erdogan's government, Turkey is embarking on a more independent foreign policy course and enlarging its room to maneuver by exploring non-Western alternatives. Guvenc said that "in ten years we are back to the Eurasia option; remember [then-National Security Council Secretary-General] Tuncer Kilic's statement in 2002, asking to give up on EU and forging alliances with Iran and Russia."[49] He observed that ten years ago the Eurasian alternative was Russia-focused; now it is on China.[50]

His view differs from Dr. Mesut Ozcan, Chairman of the Center for Strategic Research (SAM) in the Ministry of Foreign Affairs. Dr. Ozcan said that China offered the best deal in terms of price and technology transfer, and it is important for Turkey to develop indigenous capability and not be completely dependent on other countries for its defense needs.[51] Indeed, the Chinese offer was some $1 billion less than the others, including technology transfer, and a faster delivery timeframe.

Moreover, according to Yoram Evron and Gallia Lindenstrauss at the Tel-Aviv based Institute for National Security Studies, both China and Turkey share complementary interests given current circumstances. Both nations view the American and European refusal to transfer to Turkey manufacturing technology connected to the anti-missile defense system as a way to perpetuate the superiority of the developed nations over the developing nations and leave the latter in a state of dependency.[52] As such, the Chinese offer suits Turkey's desire to develop an independent, technologically advanced defense industry and increase its foreign policy freedom of action, especially in the face of increasingly divergent interests and its policy stance on the Middle East with its NATO allies.

Economic driver for further Eurasian shift – Transatlantic Trade and Investment Partnership (TTIP)?

This then begs the question of whether Turkey is fundamentally shifting away from the West. According to Guvenc of Kadir Has University, a good indicator of whether Turkey will remain tied to the EU and NATO is admission to the TTIP currently being negotiated between the EU and the United States.

Guvenc argues that Turkey is tied to the West based on two pillars. The first is the security pillar tied to NATO and US relations, and the second is the trade/economic pillar tied to EU, including the Customs Union and now TTIP. If Turkey is denied entry into TTIP, this would undermine overall Turkey-EU trade relations, Guvenc warned.

According to Kemal Kirisci at the Brookings Institution, a study by the German Information und Forschung Institute for Economic Research lists Turkey among countries that will experience a net loss of welfare from TTIP, aggravating existing grievances and creating additional pressures on Turkey to break away from the EU and the broader Western liberal order.[53] As Thomas Straubhaar analyzed in the 2013–2014 Transatlantic Academy report, "Liberal Order in a Post-Western World," one consequence of regional agreements is trade diversion from non-members to members. In the short run, he noted, countries that are geographically close to the US or to the EU (with free trade agreements), and countries that have a high trade volume with either economies, would experience trade diversion and loss. Turkey, a close EU neighbor, would lose about 2.5% of its real per capita income –an approximate $20 billion loss of income, based on Turkey's 2012 GDP. This amount is roughly equivalent to the current Turkish trade level with the US[54]

Straubhaar cautions that trade diversion would lead to discrimination against third party countries outside of TTIP, eliciting feelings of unfair treatment in these countries that could culminate in anti-liberal tendencies or even an aversion to the Western economic order.[55] Indeed, Oznur Keles from International Research Organization argued that TTIP is a struggle to protect the supremacy of the Western Bloc against new emerging powers.[56] This view, along with other grievances, helps to explain Erdogan's desire to join the SCO. In face of possible exclusion from TTIP, his economy minister, Zafer Caglayn, further criticized the EU Customs Union as "an agreement of servitude," with Turkey facing greater competition in the EU and its own domestic market, without enjoying preferential access to other markets with whom EU signs free trade agreements (FTAs).[57]

Conclusion: Turkey at a crossroads

Turkey thus appears to be at a crossroads. Already, Erdogan is tilting Turkey towards the SCO and away from the EU and NATO. Guvenc aptly warns that if Turkey is not admitted into TTIP, the economic pillar of Turkey's anchor to the West will collapse and Turkey will shift its axis away from Europe. Nonetheless, the prospects of Turkey joining TTIP in the near term are not encouraging. According to EU Trade Commissioner Karel De Gucht, asked if Turkey would receive preferential treatment under TTIP, he responded that there would be no policy change. He stated that Turkey under the EU-Turkey Customs Union enters into negotiations with EU's FTA partners separately from the EU,[58] while others point out Turkey's failure to fully comply with previous Customs Union Agreements, whereby it would normalize relations and open its ports and airports to Cyprus, as an indicator of its inability to fulfill TTIP standards.[59]

As for the security pillar of Turkey's anchor via NATO, Suat Kiniklioglu, former AKP parliamentary member from the Ankara-based think tank STRATIM, believes the Chinese missile defense deal will not be finalized at this particular juncture, when relations with the US are hanging in a delicate balance.[60] As such, it is still uncertain whether Turkey will remain anchored in the West or join the TTIP.

Notes

1. "A general speaks his mind," *The Economist*, March 14, 2002; Jon Gorvett, "Turkish General Causes Controversy with Call for Turkey to Stop Seeking European Union Membership,," *Eurasianet*, 12 March 2002; Ihsan D. Dagi, "Competing Strategies for Turkey: Eurasianism or Europeanism," *CACI Analyst*, 8 May 2002.
2. Igor Torbakov, "Eurasian Idea Could Bring Together Erstwhile Enemies Turkey and Russia," *Eurasianet*, 17 March 2002; Halil M. Karavelli, "Islamic-Western Embrace Fuels Eurasianism in the Turkish Military," *Turkey Analyst*, 13 February 2009
3. Emel Akcali, Mehmet Perincek, "Kemalist Eurasianism: An Emerging Geopolitical Discourse in Turkey," *Geopolitics*, 1 July 2009.

4. Ihsan Dagi, "Turkey's quest for a Eurasian Union," *Today's Zaman*, 27 January 2013.
5. As of August 2015, Turkey had selected a Chinese firm, but not yet finalized the deal due to NATO's continual objections.
6. Kent E. Calder, *The New Continentalism: Energy and Twenty-First-Century Eurasian Geopolitics* (New Haven: Yale University Press, 2012); Alexandros Petersen, *The World Island: Eurasian Geopolitics and the Fate of the West* (Santa Barbara, CA: Praeger, 2011).
7. Emel Akcali, Mehmet Perincek, "Kemalist Eurasianism: An Emerging Geopolitical Discourse in Turkey," *Geopolitics*, 1 July 2009, pp. 550, 560.
8. Nadir Devlet, "When Russian Eurasianism Meets Turkey's Eurasia,", German Marshall Fund of the United States's *On Turkey*, 8 March 2012, 2. http://www.gmfus.org/publications/when-russian-eurasianism-meets-turkey's-eurasia.
9. *Ibid*, p.3.
10. Ihsan Dagi, "Turkey's quest for a Eurasian Union," *Today's Zaman*, 27 January 2013; Claude Salhani, "Analysis: Eurasianism, an EU alternative?," *UPI*, 22 December 2005; Giray Sadik, "Can Euroskepticism propel Turkey toward Russia?" *Today's Zaman*, 3 March 2013.
11. Ihsan Dagi, *Ibid*.
12. "A general speaks his mind," *The Economist*, 14 March 2002.
13. Halil M. Karaveli, "Islamic-Western Embrace," *Turkey Analyst*, 13 February 2009; Igor Torbakov, 'Eurasian Idea Could Bring Together Erstwhile Enemies Turkey and Russia," *Eurasia Net*. 17 March 2002.
14. Turkish naval officer correspondence with author, 25 January 2014. While the Turkish military largely remains supportive of NATO, there exist factions within the military with an Eurasian orientation. Author discussion with Ozgur Unluhisarcikli, Director of the German Marshall Fund of the United States' Ankara office, Ankara, Turkey on 18 February 2014. However, given the shift in Turkey's defense policy to develop autonomous military production to support unilateral security actions, the Eurasian faction will likely gain additional traction in the face of the growing rift between Turkey and NATO over technology transfer issues as well as divergent Middle East interests.
15. Christian Molling, "Europe without Defence," SWP Comment 38, November 2011, 3; "Defenceless? Austerity is hollowing out Europe's armies," *The Economist*, 21 December 2013; "Needed Reform: The Case of NATO," ISN Comment, ETH Zurich, 11 January 2012.
16. Edward J. Erickson, "Turkey as Regional Hegemon—2014: Strategic Implications for the United States," *Turkish Studies*, Vol. 5, No. 3, Autumn 2004, 31.
17. *Ibid*, p.33.
18. "Japan, Turkey considering co-producing engine for Altay tank," *Today's Zaman*, 18 November 2013. However, Japan shares Germany's restrictions on potential future export licenses for the Altay to third parties such as Azerbaijan, so in March 2014 the deal with Japan fell through and Turkey continues to search for new partners to co-produce the Altay engine. Peter Lee, "Turkey a battleground for Asia arms exports," *Asia Times*, 13 December 2013; Burak Ege Bekdil, "Japan Deal Scrapped, Turkey Looking for Tank Engine,," *Defense News*, 5 March 2014; "Japan Decides Against Turkish-Azerbaijan Tank Deal,," *EurasiaNet*, 28 February 2014; "Turkey & South Korea's Altay Tank Project,,"

Defense Industry Daily, 3 March 2014; "Syrian Conflict Could Win Ankara a Saudi Order for Altay Main Battle Tanks,," *Defense Updates*, 31 May 2013.

19. Selcuk Colakoglu, "Turkish Perceptions of China's Rise," USAK Report No: 39, March 2014, 8.
20. *Ibid*, 12.
21. Dogu Perincek, "Kursat, Pekos Bill'in at usagi olur mu?" *Aydnnlik*, 21 October 2012; Selcuk Colakoglu, *Ibid.*, 12.
22. Selcuk Colakoglu, *Ibid*, 19, 25, 28.
23. Zachary Keck, "Turkey renews plea to join Shanghai Cooperation Organization," *The Diplomat*, 1 December 2013; Daniel Pipes, "Is Turkey leaving the West?" *The Washington Times*, 6 February 2013.
24. "Turkish PM in Iran amid improving relations," *Al Jazeera*, 29 January 2014; David Wagner, "Turkey and Iran's Growing Alliance – Analysis,," *Eurasia Review*, 19 February 2014; Zvi Bar'el, "As Erdogan rebuilds shattered foreign policy, Turkey moves closer to Iran,," *Ha'aretz*, 4 February 2014; Parisa Hafezi, "Turkey's Erdogan visits Iran to improve ties after split over Syria," *Reuters*, 29 January 2014; Olgu Okumus, "Why is Turkey buying more gas than it needs from Iran," *Al-monitor*, 2 February 2014; "Iran-Turkey trade to rise: Erdogan," *Zawya*, 3 February 2014.
25. Bilal Ciplak, "Turkey creates 'Eurasian Law Enforcement Organization of Military Status,," *The Muslim Issue*, 31 October 2013; "Joint Armed Forces of Turkic-Speaking Countries Created,," *Journal of Turkish Weekly*, 29 January 2013; "Turkish World Forms Joint Military Unit," *Turkish Radio and Television Corporation (TRT)*, 26 January 2013; "Turkey delivers security experience to Central Asia via TAKM," *Today's Zaman*, 2 October 2013; Nigar Orujova, "Top officials hold board meeting on Eurasia military association," Azernews, 31 January 2013; "The Association of the Eurasian Law Enforcement Forces with Military Status (TAKM)," http://www.jandarma.tsk.tr/ing/dis/takm/takm_En.htm.
26. Joshua Kucera, "Turkic Countries Create" Joint Armed Forces," *Eurasianet*, 30 January 2013.
27. "New states to join TAKM," *Azeri Press Agency*, 20 February 2013; "Turkey deepens military ties with Central Asia," *The Journal of Turkish Weekly*, 24 January 2014.
28. *Ibid*.
29. "Islamabad-Tehran-Istanbul Line boosts trade in Central Asia," *Railway Pro*, 31 August 2012; Heinz Kramer, "Will CentralAsia Become Turkey's Sphere of Influence?," 1 August 2012, http://sam.gov.tr/wp-content/uploads/2012/01/8-WILL-CENTRAL-ASIA-BECOME-TURKEYS-SPHERE-OF-INFLUENCE.pdf.
30. "Trans-Eurasian Corridor: Turkey and Azerbaijan lead revival of modern Silk 'Rail' Road," *Stratrisk*, 16 December 2013; F. William Engdahl, "China's Land Bridge to Turkey creates new Eurasian Geopolitical Potentials," *Voltairenet*, 23 April 2012; Riza Kadilar & Andrew K. P. Leung, "Possible Turkish-Chinese Partnership on a New Silk Road Renaissance by 2023" *Turkish Policy Quarterly*, Summer 2013; "Turkey realises Ottoman dream with Marmaray Underwater rail link between Europe and Asia," ABC News, 30 October 2013; Thomas Selbert, "Turkey opens its iron 'Silk Road'," *The National*, October 28, 2013; "Turkey's infrastructure: The sultan's dream," *The Economist*, October 26, 2013.

31. "Trans Eurasian Corridor," December 16, 2013; "Tbilisi, Baku see railway completed in late 2014," *New Europe*, February 8, 2013; "Railway to link Kars, Tbilisi, Baku in 2015," *Hurriyet Daily News*, February 24, 2014.
32. "Turkey offers to create the Eurasia Union," *The Railway Insider*, February 24, 2010.
33. "Trans-Eurasian Corridor," *Stratrisk*, December 16, 2013; Can Erimtan, "The New Silk Road: China looks West, Turkey looks East," *RT*, March 19, 2014; Dabvid Gosset, "The Significance of Sino-Turkish Relations," *The Huffington Post*, August 28, 2013; Zan Tao, "An Alternative Partner to the West? Turkey's Growing Relations with China," Middle East Institute, October 15, 2013.
34. Tang Yongsheng, "Actively Promoting Westward Strategy," *Beijing Xiandai Guoji Guanxi*, November 20, 2010.
35. *Ibid.*
36. "China to build Asia-Europe high-speed railway network," *Global Times*, March 8, 2010; Fu Jing, "Re-building the ancient Silk Road," *China Daily*, September 1, 2004.
37. Mu Chunshan, "China and the Middle East,' *The Diplomat*, November 9, 2010. In 2010, its security budget was $87 billion while defense was $84.6 billion; in 2011 security was $99 billion while defense was $95.6 billion; in 2012 security was $111.4 billion while defense was $106.4 billion. "China boosts domestic security spending by 11.5 pct," *Reuters*, March 5, 2012; Leslie Hook, "Beijing raises spending on internal security," *Financial Times*, March 6, 2011.
38. "China seeks further engagement from Turkey in Xinjiang region," *Today's Zaman*, April 1 2012; "Turkey and China Strengthen Relations with Historic Visit," *International Business News*, April 10, 2012; "China's PM says to welcome Turkey industrial zone in Uighur region," World Uyghur Congress, October 10, 2010; "Urumqi to build Sino-Turkish Industrial co-op base," Tianshannet, September 3, 2–11; Julia Famularom "Erdogan Visits Xinjinag," *The Diplomat*, April 14, 2012; Rafaello Pantucci, "Xinjiang: struggle to revive Silk Road," *Financial Times*, September 4, 2012.
39. Author interview with Selcuk Colakoglu, vice president of International Strategic Research Organization, USAK House, Ankara, Turkey, on February 17, 2014.
40. Liu Zhun, "Take fight to ETIM before threat grow," *Global Times*, December 22, 2013.
41. *Washington Post*, November 29, 2011; *People's Daily*, July 6, 2009.
42. "China seeks further engagemenet from Turkey in Xinjiang region," *Today's Zaman*, April 1, 2012.
43. Dogu Perincek, "Kursat, Pekos Bill'in at usagi olur mu?," *Aydinlik*, October 21, 2012.
44. Alan Cowell, "Turkey Turns Its Back on the EU', *The New York Times*, April 3, 2014; "Statement of Stefan Fule on the Blocking of Twitter in Turkey," European Commission, http://ec.europa.eu/commission_2010–2014/fule/headlines/news/2014/03/20140321_En.htm; Semih Idiz, "Erdogan's fractured ties to the West," *Al Monitor*, April 4, 2014.
45. "Who will provide truly democratic leadership for Turkey," *Hurriyet Daily News*, April 5, 2014; "Be merciful, great Sultan," *The Economist*, April 5, 2014
46. Keri Phillips, "Turkey's Erdogan weakened despite win," ABC Radio National, April 1, 2014.

47. Author interview at Kadir Has University, Istanbul, Turkey on February 20, 2014.
48. *Ibid.*
49. "China missile deal 'sign of Turks' frustration with US'," *Hurriyet Daily News*, October 21, 2013.
50. *Ibid.*
51. Author interview at Center for Strategic Research (SAM) in Turkish Ministry of Foreign Affairs, Ankara, Turkey on February 18, 2014.
52. Gallia Lindenstrauss, Yoram Evron, "Is Turkey Swerving Eastward? The Air Defense System Deal with China and the Crisis with NATO," INSS Insight No. 479, October 24, 2013.
53. Kemal Krisci, "Don't Forget Free Trade with Turkey," *The National Interest*, April 15, 2013.
54. K. Kirisci, "Turkey and the Transatlantic Trade and Investment Partnership: Boosting the Model Partnership with the United States," The Brookings Institution (September 2013); Straubhaar, "The Transatlantic Trade and Investment Partnership (TTIP): From Global to Regional Multilateralism" in *Liberal Order in a Post-Western World*, The 2013–14 Collaborative Report of the Transatlantic Academy, April 2014, p.44.
55. Thomas Straubhaar, "The Transatlantic Trade and Investment Partnership," p. 42.
56. Oznur Keles, "Transatlantic Trade Agreement and Turkey," *The Journal of Turkish Weekly*, February 14, 2014.
57. Amanda Paul and Serdar Yesilyurt, "Between a rock and a hard palce: What is Turkey's place in the transatlantic market?" *European Policy Centre*, July 9, 2013.
58. "Answer to a written question – Turkey and the Transatlantic Trade and Investment Partnership (TTIP)," Parliamentary Questions P-008279/2013, August 19, 2013,.
59. Niki Tzavela, "Written question – Turkey and the Transatlantic Trade and Investment Partnership (TTIP)," Parliamentary Questions P-008279/2013, July 10, 2013, http://money-saving4.rssing.com/browser.php?indx=3742317& item=5203
60. Author interview in Ankara, Turkey, on February 18, 2014.

4
The Perception of the 2009 Ürümqi Conflict across the Islamic World

Robert R. Bianchi

The Ürümqi riots of July 2009 were a political earthquake that jolted China's confidence and image, inflicting particular damage on Beijing's deepening ties with the Islamic world. Since then, the bloodshed from Xinjiang's ethnic and religious strife has escalated to the point that China's rulers constantly feel forced to prove that they can protect their own citizens – especially the Han Chinese – at home and around the world. As a result, China increasingly resembles a wounded Colossus – a burgeoning Great Power plagued by internal conflicts despite its looming influence in global affairs.

Because both sides in the Uyghur-Han conflict are aggressors as well as victims, it is difficult to adopt a consistent moral judgment in favor of one group and against the other (Meng and Zhu, 2003). The Han colonize Uyghurs' lands, marginalize their culture, persecute their religion, and monopolize the region's economy (Ruddelson 1997, Millward 2009, Bovington 2010). Uyghur retaliation is increasingly violent, indiscriminate, and far-flung – including suicide attacks against unarmed civilians not only in Xinjiang, but in distant targets such as Kunming, Guangzhou, and the heart of Beijing.

The inherent injustice and brutality of the conflict have split the Han and Uyghur communities in China and paralyzed foreign audiences who want no part of the quarrel. China's ruling establishment is filled with critical voices who argue that force alone will merely enflame ethnic and religious protest (Li 2007, Ma 2010, Liebold 2012). The government's Uyghur opponents realize that terrorism and separatism are hopeless causes that can aggravate their subjugation and hasten their extinction as a people. Neither side has found reliable backing abroad. Uyghurs hear ready expressions of sympathy, but little concrete support for armed struggle and none for independence. Beijing has learned that official endorsements of its territorial claims and anti-terrorist rhetoric are routinely coupled with denunciations of its human rights violations and discriminatory social policies. The global Islamic community is divided just as deeply as China and the rest of the world over the conflicts in Xinjiang. The issues are too complex, the blame is too widely shared, and the solution is too uncertain for Muslim leaders and citizens to rally behind a common position. China is too powerful to be demonized like Israel, India or Serbia. And the Uyghurs are too capable of retaliation to be seen as a vanquished people such as the Palestinians, Kashmiris or Bosnians.

Some of the most intense disagreements over Xinjiang have arisen in Turkey, Pakistan, and Indonesia – the handful of countries where Muslim politicians tried to manipulate the 2009 Ürümqi riots and subsequent conflicts for domestic benefit only to pave the way for diplomatic countermeasures that strengthened Beijing's hand while isolating Uyghur extremists more than ever. In each nation, the ruling coalition eventually agreed that their long-term strategic and economic relations with China were too important to jeopardize even if local voters and media were eager to imagine Xinjiang as a reflection of their own racial and religious passions at home (Bianchi 2013a, 2013b).

Turkey: Recalling the lessons of Timur and Beyazit

Turkey launched the earliest and most aggressive attack on China's suppression of the Ürümqi protests. Prime Minister Recep Tayyip Erdoğan accused Beijing of genocide and threatened to censure China in the United Nations Security Council. In fact, this bitter exchange had surprisingly little effect on Sino-Turkish relations because Turkey quickly abandoned efforts to change the status quo in Xinjiang so that it could win greater economic and diplomatic concessions from China (Mo 2009, Torbakov and Nojenen, 2009, Usla 2009).

By 2009, Turkey had already committed to a major retrenchment of its ambitions in Central Asia after nearly two decades of disappointing efforts to exploit the anticipated vacuum in the former Soviet republics. Just a few months before the Xinjiang riots, it became clear that China and Turkey were making progress on a package of trade, investment, and security agreements that were far more valuable to Ankara than to Beijing. Realizing that economic gains at home required political retreat in Central Asia, Erdoğan's government decided to endorse Chinese policies in Xinjiang and even to curtail the freedom of Uyghur nationalists in Turkey itself.

At the height of Ankara's pan-Turkic enthusiasm in the 1990s, nation-alist leaders thought their leverage might extend all the way to China because of their long association with Uyghur refugees around the world. They did not expect China to react so negatively and so effectively to their unwelcome interest in Xinjiang and its neighbors. Chinese diplomats focused on multiple pressure points where they knew Turkey was vulnerable, steadily increasing the tension until Ankara felt over-whelmed and was forced to admit defeat (Adıbelli, 2008).

The most sensitive issue was China's growing influence with Kurdish leaders in the newly autonomous region of northern Iraq. Chinese oil companies were some of the first international firms to court Erbil as it sought to negotiate production contracts independently of the central government in Baghdad (Cordoba, 2013). By acquiring a foothold in Iraqi Kurdistan, China sent Turkey several messages at the same time.

Chinese companies could not only lock Turkish firms out of Xinjiang and outmaneuver them throughout Central Asia, they could even beat them to the punch in their own back yard where the Turks thought they had an unassailable advantage. Worse yet, China now had direct influence with long-time allies of the Kurdish rebels who were enjoying safe havens just across the border with Turkey. Beijing left no doubt about its intentions – if Ankara encouraged troublemakers in Xinjiang, it could expect to see Chinese-supported Kurds moving into Turkey's southeastern provinces (Adıbelli, 2007).

On the Mediterranean front, China reminded Turkey of its growing leverage in Cyprus and Greece. Ankara was under constant attack in the United Nations (UN) for its military occupation of northern Cyprus and it was desperate to keep China out of the argument. At the same time, the debt-ridden Greek government was inviting China to spend millions of dollars to transform the port of Piraeus into its European shipping hub. Not only was China becoming a virtual neighbor of Turkey, it also was serving as the leading patron of an archenemy that was still deter-mined to settle old scores in Turkish-controlled Cyprus (Smith, 2014).

To the north, China could pressure Turkey in Bosnia and the Balkans. Turkish settlers and refugees from Eastern Europe form powerful constit-uencies throughout Thrace and western Anatolia. They are far more numerous than the descendants of Central Asians and more deeply concerned about the fate of their European relatives than of distant groups that speak Turkic languages they do not understand. For right-of-center politicians, Balkan Turks are particularly important swing voters because they are most concentrated in districts that are strongholds of the secularist parties.

Erdoğan and his right-wing rivals are more likely to attract these voters with racial issues than with religious appeals, but not if Ankara appears impotent in Balkan affairs. China's bitter opposition to the North Atlantic Treaty Organization's (NATO) involvement in the former Yugoslavia made it difficult for Turkish governments to assert influence in the Balkans and it made a mockery of their ambitions in Xinjiang. How could Ankara expect voters to back pro-Uyghur efforts in Xinjiang when China obstructed its efforts to help kinsmen much closer to home? In the Balkans – just as with Iraq and Cyprus – Beijing showed it could punish any incursion into Chinese lands by moving at will on all of Turkey's borders.

A few years after the 2009 riots in Xinjiang, a leading Turkish diplomat told me that Erdoğan's accusations of Chinese genocide reminded him of Beyazit I, the Ottoman Sultan who was trounced by Timur at the Battle of Ankara in 1402. In his opinion, Beyazit was consumed with arrogance – so convinced he would soon surround Constantinople that he ignored his eastern flank and taunted Timur with insults, never imagining that his rival's army could march all the way from Samarkand to defeat the Ottomans and capture the Sultan in his Anatolian heartland (Kinross, 1979, Gibbons, 2013). The Chinese, this diplomat contended, were the modern-day equivalent of three Timurs because they knew how to threaten Turkey from several directions at once. Like Timur, China had taught Turkey's leaders a harsh lesson in humility as well as in geostrategy.

Some of Erdoğan's closest allies grasped these lessons and helped to limit the damage to Sino-Turkish relations. Before and after the Ürümqi protests of 2009, two men ensured that negotiations with China stayed on track – Abdullah Gül, Erdoğan's old comrade in the ruling party leadership, and Ahmet Davutoğlu, the government's chief foreign policy advisor. Thanks to the persistence of Gül and Davutoğlu, Beijing and Ankara made mutual concessions on Xinjiang, allowing them to move rapidly toward major economic deals and even toward military and strategic measures that had seemed inconceivable just a few years earlier.

The turning point was a deft agreement that Turkey would not harbor pro-independence groups from Xinjiang if the Chinese embassy in Ankara would hold regular meetings with Turkish opposition party leaders who would speak on behalf of Uyghur interests (*Haberx.com*, 2010). In an added measure of goodwill, China also pledged to halt all sales of hajj related products to Turkey – particularly travel gear, clothing, prayer rugs, and religious souvenirs – so that local manufacturers could rebuild a lucrative and symbolically important market they had lost to Chinese competition (Becerekli, 2010, *World Bulletin,* 2011a, 2011c).

China coupled political flexibility with economic incentives to convince Turkey that partnership was wiser than confrontation. Beijing's trump card was its huge trade surplus with Turkey and Ankara's urgent desire to offset the burden with new Chinese investments in industry and infrastructure (*Global Times,* 2009, *Türkiye Gazetesi,* 2010). China was eager to expand its economic presence in Turkey because it could serve as a convenient platform for re-exporting Chinese products to the European Union (EU) – where Ankara enjoyed privileged trade access – as well as to the Middle East and Africa (*Dunya Ekonomisi,* 2012, Özyürek and Abbak, 2012). When Turkey received assurances that it could make similar investments in China, including Xinjiang, the bargain was sealed (Parkinson, 2012, *Sunday's Zaman,* 2012).

Eventually, contracts were signed in several other fields, including high-speed railways, nuclear power plants, and clean energy development (Parkinson, 2010, Erol, 2012, Bayraktar, 2012). Many of these deals had been on the drawing board for years, but the most surprising progress came in discussions on military and geostrategic planning – areas where Western powers had long assumed they enjoyed an unassailable priority in Turkey's calculations (*World Bulletin,* 2011b, Barriaux, 2012).

As early as September 2010 – only 15 months after the Ürümqi riots – Turkey invited China's air force to join military exercises that previously had included only NATO and Israeli partners. Turkey decided to bar Israeli participation because of their bitter clashes over the blockade of Gaza, and American pressure prompted many NATO countries to cancel their appearances in sympathy with Israel. In response, Turkey promptly invited China to fill the vacancies, giving the Peoples Liberation Army (PLA) its first opportunity to fly missions outside of its own territory (Pfeffer, 2010, Wolf, 2010). Nearly 60 years after Turkish and Chinese troops had faced off in Korea, their pilots were flying joint missions over Konya. The Turks assured the Pentagon that they would keep the most recent US technology in hangers far from Chinese view, but the psychological impact was irreversible. The speedy growth of Sino-Turkish cooperation stunned the NATO alliance and threatened to upset military balances from one end of Eurasia to the other (Megalommatis, 2008, McCauley, 2009, Feffer, 2010).

In 2013, Erdoğan hinted that he had an even bigger card up his sleeve. In a live television interview, he threw everyone off balance by saying he was ready to forget about the EU if Russia and China invited Turkey to join the Shanghai Cooperation Organization (SCO). Responding to the subsequent uproar, Erdoğan shrugged off the incident, claiming that he was merely describing the teasing sessions he enjoyed with Vladimir Putin. For years, Putin had needled him about Turkey putting up with mistreatment from the EU and getting nothing in return. This time, Erdoğan said, he wanted to give Putin a dose of his own medicine by daring him to make a better offer – an offer everyone knew was premature and perhaps impossible given the difficult Sino-Russian negotiations over expanding SCO membership (*Anadolu Ajansi,* 2013).

Pakistan: mullahs are better than ransom

Unrest in Xinjiang has long strained Sino-Pakistani ties because Beijing believes that Uyghur insurgents operate from bases in northwest Pakistan near the border with Afghanistan. China repeated these accusations with growing intensity after the 2009 Ürümqi riots and in response to subsequent clashes in Xinjiang, Beijing, and Kunming (*Agence France Presse,* 2011, Wines and Walsh, 2012). In addition, China has criticized Pakistani authorities for failing to protect Chinese civilians working throughout the country, particularly near Islamabad where religious radicals held several Chinese hostage and in Baluchistan where tribal insurgents regularly attack and kidnap foreigners building energy-related infrastructure and the new deep-water port at Gwadar (French 2007, *Indian Express,* 2011).

Nonetheless, Chinese and Pakistani leaders realized that history was drawing them closer together and neither side wanted to jeopardize that process. The Obama administration's frustrations in the Afghanistan war led it to push the fighting into Pakistan with catastrophic results for the civilian population and their already negative feelings toward the US (Lakshmanan, 2012). Meanwhile, Washington was tilting more openly than ever toward New Delhi – a strategy that most Asian commentators interpreted as aiming to counterbalance China's growing power (Asghar, 2010, Bajoria, 2010).

In this context, Beijing and Islamabad expected that America's withdrawals from Afghanistan and Iraq would create countless dangers that neighboring countries would have to manage by themselves. For China and Pakistan, the stakes were far greater than the fate of the two war-ravaged semi-colonies of the United States. The same problems that connected China and Pakistan in Xinjiang also pointed to their vital joint interests in the future of a more integrated Eurasia – not only in South Asia, but also in Central Asia and the Middle East (Rahman and Hameed, 2010).

Like the United States, China was often vexed by Pakistan's seemingly intractable disorder and poverty, which made it impossible for any Great Power to protect its citizens abroad. However, because Chinese diplomats placed a higher value on long-term relations with Pakistan, they tried to devise more creative and productive solutions than their American competitors, who focused on safeguarding and extracting their troops instead of improving the lives of the people in the region. Beyond routinely shaming and rebuking Islamabad's security forces, China stepped up its economic assistance and political support at many times that pointedly coincided with America's deepening estrangement from Pakistan and its steady drift toward India.

While most foreign donors focused on shoring up Pakistan's short-term finances, China's aid targeted infrastructure, military hardware, and disaster relief – efforts that encouraged development instead of deeper indebtedness. Many of the showcase projects were explicitly designed to create a transnational transport network connected to Xinjiang. From the Himalayas to the Arabian Sea, Chinese engineers led work on highways, railways, dams, pipelines, and ports, all destined to spur the flow of energy and trade throughout China and Central Asia (Haider, 2005 a, Khan, 2009, MacDonald, 2011).

Gwadar was to become a key hub bringing Persian Gulf oil and gas overland and easing China's exposure to long maritime routes and chokepoints dominated by the US Navy (Zeng. 2009, Singh. 2013). For both China and Pakistan, the combined economic and military benefits justified the huge costs and dangers that constantly plagued their efforts (Itamar Lee, 2009, Bokhari and Hille, 2011). When Baluchi nationalists ratcheted up campaigns of sabotage and kidnapping, Beijing and Islamabad blamed American and Indian intelligence agencies for the violence (Escobar, 2009). The Afghanistan war had thwarted America's ambitions to build pipelines connecting the Caspian Sea with India while excluding both Iran and China. Many Pakistanis believed that the US was venting its frustrations on their country and deliberately undermining its plans to profit from opening direct links for trade between Iran and China (Haider, 2005b, Kaplan, 2009).

As US-Pakistani relations deteriorated, China strengthened its military ties with Islamabad (Bokhari, 2011, Perlez, 2011). They started a joint venture to build fighter jets and coordinated operations near disputed territories along their borders with India (Harrison, 2010). When Washington agreed to support India's nuclear power development, Beijing offered to build more reactors in Pakistan (Mirza, 2010, Ahmed, 2010, Haniffa, 2011). The inter-Asian arms race surged to higher levels as New Delhi tested new long-range missiles – dubbed "China killers" – and touted its rapid naval build-up as proof that India had become a Pacific power (*Daily Times*, 2010, Deen, 2010, Patranobis, 2012).

The perception of common enemies encouraged Beijing and Islamabad to contain their disagreements as much as possible, but it did not remove the threats to Chinese citizens in either Xinjiang or Pakistan. Sporadic attacks on terrorist camps near the Afghanistan border and against Baluchi insurgents failed to end the problem. Eventually, Chinese leaders realized that the official channels would never be able to deliver the security they demanded. Quietly, the Chinese embassy began to try a more direct approach to local religious groups with ties to outlaws and dissidents that the government could not reach (Peter Lee, 2009).

Of course, much of the anti-Chinese violence was motivated not by religion, but by ethnic and nationalist grievances or by simple extortion. Nonetheless, China saw multiple benefits in cultivating some of Pakistan's mainstream mullahs and preachers. China could show that, in contrast to Pakistan's Western and Indian critics, it was an Islam-friendly country – indeed that it was an integral part of the Muslim world.

At the same time, Beijing hoped that capitalizing on the prestige of cooperative religious leaders would help to ward off kidnappings in Pakistan and discourage deviant teachings in China. When Chinese citizens were threatened, Pakistani preachers were asked to intercede on their behalf. Several Pakistani scholars were invited to China to teach in Islamic schools and the previously banned Jama'at Tabligh was allowed to resume its work in several Hui communities (Ali, 2009).

Beijing's security problems – both foreign and domestic – pushed it to ever growing displays of its capabilities for rescue and deterrence. These were aimed at multiple audiences, signaling both defensive and offensive powers. From this perspective, China's growing global reach created greater vulnerabilities which, in turn, justified nationalistic demands to project stronger military force.

Somali pirates paved the way for Chinese warships to launch regular patrols in the Indian Ocean and the Persian Gulf. Libyan rebels set the stage for a grand airlift and naval rescue of 30,000 Chinese citizens that rushed PLA assets to the Mediterranean and placed them on Europe's doorstep. A rising tide of attacks on overseas Chinese has swept across Asia, Africa, Europe, and Latin America, creating a compelling argument that China's military presence needs to catch up with its sprawling commercial and security interests (Duchâtel and Gill, 2012). Ironically, China's hard-line American critics have encouraged its military expansion by complaining about Beijing's supposed free-riding on the global security that Western nations provide at their own expense.

Indonesia: Muslim power and the overseas Chinese

In the aftermath of the 2009 Ürümqi riots, the most chilling threats against China came not from terrorists or religious fanatics but from a mainstream Muslim politician in Indonesia. Din Syamsuddin was the leader of Muhammadiya, Indonesia's second largest Islamic movement with over 30 million members throughout the archipelago. He accused Beijing of "ethnic cleansing" in Xinjiang and implied that such crimes could provoke attacks against Chinese citizens in Indonesia (Widhi, 2009).

Syamsuddin and other Muslim leaders deliberately avoided specifying whether they were referring merely to mainland citizens carrying PRC passports or to the nearly ten million overseas Chinese who were native-born Indonesians (*indonesiamatters.com*, 2009). The ambiguity quickly raised the specter of the anti-Chinese riots during the final months of Suharto's rule in 1998 and, more ominously, the mass bloodbath of 1965 in which thousands of Indonesians of Chinese descent were murdered because they were accused of conspiring with Communist insurgents.

A major row with Jakarta would have been even more threatening to Beijing's interests than the spats with Ankara and Islamabad. Turkey and Pakistan were China's overland gateways to Europe and the Middle East, but Indonesia stood squarely astride China's maritime lifeline – the crowded and narrow sea lanes connecting the Pacific and Indian Oceans (Sukma, 2009a, Laksmana, 2011). In addition, Indonesia was the decisive voice in the Association of Southeast Asian Nations (ASEAN), which had emerged as the regional broker for Great Power competition throughout the Western Pacific (Hadi, 2010, Pattiradjawane, 2010). Indonesia would shape any proposal for settling the territorial disputes that were breaking out between China and its neighbors and for creating a wider Asian security community that might try to balance China against rival powers, including the US, Russia, Japan, and India (Sukma, 2009b).

When the Ürümqi riots erupted, Indonesia's Chinese community was enjoying a commercial and cultural renaissance after decades of isolation and discrimination under Suharto. Their family-run firms were more integrated than ever into the vast network of overseas Chinese businesses that ran Asia's financial hubs and linked them to mainland China (Suryadinata, 2006). Chinese festivals were celebrated openly for the first time in years and the once-banned Chinese language was making a comeback in print and electronic media. Coming from one of Indonesia's most powerful Muslim politicians, Syamsuddin's remarks put all of this at risk, threatening to turn back the clock to Cold War days of conflating Chinese heritage with disloyalty (Suryadinata, 2008, Glionna, 2010).

Beijing wisely responded to Syamsuddin as though he was an opportunist rather than an old-fashioned racist and anti-Communist. Everyone knew that he was no friend of the US, notwithstanding his doctorate from the University of California, Los Angeles (UCLA). Indeed, he was famous for his long-running feud with the American government, which he regularly described as anti-Muslim because of its accusations that Indonesia was coddling Islamic terrorists (Martin, 2007).

Like other Muhammadiya leaders before him, Syamsuddin tried to represent the grievances of Muslim businesses that were battling what they viewed as unfair competition from foreign multinationals and from the well-connected Chinese firms they often preferred as partners in Indonesia. Muhammadiya had considerable success in lobbying Jakarta for preferential treatment to Muslim entrepreneurs, but they were frightened that the new ASEAN-China free trade agreement would decimate that vulnerable constituency (Amirrachman, 2007).

Bearing such political and commercial interests in mind, Beijing could pragmatically approach Muhammadiya and its followers not as enemies, but as rent-seekers or would-be tributaries. Accordingly, China set out to defuse tensions with Indonesia's Muslims through a combination of economic incentives and cultural diplomacy.

China is probably the only country in the world capable of tackling Indonesia's massive needs for rapid infrastructure development. Indonesian planners are eager to integrate the internal markets of the largest islands where overland transport and communications are often dilapidated or non-existent. Such integration requires a level of capital, technology, and commitment that Jakarta has never obtained from its long-time trading partners in Japan, the US, or Europe. China, in contrast, has offered to undertake many of the most costly projects because it regards Indonesia's resources, markets, and goodwill as indispensible to its own prosperity and security. Hence, there was little surprise when Beijing increased its already impressive loans and trade benefits after the incidents in Xinjiang (Baskoro and Bisara, 2010, Bisara and Agustiyanti, 2012).

Responding directly to the fears of weaker Muslim businesses, China also carved out several exemptions for Indonesian producers in the regional free trade agreement that was due to take effect in 2010 (*Jakarta*

Globe, 2010, Safrina 2010, Fung 2011). Smaller firms were temporarily protected from tariff reductions. Most of them qualified for adjustment loans during the early years of the treaty. And several received long-term supply contracts with Chinese state enterprises, including special procurement deals with the PLA for uniforms and non-combat equipment (Blake, 2010, Ekawati, 2010).

Beijing also launched several initiatives to identify China's history and culture with Indonesian Islam. The Chinese embassy sponsored a grand exhibit in Jakarta showcasing Islamic arts from China, including a wide assortment of manuscripts, calligraphy, and hajj memorabilia. (Hew, 2009, *Purwoko*, 2010) Chinese scholars and media celebrated the role of Zheng He, the Muslim admiral who commanded the 15th-century armadas of the Ming emperor that sailed from the Pacific to the Persian Gulf and on to East Africa (Marsahid, 2013, Karsono, 2010).

Zheng He and his Chinese crews were described as some of the earliest bearers of Islam in Indonesia. Their descendants were traced to well-known communities of Chinese Muslims who had lived for centuries in Surabaya and other coastal cities (Lombard and Salmon, 1994, Kong, 2008). Historians in China and Indonesia increasingly portrayed the Islamization of Southeast Asia as a complex blending of Chinese, Arabian, and Indian influences. Zheng He has become a multivalent icon of China's solidarity with Afro-Asian peoples and the Islamic world, but he enjoys a special role as a patriarch of all Chinese Indonesians – Muslim and non-Muslim alike. In this narrative, Islam will help to unite Chinese and Indonesians in the future as Communism once divided them in the past (Muazkki, 2010, Zhuang, 2011).

China has benefitted greatly from its sensitivity to Indonesia's growing influence in regional and global affairs (Darusman, 2010, Padden, 2010, Raslan, 2010). Indonesian diplomats have repeatedly foiled Washington's efforts to participate in negotiations on maritime disputes between China and ASEAN member states. Indonesia continues to balance Great Power ambitions in the Pacific, avoiding formal alliances while steadily leading ASEAN's economic integration with mainland China (Laksmana, 2010, Brown, 2011). This sort of diplomatic hedging suits China's interests admirably because it encourages a fluid, multipolar international order instead of an American-dominated Pacific or a return to the treaty blocks of the Cold War. Hence, China can credibly claim to uphold the Western Pacific status quo in principle while gradually expanding its influence in practice (Goh, 2008, Laksmana, 2009).

Common techniques of damage control – and their diminishing returns

In dealing with the fallout of the Xinjiang protests, Chinese leaders used three interrelated approaches that helped to steady and improve their relations with Turkey, Pakistan, and Indonesia. In each case, they recognized grievances and offered compromises to ameliorate them. They also tried explicitly to identify China with the Islamic world, either as a sister civilization or as an integral member. In addition, they shrewdly distinguished or combined the issues of race and religion, depending on the apparent demands of the circumstances.

Chinese diplomats seldom discussed Xinjiang in a vacuum. Even when they blamed others for contributing to the violence, they offered attractive incentives for isolating Uyghur nationalists. In Turkey, they even agreed to discuss China's domestic problems with foreigners as long as the conversations were private and limited to Xinjiang. Whenever possible, Beijing found important economic grievances that it could address as trade-offs for sympathizing with its predicament in Xinjiang. China also stressed the wider geopolitical perspective, treating each country as a key member of an emerging global order that would improve its status and well-being.

China's negotiators made concrete efforts to identify with Islam as a civilization and to disavow accusations that Beijing was hostile to any world religion. Every package of incentives included symbolic religious measures that were calculated to produce lasting emotional effects – deference to the hajj, respect for religious scholars, shared artistic traditions, even kinship with the earliest Muslim missionaries. The more China portrayed itself as a Muslim-friendly country, the more it could cast the Uyghur protestors as separatists and extremists who were pressing ethnic and nationalist demands instead of as pious victims defending their religion and traditions.

The Chinese emphasized racial identities when they thought doing so would strengthen their case. In Turkey, they portrayed the Uyghurs as only remotely connected to the people of Anatolia, especially compared with Muslims in the Balkans. In Indonesia, the Chinese highlighted common Muslim ancestors and touted China as a source of Southeast Asian Islam. In Pakistan, however, China focused on common religious concerns, arguing that Pakistani scholars could help to elevate Islamic learning and practice in China itself (Ali, 2009).

All of these damage-control efforts are being rapidly overtaken by mounting eruptions of carnage in Xinjiang and their reverberations in all corners of China. No amount of nimble and shrewd diplomacy can end the bloodshed that shocks China's citizens at home and disgraces them around the world. The spillover from Xinjiang threatens to aggravate many other festering ethnic divisions – not only in Tibet and Inner Mongolia, but also among the Chinese-speaking Hui Muslims that Beijing depicts as the loyal face of a domesticated and nationalist Islam (Iredale, Bilik and Guo, 2003, Jia and Mi, 2007). Nor can the party-state count on support from the over-stressed Han majority (Wei, 2010, Blanchard, 2011). Increasingly divided by social inequality and disillusioned by corruption, why would they stand by a fractured police state that cannot even protect their families in schools and clinics or in markets and train stations?

The party, police, and army cannot agree on effective remedies for Xinjiang's troubles – just as they can't agree on the root causes. The muscular approach continues the centuries of conquest, rebellion, and re-conquest, viewing the province as a perpetual war zone that China's rulers must subdue and repopulate lest their enemies turn it against them (Forbes, 1986, Millward, 1998). The developmental approach imagines Xinjiang as a global crossroads that makes China more than the sum of its parts while linking it to continents far beyond (Tian, 2008, Fisher, 2009, *The Economist,* 2011).

The fatal flaw of the developmental strategy is that it remains just another form of colonization. Uyghurs and other Muslim inhabitants might survive as diminished minorities in their homelands, but they cannot share in the vision of a modern and multi-cultural society that Beijing advertises (Cao, 2010, Gladney, 2009, Zang, 2012). The marginalized non-Han residents of Xinjiang see a future of apartheid disguised as ethnic pluralism – and for the most desperate among them, that is a reason to expand the zone of battle to all of China.

Festering Sino-Turkish tensions and the Arab spring

Repeated flare-ups of violence in Xinjiang and their repercussions throughout China have put greater strains on Sino-Turkish relations. More than any other country, Turkey retains the most abiding involvement in Uyghur affairs and suffers from the greatest contradiction between popular and official attitudes toward China. For a few years, the Arab Spring and challenges to the blockade of Gaza gave Turkey and China an unexpected cooling off period in which Middle Eastern conflicts overshadowed Central Asian geopolitics. Erdoğan garnered enormous popularity by engaging in constant quarrels with Israel and by identifying with Arab aspirations for democracy (Al- Marzuqi, 2010, Shadid, 2011, Samir, 2012).

From Ankara's perspective, these Middle Eastern arenas appeared far more promising and less costly than earlier run-ins with China and Central Asian governments who had accused Turkey of pursuing pan-Turkist and pan-Islamic agendas (Tuğal, 2012, Pantucci, 2015). In Turkey, pro-Uyghur causes were eclipsed by the AK Party's electoral victories in 2011 and Erdoğan's successful campaign to assume the Presidency in 2014. Annual commemorations of the "East Turkestan Ürümqi massacres", anti-China hackers pasting Turkish flags on Chinese websites, and nationalist politicians' complaints during public visits to the Chinese embassy – all these continued, but with less and less fanfare (HaberVakti, 2010, Haberx, 2010).

However, Erdoğan's triumphs were short-lived. As president, he quickly found himself fighting off challenges on several fronts at the same time: from the fallout of long civil wars in Syria and Iraq, from more defiant Kurdish groups in the southeastern provinces, and from new waves of secularist and leftist protests in the major cities (Grunstein, 2011, Manthorpe, 2012, Shafak, 2013). Before long, Xinjiang returned to the crisis list as well.

In 2014, police in Thailand announced that they had rescued hundreds of Chinese Uyghur refugees who had fallen into the hands of human traffickers after fleeing the deepening violence in Xinjiang. Turkey and China traded accusations and insults over their plight, with Ankara claiming they were victims of racial and religious persecution who should be given asylum in Turkey and Beijing insisting they were fugitives who should be extradited to China for interrogation and trial (Martina, 2014). Bangkok rejected both countries' demands and kept most of the Uyghurs in Thai custody. Nonetheless, several refugee families managed to enter Turkey and resettle in Kayseri. Before long, the Uyghur detainees in Thailand began a hunger strike to attract international attention to their cause (HaberVakti, 2015, Gerin, 2015).

These quarrels opened the door for Rebiya Kadeer to return to center stage, aggravating old ulcers in Ankara and Beijing alike. Kadeer is the head of the World Uyghur Congress that China accused of organizing the 2009 Ürümqi protests and many other incidents. She claimed that Turkish diplomats were dragging their feet in the refugee matter, pretending to stand up for the Uyghurs while intentionally doing nothing that might antagonize the Chinese. Kadeer charged that for years Turkish leaders had made many promises to China about expelling

Uyghur activists, restraining pro-Uyghur demonstrations, and barring her from her "second homeland" in Turkey (Elveren, 2014).

Now, she asked, why was Turkey's government stalling over a few hundred Xinjiang refugees while accepting tens of thousands from other countries such as Syria, Iraq, Palestine, Libya, and Somalia? "If Turkey is taking in so many Syrians because they are Muslims," she said, "then Turkey should lend a helping hand to the Uyghurs, who nobody looks after, because they are both Turks and Muslims." (Elveren 2014) Kadeer's accusations resonated widely in Turkey, particularly in Central Anatolia where Erdoğan's party is most vulnerable to rival right-wing parties with a long history of pan-Turkist and anti-China activities (Milli Gazete, 2010). Just as Ankara and Beijing were looking forward to a decade of cooperation in building a "New Silk Road" traversing Eurasia and linking London with Shanghai, both countries were again locked in prolonged and bitter exchanges over Xinjiang's Uyghurs (Ermintan, 2014).

The current stand-off over the Xinjiang refugees illustrates the inherent weakness of the tacit Sino-Turkish strategy of indefinite damage control. Diplomats on both sides want to improvise formal exchanges that will allow their leaders to fend off criticism from ultranationalists at home while conducting business as usual on every other issue. Xinjiang's eruptions are growing in frequency and magnitude. But Ankara and Beijing are just beginning to realize that the Uyghurs' predicament jeopardizes their own destinies, particularly their grand vision of Eurasian integration.

References

Adıbelli, Barış (2007). "Kürt liderlerin Çin'le flörtü" (Kurdish leaders flirtation with China), *Radikal*, July 4.
Adıbelli, Barış (2008). "Türkiye'nin Avrasya politikası çöktü!" (Turkey's Eurasia policy has collapsed!), *Radikal*, August 16.
Agence France Presse (2011). "Pakistan vows to work with China on terror: Xinhua", August 31.
Ahmed, Issam (2010). "China-Pakistan deal raises fears of nuclear proliferation", *Christian Science Monitor*, July 1.
Al-Marzuqi, Munsif (2010). Erdoğan Hadha al-Za'im al-'Arabi al-Muntazir ("Erdoğan: the Arab Leader We've Been Hoping For"), *al-Jazeera*, June 5.
Ali, Zulfiqar (2009). "Jamaat to preach Islam in China, says Qazi", *Dawn*, April 4.
Amirrachman, Alpha (2007). "Din Syamsuddin: A Man to Watch", *Jakarta Post*, July 11.
Anadolu Ajansi (2013). "Şangay Beşlisi'ne Alın, AB'yi Unutalım" (Take Us into the Shanghai Cooperation Organization and We'll Forget About the E.U.), January 25.
Asghar, Nauman (2010). "Moving closer: the development of Sino-Pakistani ties has been shaped by regional geopolitical dynamics", *The News*, July 10.

Bajoria, Jayshree (2010). "Interview with Andrew Small on Intensifying China-Pakistan ties", *Council on Foreign Relations*, July 7.

Barriaux, Marianne (2012). "Turkey PM oversees nuclear agreements with China", *Agence France Presse*, April 9.

Baskoro, Faisal Maliki and Dion Bisara (2010). "There is both happiness and concern about a commitment by China to invest more in Indonesia's infrastructure", *Jakarta Globe*, June 27.

Bayraktar, Arıf (2012). "Çin'le üç günde 4,3 milyar dolarlık anlaşma" (4.3 Billion Dollar Deal With China in Three Days), *Zaman*, February 23.

Becerekli, Uğur (2010). "Diyanet'ten Çin'e çalım: Hac malzemeleri yerli olacak", (A blow from the Religious Affairs Directorate to China: hajj accessories will be locally produced), *Sabah*, June 24.

Bianchi, Robert R. (2013a). "China-Middle East Relations in Light of Obama's Pivot to the Pacific", *China Report*, November .

Bianchi, Robert R. (2013b). *Islamic Globalization: Pilgrimage, Capitalism, Democracy, and Diplomacy*. Singapore and London: World Scientific Publishers.

Bisara, Dion and Agustiyanti (2012). "Experts weigh in on Indonesia's infrastructure needs", *Jakarta Post*, January 19.

Blake, Chris (2010). "Small-scale Indonesian garment factories among biggest losers in free trade with China", *Jakarta Globe*, April 26.

Blanchard, Ben (2011). "China says lessons to learn in Xinjiang from Mideast unrest", *Reuters*, March 8.

Bokhari, Farhan (2011). "With U.S. military aid cut, Pakistan eyes China", *CBS News*, July 10.

Bokhari, Farhan and Kathrin Hille (2011). "Pakistan turns to China for naval base", *Financial Times*, May 22.

Bovington, Gardner. 2010. *The Uyghurs: Strangers in Their Own Land*. New York: Columbia University Press.

Brown, Jessica (2011). "Jakarta's juggling act: balancing China and America in the Asia- Pacific", *Foreign Policy Analysis* (Australia), February 3.

Cao, Huhua (2010). "Urban-Rural Income Disparity and Urbanization: What Is the Role of Spatial Distribution of Ethnic Groups? A Case Study of Xinjiang Uyghur Autonomous Region in Western China", *Regional Studies*, October.

Cordoba, Armando (2013). "China Looks to Kurdistan as Growing Oil Partner", *rudaw.net*, July 29.

Daily Times (Pakistan) (2010). "Beijing will 'never give up' Islamabad: Wen", December 19.

Darusman, Taufik (2010). "A northern paragon", *Jakarta Globe*, April 25.

Deen, Thalif (2010). "China: 'Pakistan is our Israel'", *al-Jazeera*, October 28.

Duchâtel, Mathieu and Bates Gill (2012). "Overseas Citizen Protection: A Growing Challenge for China", *Stockholm International Peace Research Institute*, Februrary 12.

Dunya Ekonomi (2012). "Türkiye Çin üssü oluyor" (Turkey is Becoming China's Base), September 19.

Ekawati, Arti (2010). "Indonesian furniture makers mapping out strategy for China", *Jakarta Globe*, May 20.

Elveren, Muammer (2014). "Turkey Should Look After Uighur Turks in Thailand, Says Head of Uighurs", *Hürriyet Daily News*, December 22.

Ermintan, Can (2014). "The New Silk Road: China Looks West, Turkey Looks East", *RT News*, March 19.

Erol, Osman (2012). "Çin ile Türkiye arasında milyar dolarlık enerji anlaşmaları imzalandı" (Million Dollar Energy Agreements Signed between China and Turkey), *cihan.com*, April 10.

Escobar, Pepe (2009). "The shadow war in Balochistan", *Asia Times Online*, June 4.

Feffer, John (2010). "Stealth superpower: how Turkey is chasing China in bid to become the next big thing", *TomDispatch.com*, June 13.

Fischer, Andrew (2009). "Why economic boom failed to prevent unrest in Xinjiang", *ftchinese.com*, July 23.

Forbes, Andrew D. W. (1986). *Warlords and Muslims in Chinese Central Asia: a political history of Republican Sinkiang 1911-1949*. Cambridge University Press.

French, Howard W. (2007). "Letter from China: mosque siege reveals the Chinese connection", *New York Times*, July 12.

Fung, Esther (2011). "Wen pledges more trade with Indonesia, Malaysia", *Wall Street Journal*, April 30.

Gerin, Roseanne (2015). "Uyghur Refugees Go on Hunger Strike in Thai Detention Center", *Radio Free Asia*, January 22.

Gibbons, Herbert Adam (2013). *The Foundation of the Ottoman Emprire: A History of the Osmalis Up to the Death of Bayezid I 1300-1403*. Routledge.

Gladney, Dru (2009). "Uighurs and China's social justice problem", *China Digital Times*, July 18.

Glionna, John M. (2010). "In Indonesia, 1998 violence against ethnic Chinese remains unaddressed", *Los Angeles Times*, July 8.

Global Times-Xinhua (2009). "Chery to start Turkey plant construction by year end", October 12.

Goh, Evelyn (2008). "Power, Interest, and Identity: Reviving the Sinocentric Hierarchy in East Asia", *Asia Policy*, July.

Grunstein, Judah (2011). "Turkey and the Arab Spring", *World Politics Review*, May 6.

HaberVakti (2010). Çin Sitelerini Kuşattılar ("They Shut Down Chinese Wesbsites"), July 15.

HaberVakti (2015). Çin Zulmünden Kaçan 500 Uygur Türkü Kayseri'de ("500 Uyghur Turks Who Fled Chinese Oppression Are in Kayseri"), January 15.

Haberx.com (2010). "BBP Genel Sekreteri Destici, Çin Büyükelçiliği 1. Müsteşari Junzheng ile Görüştü" (BBP General Secretary Destici Speaks with Chinese Embassy First Deputy, Junzheng), June 24.

Hadi, Syamsul (2010). "Engaging the dragon: the dynamics of Indonesia-China relations in the post-Soeharto era", *Indonesian Social Science Review*, vol. 1, no. 1.

Haider, Ziad (2005a). "Baluchis, Beijing, and Pakistan's Gwadar port", *Georgetown Journal of International Affairs*, Winter/Spring.

Haider, Ziad (2005b). "Sino-Pakistan relations and Xinjiang's Uighurs: politics, trade, and Islam along the Karakoram highway", *Asian Survey*, July-August.

Haniffa, Aziz (2011). "U.S.-Indian bonhomie driving Pakistan deeper into China's arms", *Rediff.com*, April 19.

Harrison, Selig S. (2010). "China's discreet hold on Pakistan's northern borderlands", *New York Times*, August 26.

Hew, Wai-Weng (2009). "Marketing the Chinese face of Islam", *Inside Indonesia*, December 1.

Indian Express (2011). "After pointing fingers, China lauds Pak coop against terror", August 3.

indonesiamatters.com (2009). "Chinese Uyghurs and Xinjiang province riots", July 16.

Iredale, Robyn, Naran Bilik, and Fei Guo (2003). *China's minorities on the move: selected case studies*, M.E. Sharpe.

Jakarta Globe (2010). "China trade deal fix levels playing field for Indonesians", April 6.

贾东海 与 米娟婷, 新世纪西部边疆民族宗教问题对中国民族关系的影响, 社科纵横, 2007 年 2 月, 第 2 期 (Jia Donghai and Mi Juanting (2007). "The religious problem of western border nationalities and its influence on China's nationalities relations in the new century", *Social Sciences Review*, no. 2, February.)

Kaplan, Robert (2009). "Pakistan's fatal shore", *The Atlantic*, May.

Karsono, Ong Mia Farao (2007). "Chinese tradition practices by the Chinese Muslim community of Surabaya", *Humanity and Social Sciences Journal*, no. 2.

Khan, Hamayoun (2009). "President Zardari's fourth trip to China", *Institute of Strategic Studies, Islamabad*, August.

Kinross, Lord (1979). *Ottoman Centuries: The Rise and Fall of the Turkish Empire*. Harper Collins.

Kong, Yuanzhi (2008). "On the Relationship between Cheng Ho and Islam in Southeast Asia", *Kyoto Review of Southeast Asia*, August.

Lakshmanan, Indira A.R. (2012). "Obama increases Pakistan drone strikes as relations sour", *Bloomberg*, June 8.

Laksmana, Evan A. (2009). "Indonesia's pivotal role in the U.S.'s grand strategy", *Jakarta Post*, October 6.

Laksmana, Evan A. (2010). "Indonesia's dance with the titans", *Today Online* (Singapore), March 27.

Laksmana, Evan A. (2011). "Dimensions of ambivalence in Indonesia-China relations", *Harvard Asia Quarterly*, Spring.

Lee, Itamar (2009). "Deepening Naval Cooperation Between Islamabad and Beijing", *China Brief*, June 24.

Lee, Peter (2009). "Taliban Force a China Switch", *Asia Times*, May 6.

李先荣 (2007). 新疆周边民族宗教问题对新疆的影响, 民族宗教, 2007 年, 第 3 期 (Li Xianrong, "The influence of nationality and religious problems in the Xinjiang periphery on Xinjiang", *Nationalities and Religion*, no. 3).

Liebold, James (2012). "Toward a Second Generation of Ethnic Policies?" *China Brief*, July 7.

Lombard, Denys and Claudine Salmon (1994). "Islam and Chineseness", *Indonesia*, 57 April.

Ma, Rong, (2010). "The Soviet Model's Influence and the Current Debate on Ethnic Relations", *Global Asia*, June 22.

Manthorpe, Jonathan (2012). "Arab Spring Awakens Kurdish Dreams of Autonomy", *Vancouver Sun*, August 2.

Martina, Michael (2014). "China Rebukes Turkey for Offer to Shelter Uighur Refugees", *Reuters*, November 28.

MacDonald, Myra (2011). "China-Pakistan-Afghanistan building economic ties", *Reuters*, April 27.

Marsahid, Choirul Mahfud (2013). The Role of Cheng Ho Mosque: The New Silk Road Indonesia-China Relations in Islamic Cultural Identity

66   *Robert R. Bianchi*

Martin, Di (2007). "Indonesia: Leadership Candidate Warns West is to Blame for Terrorism", *Australian Broadcasting Corporation*, October 8.
McCauley, Martin (2009). "China and Turkey increase their military cooperation: what is behind it?" *Stirring Trouble Internationally*, April 23.
Megalommatis, Muhammad Shamsaddin (2008). "The Asiatic landmass and the geo- strategic alliance between China and Turkey", *American Chronicle*, Sep. 21.
孟建国 与 朱建 (2003). 新疆地区的跨文化交际问题 – 有关维吾尔族与汉族交往的一份问卷调查与分析，新疆教育学院学报，2003 年 3 月，第 1 期 (Meng Jianguo and Zhu Jian, "Cross-cultural communication problems in the Xinjiang region – a survey and analysis of Uighur and Han contacts", *Journal of Xinjiang Education Institute*, no. 1, March).
Milli Gazete (2010). Kayseri Mazlum Der'den Çin Zulmüne Protesto ("Kayseri Human Rights Association Protests China Oppression"), July 14.
Mo, Lingjiao, (2009). "Turkey, another axis of evil!?" *Global Times*, July 10.
Millward, James (1998). *Beyond the pass: economy, ethnicity, and empire in Qing Central Asia, 1759-1864*. Stanford University Press.
Millward, James (2009). *Eurasian crossroads: a history of Xinjiang*. Columbia University Press.
Mirza, Nusrat (2010). "Pak China atemi mu'ahada" (Pak-China nuclear agreement), *Daily Jang*, July 9.
Mo Lingjiao (2009). "Turkey, another axis of evil?" *Global Times*, July 10.
Muzakki, Akh (2010). "Ethnic Chinese Muslims in Indonesia: an unfinished anti-discrimination project", *Journal of Muslim Minority Affairs*, vol. 30, no. 1.
Özyürek, Musa and Betül Abbak (2012). "Niğde'de Çin'in üretim üssü oluyor" (Niğde Becomes a Production Base of China), *Milliyet*, September 12.
Padden, Brian (2010). "Some Indonesian Islamic groups prefer China over America", *Voice of America*, April 1.
Pantucci, Raffaello (2015). "Central Asia: The View From China", *European Union Institute for Security Studies*, January 23.
Parkinson, Joe (2010). "Turkey, China shun the dollar in conducting trade", *Wall Street Journal*, October 8.
Parkinson, Joe (2012). "Minister says 'Door's open' to Chinese banks in Turkey", *Wall Street Journal*, February 22.
Patranobis, Sutirtho (2012). "Beijing's enemies are Islamabad's enemies: Pakistan PM", *Hindustan Times*, April 2.
Pattiradjawane, Rene L. (2010). "Doktrin Natalegawa: Indonesia dalam Politik Globalisasi" (The Natalegawa Doctrine: Indonesia in Political Globalization), *Kompas*, May 5, 2010
Perlez, Jane (2011). "China gives Pakistan 50 fighter jets", *New York Times*, May 19.
Pfeffer, Anshel (2010). "Growing ties between Turkey, China, Iran worry Israel and U.S.", *Ha'aretz*, October 7.
Purwoko, Krisman (2010). "Pameran Islam Cina pererat hubungan Indonesia-Cina" (Exhibit ofChinese Islam strengthens Indonesia-China relations), *Republika,* July 20.
Rahman, Khalid and Rashida Hameed (2010). "Sino-Pak Relations and Xinjiang: Writings of Pakistani Scholars", *Institute of Policy Studies, Islamabad*, February 4.

Raslan, Karim (2010). "Shanghai love letter", *Jakarta Globe*, May 5.

Rudelson, Justin Jon (1997). *Oasis Identities: Uyghur nationalism along China's silk road*. Columbia University Press.

Safrina, Magda (2010). "Indonesia-China relations: rethinking trade policy", *Jakarta Post*, April 5.

Samir, Salwa (2012). "Erdogan's Enthusiatic Visit to Cairo", *Egyptian Gazette*, November 18.

Shadid, Anthony (2011). "In Riddle of Mideast Upheaval, Turkey Offers Itself as an Answer", *New York Times*, September 26.

Shafak, Elif (2013). "The View From Taksim Square: Why Is Turkey Now In Turmoil?", *The Guardian*, June 3.

Singh, Abhijit (2013). "Gwadar: A New 'Pearl' or a Step in China's 'March West'?", *World Politics Review*, February 11.

Smith, Helena (2014). "Chinese Carrier Cosco is Transforming Piraeus – and has eyes on Thessaloniki", *The Guardian*, June 29.

Sukma, Rizal (2009a). "Indonesia-China relations: the politics of re-engagement", *Asian Survey*, July/August.

Sukma, Rizal (2009b). "A post-ASEAN foreign policy for a post-G8 world", *Jakarta Post*, October 5.

Sunday's Zaman (2012). "Turkey-China ready to strengthen already close ties", February 5.

Suryadinata, Leo, ed. (2006). *Southeast Asia's Chinese businesses in an era of globalization: coping with the rise of China*. Singapore: Institute of Southeast Asian Studies.

Suryadinata, Leo, ed. (2008). *Ethnic Chinese in contemporary Indonesia*. Singapore: Chinese Heritage Center and Institute of Southeast Asian Studies.

The Economist (2011). "Let them shoot hoops: China's turbulent west is unlikely to be calmed by plans for economic development", July 30.

Tian, Robert Guang (2008). "Xinjiang and its role in greater Central Asian regional economic cooperation", *Central Asia and the Caucasus*, no. 1.

Torbakov, Igor and Matti Nojonen (2009). "China, Turkey, and Xinjiang: a frayed relationship", *Australia.to*, July 31.

Tuğal, Cihan (2012). "Democratic Janissaries? Turkey's Role in the Arab Spring", *New Left Review*, July-August.

Türkiye Gazetesi (2010). "Çinli tekstilcinin ağlaması sadece timsah göz yaşı" (Chinese textile producers are merely crying crocodile tears), July 15.

Uslu, Emrullah (2009). "Are China's Uyghurs operating an al-Qaeda network in Turkey? Ankara and Beijing discuss cooperation against terrorism", *Terrorism Monitor*, October 1.

Wei, Shan (2010). "Comparing Ethnic Minorities and Han Chinese in China: Life Satisfaction, Economic Well Being and Political Attitudes", *East Asia Policy*, April–June.

Widhi, Nograhany (2009). "Din Syamsuddin: Kerusuhan di Xinjiang Genosida, Pelanggaran HAM Berat" (Din Syamsuddin: The Riot in Xinjiang is Genocide, a Grave Human Rights Violation), *news.detik.com*, July 12.

Wines, Michael and Declan Walsh (2012). "China says wanted militants use nearby countries to stage attacks", *New York Times*, April 6.

Wolf, Jim (2010). "China mounts air exercise wih Turkey, U.S. says", *Reuters*, October 8.

World Bulletin (2011a). "Chinese Muslims can attend Islamic schools in Turkey", February 17.

World Bulletin (2011b). "China to launch Turkey's first intelligence satellite in December," June 6.

World Bulletin (2011c). "Turkey signs cooperation deal with China's Islamic Association", June 22.

Zang, Xiaowei (2012). "Age and the cost of being Uyghurs in Ürümchi", *China Quarterly*, June.

曾祥裕 (2009). 巴基斯坦瓜达尔港对国际安全态势的影响 (Zeng Xiangyu, "The Influence of the Gwadar Port on International Security"), *South Asia Studies Quarterly*.

Zhonghua.yuku.com (2009). "Chinese-Indonesian Muslims criticize China over Urumqi unrest", July 10.

庄吴斌(2011). 印尼华人回教徒 - 摄影画册 (Zhuang, Wubin. *Chinese Muslims in Indonesia*. Select Books).

5

China's Dual Diplomacy: Arab Iraq and the Kurdistan Region

Mohammed Shareef

Iraq's foreign relations consist of three major intersecting loops – the East, the West, and international institutions. The first circle of Iraq's interactions deal with neighbouring, regional, and eastern powers, China being Iraq's most important trade partner in the Eastern hemisphere. Iraq is also influenced by its relations with the Western powers – especially the United States, which has the greatest leverage with Iraq. Finally, Iraq interacts with international institutions.

Iraq has always aspired to an active foreign policy within the international community. The Saadabad Pact in 1937 and the Baghdad Pact created in 1955 are testimony to this role.[1] Iraq was one of the founding members of the United Nations in 1945, OPEC was established in Baghdad in 1960, and Iraq was also a founding member of the Non-Aligned Movement in 1961. Baghdad historically asserted its role as a Middle Power, that is, as a potentially "system-affecting" state; it is not able to influence major powers alone, yet can have an impact if allied with a group of other nations pursuing similar interests. During the monarchy (1921–1958) Iraq was mostly restricted by the Anglo-Iraqi treaties of 1922 and 1930 in which Baghdad's foreign relations were guided from London. As for the republican post-monarchy military rule from 1958 onwards, Iraq's foreign relations were characterized by a tendency to largely dissociate from the West and embrace an Arab nationalist and pan-Arab agenda. This tendency continued under the ruling Baath Party up to the toppling of Saddam Hussein during the US-led invasion in 2003. The Baath Arab Socialist Party subscribed to a pan-Arab nationalist ideology with a socialist agenda. It was established in Syria by Arab nationalist Michel Aflaq. The ideology behind the party was the unification of all Arabs and the return of Arabs to their former glory and freedom from Western influence. However, after 2003

Iraq's foreign relations reverted to a broader international outlook and an appetite for enhanced relations with all regional and international powers.[2] After Saddam's overthrow, the West re-emerged as an important foreign player in the new Iraq even though successive governments in Baghdad were cautious not to be seen as too pro-Western – thus lacking sovereignty –it is within this conceptual framework that Iraqi relations with China developed.

Iraq is both influenced by and contributes to a rapidly changing Middle East, especially so after the Arab Spring that started in December 2010. In order to revive Iraq as an effective and healthy actor in the international system, a competent foreign policy has to be achieved. As foreign policy is an extension and reflection of domestic policy, Iraq will need to tackle many obstacles to achieve this goal: primarily the settlement of its domestic instability, largely a consequence of its geopolitical location and population structure, and ultimately the regaining of sovereignty over its national territory. The radical Islamist organization known as the Islamic State (IS) that captured and controlled huge parts of northwestern Iraq in June 2014 is only one of several extra-governmental groups to which Iraq has lost territory since 2003. Geopolitically, Iraq arguably enjoys a strategic location; however, it is also geographically flawed. It is an almost landlocked country surrounded on six sides by states that are, on most occasions, hostile to Iraq's interests. Moreover, as a result of Saddam's occupation of Kuwait in 1990, Iraq suffered a great blow in terms of isolation and marginalization on the world stage. Additionally, the impact of the sanctions on Iraq's infrastructure was hugely detrimental to its progress. Therefore, re-establishing healthy international relations has been indispensable in order to emerge as a prosperous, influential, and respected actor in the international community. Establishing good relations with neighbouring, regional, and East Asian powers, especially China, which this chapter highlights, is only one of the many tasks. Maintaining healthy relations with European powers and the US are also objectives, as well as achieving influence in international institutions.

This task, however, is a major challenge for an Iraq fragmented along ethnic (Arab and Kurd) and sectarian (Sunni and Shi'a) lines. Iraq entered a new phase of international politics on 9 April 2003 when United States-led coalition forces toppled the Baath regime. When the US civil administrator in Iraq Paul Bremer handed over sovereignty on 28 June 2004 to a weak interim government, security and economic difficulties were only two of the many problems the Iraqi government faced. During this time, Chinese state-owned oil companies seized the opportunity, showing a willingness to play by the new Iraqi government's rules and to accept lower profits to win contracts.[3]

The new Iraq, post–Saddam Hussein, was faced with huge debts, regional and international isolation, and external scepticism. For this reason, the Chinese were welcome: the Iraqi government needed investment, especially in the oil sector, as oil remained at the heart of the political and economic future of the Iraqi state. States define their foreign policy interests according to and in large part based on their economic interests and energy interests, so the Chinese also needed Iraq. The US did not interfere in Iraq's attempts at reviving its economy and the oil sector behind it. This inadvertently opened up Iraq to many international players, including China.[4]

China, with its consumption on the rise, became the world's largest oil importer in 2013. To this end, China made energetic moves to expand its role in Iraq through both Arab Iraq and the Kurdistan region. For this reason, gaining a foothold in Kurdistan became an aspect of China's foreign and economic policy. However, Baghdad was increasingly opposed to oil companies that cut separate deals with Iraq's semiautonomous Kurdistan region. Essentially, Iraq incorporates two political entities: a Shi'a dominated Arab Iraq and an increasingly independent Kurdistan region, each with its own distinct approach in its dealings with China, which is the focus of this study.

China's Policy toward the Middle East

China's policy toward Iraq is part of its Middle East policy, an important part of Chinese foreign policy at the global level. China's policy in the Middle East has a number of goals. First, China wants to maintain a positive image and reputation in the Arab world, which it generally attempts to do with people and countries where it has mutual interests, especially in third world and developing countries, including those in the Arab world.[5]

Second, China wishes to secure a continued supply of oil and gas, particularly from the Persian Gulf, to help meet China's vast energy needs.[6] The Middle East region is one of the greatest sources of energy in the world, and China's increasing levels of industry are directly dependent on energy supplies.[7]

China is the world's second largest economy after the United States; it is also the world's second largest consumer of oil, consuming 11.1 million barrels per day (MBD). However, although it is also the fourth largest producer of oil (4.19 MBD), accounting for 4.7% of world production, China is also the world's top importer of oil, having over-taken the United States in 2013, as previously mentioned.[8]

For China, Iraq is one of several countries it increasingly relies on to keep its growing economy running. With China's consumption constantly growing, it is investing heavily in oil and gas fields around the world – 157.5 billion US dollars (USD) between 2005 and 2014 alone.[9] Over 50% of China's oil imports come from the Middle East, even though imports from Iran have been reduced in recent years as a consequence of the sanctions.[10] China's third objective is to diversify its sources of energy, as it is acutely conscious of the security of supply.[11] China's fourth foreign policy objective lies in continued trade and economic partnership with the Arab world, especially as a major market for Chinese goods.[12]

Finally, and most importantly, the Chinese Communist Party's (CCP) legitimacy and continuity rests on continued economic growth, its domestic modernization programs and the ability to deliver a rising standard of living for the Chinese population.[13] The continued growth of the Chinese economy is regarded as a necessity rather than a luxury and requires the development of economic relations with various countries, including those in the Middle East and the Arab world.[14]

China's Strategy in the Middle East

In order to achieve its goals in the Middle East, China subscribes to a host of strategies. Since the 2003 US intervention in Iraq, China has become more active in pursuing a counter-encirclement strategy against perceived US hegemony in the Middle East. China believes that Washington's Middle East strategy entails advancing the encirclement of China and instituting regime change against undemocratic states, which implicitly challenges CCP legitimacy at home.[15]

To confront this perceived US strategy, China has embarked on the construction of a new twenty-first century Silk Road, a network of pipes, roads, and railways extending from China to Central Asia and the Middle East. It has also changed its defensive posture from coastal defense to far seas defense.[16] Both follow from the fear of possible suffocation and obstruction of its energy supply lines; their vulnerability is most visible at the Strait of Malacca, where US blockades may occur. The strait is the main shipping channel between the Indian Ocean and the Pacific Ocean and about a quarter of all the world's oil carried by sea, mainly from the Persian Gulf, passes through the strait.

The second Chinese strategy is to actively pursue good relations with all Middle Eastern states and refrain from involvement in Middle Eastern disputes. Another Chinese strategy is that it has neither the intention nor the capability to challenge the role of the US in the Middle East. The Chinese leadership avoids any confrontation with the US; it also coordinates with the US in various issues so as to keep Sino-US relations stable. To this end, it has been China's strategy not to contribute militarily to regional stability and security in the Gulf/Middle East region to avoid infringement on US domination of the area. Furthermore, as a developing power, China finds itself still short of strength and the means to participate more fully in Middle East affairs. The US Fifth Fleet and air force are the major security guarantors of the gulf region and international energy supplies.[17] Although China is a major economic competitor with the US, ironically it benefits heavily from free riding and US protection in the Persian Gulf.

China's tactics in the Middle East

China pursues pragmatism (i.e., deals with unsavoury regimes) to meet its energy demands. China also provides other services in addition to oil production, such as building roads and other infrastructure that the host nation may not be able to provide. The prime goal of China's state-owned oil companies is not profit but simply to procure more fuel for China's growing economy. This situation gives them a competitive advantage over all the other commercial international oil companies. Notably, the Chinese are not complaining: unlike the executives of Western oil giants like ExxonMobil, Chevron, or Total and others, the Chinese happily accept the strict terms of Iraq's oil contracts, which yield only minimal profits. China is more interested in energy to fuel its economy than profits to enrich its oil companies. Chinese companies do not have to answer to shareholders, pay dividends, or even generate profits. They are tools of Beijing's foreign policy of securing a supply of energy for its increasingly prosperous and energy-hungry population.[18]

China's policy toward Iraq

For China, oil supply is a major consideration. Since the 2003 American-led invasion of Iraq, that country has become one of the world's top oil producers. In 2014, Iraq was the second-leading contributor to global oil supply growth, behind only the United States,[19] and China is now one of its biggest customers (see Table 5.1). The Chinese

Table 5.1   Chinese oil imports from Iraq (Post-Saddam, 2004–2014)

Year	Kilograms of Oil	Value / USD
2004	1,306,510,611	312,552,121
2005	1,170,434,115	388,086,536
2006	1,045,842,405	463,109,182
2007	1,412,107,915	690,304,357
2008	1,860,079,990	1,311,305,919
2009	7,162,811,054	3,306,284,126
2010	11,237,565,209	6,272,767,556
2011	13,773,637,131	10,438,936,463
2012	22,075,200000	15,745,924,800
2013	22,892,800000	16,329,107,200
2014	31,831,000000	21,054,000,000

Note: Data obtained from the annual report produced by the Iraqi Embassy in Beijing in late 2014 covering up to the end of 2014.[30]

are the biggest beneficiary of this post-Saddam oil boom in Iraq. China needs energy and wants to get into the market.[20]

The Chinese had nothing to do with the 2003 Iraq invasion, but from an economic standpoint they are benefiting from it. Chinese state-owned oil companies seized the opportunity, pouring more than 2 billion USD a year and hundreds of workers into Iraq. Just as important, China is willing to play by the new Iraqi government's rules and to accept lower profits to win contracts.[21] China has even built its own airport, in the desert near the Iranian border, to ferry workers to Iraq's southern oil fields. PetroChina opened its special airport on 7 January 2015 in the Kahala area to assist with work on the Hilfaya oilfield.[22] There are plans to begin direct flights from Beijing and Shanghai to Baghdad.[23]

If the US invasion and occupation of Iraq ended up benefiting China, the unforeseen turn of events is not unfavorable to US interests either. The increased Iraqi production, much of it pumped by Chinese workers, has shielded the world economy from a spike in oil prices resulting from Western sanctions on Iranian oil exports. A second US interest is also served, as oil gets produced and Iraq makes money.[24] And, although China is a major beneficiary of postwar Iraq, a diminished American role would be perceived even more favorably by the Chinese, as it would increase China's ability to further penetrate the country.[25]

China is eager to reduce superpower influence in Iraq. Because of China's skepticism concerning the US-led invasion of Iraq, it was not until February 2014 (ten years after the invasion) that China's foreign minister Wang Yi visited Baghdad, the most senior Chinese official to do so since the US intervention.

China's interests in Iraq could also help stabilize the country as it faces a growing sectarian conflict.[26] Although China does not have political objectives in Iraq, China's oil interests help develop close links between China and Iraq. As China is heavily involved in Iraq, it has a stake in assuring the continuity of the regime that facilitates its investments.

China has a major competitive advantage over Western oil companies working in Iraq. The Iraqis appreciate that the Chinese, unlike many Western oil companies, are willing to accept service contracts at a very low per-barrel oil fee without the promise of rights to future reserves, while private oil companies need to list oil reserves on their books to satisfy investors demanding growth. An additional advantage is that the Chinese do not have to answer to shareholders.[27] The investment necessary in Iraq's oil sector has required contracting the services of foreign oil companies that are not always enthusiastic about Iraq's nationalistic, tight-fisted terms or the unstable security situation that can put employees' lives in danger. Life insurance is also a major issue for the Western oil companies – it is very costly to buy coverage for their employees.[28]

Some companies, like Statoil of Norway, have left or curtailed their operations. Furthermore, the Chinese do not interfere in local issues. China takes a pragmatic position. It does not interfere in the politics or religion of Iraq, which the Iraqi government appreciates.[29]

Apart from oil, the Chinese have other import interests. The private purchase of sulphur by Chinese businessmen annually is in the region of half a million USD. Dates are another commodity that China consumes, at the rate of approximately 2.5 million USD per annum.[31]

Furthermore, the consumption of Chinese manufactured goods is another major objective. Though China is happy with its active presence in Iraq's oil sector, it pushes for investment opportunities in other areas (besides the oil sector) that strict Iraqi investment laws deny; it wants to substitute contracts for investment opportunities and participate in Iraq's development projects.[32]

In terms of economic and trade relations, Iraq is the third largest Arab trade partner with China after Saudi Arabia and the United Arab Emirates (UAE) (see Table 5.2); and the fifth largest supplier of oil to China at the global level. Iraq accounts for 10% of Chinese oil imports.[33] Imports from Iraq for 2014 reached 21.054 billion USD and are predicted to rise over the coming years (see Table 5.3). In 2014, China bought nearly a third of the oil that Iraq produced, nearly 850,000 barrels a day.[34] In

Table 5.2 Rise in import rates between China and Iraq

Total Billions USD	Imports from Iraq Billions USD	Imports from China Billions USD	Year
5.1	3.3	1.8	2009
9.865	6.275	3.589	2010
14.268	10.443	3.824	2011
17.570	12.660	4.910	2012
24.870	17.970	6.900	2013
30.259	23.159	7.100	2014

Note: A growth rate of 97% is shown in Iraqi imports from China in 2014 compared with 2010, and a 269% growth rate in Chinese imports from Iraq in 2014 compared with 2010 is also shown. Data obtained from the annual report produced by the Iraqi Embassy in Beijing in late 2014 covering up to the end of 2014.[36]

Table 5.3 Substantial increase in trade between China and Iraq

Total USD billions	Imports from Iraq USD billions	Imports from China USD billions	Year
0.056	0.00032	0.056	2003
30.259	23.159	7.10	2014

Note: Increase in volume of trade between China and Iraq since the toppling of Saddam Hussein's regime. Data obtained from the annual report produced by the Iraqi Embassy in Beijing in 2014 covering to the end of 2014.[40]

2014, China was the largest importer of Iraq's crude oil, followed by India and the United States.[35]

Following the toppling of the Baath Regime, as a gesture of good will, a substantial amount of Iraq's debts owed to China incurred by Saddam Hussein's regime were cancelled in a memorandum of understanding signed in 2007: 2.85 billion USD of governmental debts were written off, as well as 80% of 8.48 billion USD owed to Chinese companies only to be repaid in installments over a period of 17 years from 2010 onwards.[37]

With regard to furthering economic and cultural relations, China re-established consular relations by reopening its consular and visa services in Baghdad in December 2012. In 2013 alone, 24,000 visas were issued to Iraqis – which included businessmen, students, tourists, and individuals seeking medical treatment. Iraq also purchases weaponry from China; so far several contracts have been signed to procure military hardware from China.[38] Additionally, two major contracts were signed with Shanghai Electricity and the China National Machinery Import and Export Corporation (CMC) in 2008 and 2011 to build new thermal and steam power stations, in the provinces of Wasit and Salahaddin, which will boost electricity supplies in Iraq.[39]

China's policy toward Kurdistan

China's policy toward the Iraqi Kurds is part of China's overall policy on Iraq, which is part of China's policy towards the Middle East, which in turn is part of Chinese foreign policy at the global level. China's firm support for Arab anti-imperialism, anti-colonialism, and national independence movements won widespread acclaim around the Arab world and also in Kurdistan, which was in an armed struggle against Baghdad. It was during this period that China established diplomatic relations with Iraq on 25 August 1958. China had sent a letter recognizing the new revolutionary republic on 16 July 1958, almost immediately after the overthrow of the pro-Western Iraqi monarchy; it was the first step in establishing diplomatic ties between the two sides.[41] On 27 April 1960 Abdulhaq Fadhil, the first Iraqi ambassador to China, submitted his diplomatic credentials in Beijing.

China is now making assertive moves to expand its role, as Iraq is increasingly at odds with oil companies that have cut separate deals with Iraq's semiautonomous Kurdish region.[42] China's increasing involvement with the Kurds is motivated by several interests. First, they are used as leverage against Turkey, which still hosts Uyghur separatist activists and organisations. Since the mid-1990s, Beijing has been applying pressure on Ankara to curb Uyghur separatist activity in its territory. Fully aware of the Kurdish issue in Turkey's domestic politics and foreign policy, Beijing could use its relations with the Kurds, who claim southeastern Turkish territory, as leverage against Ankara. Beijing uses Uyghur and Kurdish separatism, implicitly threatening that if Ankara continues to support Uyghurs, Beijing will support the Kurds. Alluding to the Kurds, during President Jiang Zemin's visit to Turkey, he commented that both countries were faced with the task of protecting national unity and territorial integrity and both opposed all kinds of international terrorism, national separatism, and religious extremism.[43]

A second policy objective is for China to outflank the US in Iraq by gaining a foothold in the Kurdish north.[44] Third, and most important, Beijing is interested in Iraqi Kurdistan's rich oilfields in order to diversify its oil supplies. Sinopec, the largest of China's three state owned oil giants, paid 8.9 billion USD to purchase the Swiss-Canadian firm Addax, which had holdings in the Kurdistan region of Iraq.[45] According to official sources in the Kurdistan Regional Government (KRG), Iraqi Kurdistan is estimated to have approximately 45 billion barrels of oil reserves, the sixth largest in the world.[46] Finally, China's Kurdish policy does not mean that the Chinese are interested in Iraq's disintegration, hoping to benefit from a new and independent Kurdish state. Rather, in addition to unleashing regional instability that would be detrimental to China's interests, Kurdish independence would encourage other separatist movements (notably the Uyghur and the Tibetan). On the other hand, Kurdish dependence on the "new" Iraq would surrender complete control over the north (and its oilfields) not only to Baghdad but, furthermore, to Washington, which would not be in China's interest.[47]

Thus, the existing situation in northern Iraq, with increased Kurdish autonomy within a weak Iraqi state, is optimal for Beijing's interests and conforms to its views on limited self-determination.[48] This position parallels China's own attitude towards domestic issues regarding self-determination. China dismisses Baghdad's objections to bilateral Sino-Kurdish relations as it is aware that Iraq is fragmented and weak, and is conscious that Arab Iraq needs China at the political and economic level. The Chinese government knows that Iraq is unstable and in transition with security conditions constantly changing on the ground, allowing it the luxury of enhanced interaction with the Kurdish region.

Ironically, Beijing's overtures towards Iraqi Kurdistan, which it treats almost as an independent nation, undermine its own policies and contradict its own principles on separatism. In no way would Beijing permit another country to treat China's Uyghurs, Tibetans, or Mongols likewise: to sympathise publicly with their plight, invite their leaders, send delegations, hold negotiations, or sign agreements with them behind Beijing's back.[49]

China seeks better relations and trade with Iraq's Kurdistan region, particularly in the oil sector. Kurdistan is officially autonomous, but foreign relations predominantly remain the prerogative of the Iraqi national government in Baghdad, so the Kurds' dealings with China are handled through both the dominant Kurdish political parties and the Kurdistan Regional Government. The main oil fields in northern Iraq lie in the Kirkuk Province, over which the Kurds have *de facto* control since 11 July 2014, as a result of the IS incursion into Mosul on 10 June 2014 the concurrent, sudden collapse of the Iraqi army. The Kurds seek to incorporate Kirkuk into Kurdistan formally; however, Kirkuk is officially outside the autonomous Kurdistan region, and this potential inclusion of Kirkuk within the official borders of the KRG is a matter that increasingly draws China towards Kurdistan.

Kosrat Rasool Ali, deputy secretary general of the Patriotic Union of Kurdistan (PUK), who led a PUK delegation to Beijing in October 2005, stressed that the visit was at the invitation of the CCP, an invitation extended to the PUK leadership during a visit to Kurdistan in May 2005. According to Kosrat, the Chinese addressed two issues during the visit: first, to mend fences with Iraq and the Kurds after having been previously staunch supporters of Saddam Hussein, and second, to increase trade opportunities for China.[50] Senior Kurdish leader Nawshirwan Mustafa (coordinator general of the Gorran movement) explained that the Chinese were trying to redress and reset their diplomatic relations with Iraq, a consequence of China's close ties to Saddam. Nawshirwan stated that the Chinese specifically wanted oil and telecommunications contracts, but also other wide-ranging trade and business opportunities with Kurdistan.[51] In April 2014, another delegation from the CCP visited the Kurdish capital of Erbil at the invitation of the Kurdistan Democratic Party (KDP); the main purpose of the visit was to improve bilateral Sino-Kurdish relations. The visit was reciprocated by a delegation from the KDP to China two months later. The PUK, which is dominant in Sulaimani, and the KDP, which runs Erbil and Dohuk, are actively promoting trade and investment, with some success. Kurdistan is significantly more secure than most of Iraq, and between them, the PUK and KDP have been firmly in control of the Kurdistan region since October 1991, thanks to the protection of the US-UK northern no-fly zone until 2003. The autonomy of the Kurdistan region is now legally and internationally recognised, a fact acknowledged by China, enshrined initially in the Transitional Administrative Law (the temporary constitution adopted after Saddam's overthrow in 2004) and then the permanent constitution embraced in a national referendum in October 2005.[52]

Iraq's Policy toward China

The Iraqi government needs oil investment, as oil remains at the heart of its economy. The oil sector provides about 95% of its national revenues,[53] and the Iraqi government depends on these revenues to finance its military and social programs. During his visit to Beijing in July 2011, the very first by an Iraqi prime minister, Nouri al-Maliki stressed the importance of Chinese investments in Iraq and called for the two sides to expand cooperation in such fields as oil and gas, electricity, transportation, housing, telecommunications, and agriculture.[54] In 2014, Iraq was OPEC's second largest oil producer after Saudi Arabia with oil production at 3.5 MBD. The Iraqi Oil Ministry has projected the country's export capacity to reach 7 MBD by the end of 2017;[55] Iraq has also set in place an ambitious plan for oil production to reach 9 MBD by 2020.[56] Iraq estimates that its oil fields, pipelines, and refineries need 30 billion USD in annual investments to reach production targets that will make it one of the world's premier energy suppliers for decades to come. Chinese state-owned companies have already invested 10 billion USD in Iraq.[57] The substantial revenue this investment would produce could possibly help reduce tensions between Kurds, Shi'as, and Sunnis if equitably distributed. China's interest in Iraq could help stabilize the country as it faces a growing or even worsening sectarian conflict as those competing camps fight over the spoils.

Iraq knows that China is an important and influential power in the international system. Thus, it wants to gain China's support as a permanent member of the UN Security Council as well as China's favorable influence on friendly East Asian states allied to the People's Republic of China. Iraq is also acutely conscious of maintaining a balance between the West and the East and the negative impact the 2003 US invasion has had on China's perceptions of the country as a US puppet state. China is also actively encouraged by the Iraqi government to have greater involvement in Arab Iraq. A major reason for this encouragement is Iran's excellent relations with China in consequence of its animosity towards the West, and Shi'a-ruled Iran's influence on the Shi'a-dominated government in Baghdad. For this reason, Iraq wants China's active participation and involvement in its rebuilding; and, in order to maintain healthy relations with China, Iraq supports the One-China policy. Iraq's relations with China, however, are mostly restricted to economic and trade relations.

China is Iraq's top trading partner. Imports by Iraq from China for 2014 were 7.1 Billion USD, the total volume of trade between the two countries amounting to 30.259 billion USD in the same year. Two major Chinese oil companies, CNPC and CNOOC, were awarded Service Contracts by the Iraqi government to develop the Iraqi oil sector; PetroChina is involved in the development of the Rumaila field and is the operator of the Halfaya and Al-Ahdab fields, while CNOOC operates the Missan oilfield.[58]

Chinese telecommunications giants Huawei and ZTE are largely responsible for the Iraqi telecommunications sector; the Chinese are also heavily involved in sanitation and water treatment through CGGC in the Province of Wasit. Iraq is the largest importer of Chinese manufactured electrical appliances in the Middle East. In terms of consular relations, in 2012, 4,000 visas were issued to Chinese workers and businessmen. By 2013 there was a 150% increase to 10,000 visas issued;[59] this increase excludes visas issued to Chinese businessmen granted at the Iraqi embassy in Abu Dhabi. This number, however, has declined in 2014 as a result of the security situation in Iraq, a consequence of the IS incursions deep into Iraqi territory.

In the field of cultural relations, China wants to increase exchanges and advocate dialogue with the Arab world. Since cultural ties are an important factor towards the advancement of Sino-Arab relations, China pays great attention to cultural exchange and cooperation with Arab countries and has already signed agreements on cultural cooperation. China has agreed to open a branch of the Confucius Institute in Baghdad to encourage the teaching of the Chinese language and culture. Iraqi higher education authorities are also planning to arrange the enrollment of Chinese undergraduate students to study the Arabic language.[60]

Mutual visits within the framework of these agreements and plans are increasing; official and private cultural exchanges are on the rise and so are projects of cultural cooperation with the Arab region of Iraq. China has held several large-scale and comprehensive cultural events such as the "Quanzhou and the Silk Road on the Sea Cultural Festival" in Fujian Province, "Chinese Culture Expo in North Africa," and "China Cultural Week in the Gulf." There are currently 150 Iraqi postgraduate students in China, 30 of them on scholarships awarded by the Chinese government, and 5,000 Iraqi residents (businessmen and students with families), in addition to 3,000 non-resident Iraqi businessmen.

Most of these Iraqis are based in the major commercial and financial centers, including Shanghai, Beijing, Wuhan, and Shenzhen. Moreover, the majority of the Chinese companies are based in Arab (central and southern) Iraq in joint ventures, as stipulated by strict Iraqi law.[61]

Kurdistan's policy toward China

From a purely political perspective, a key reason for Middle Eastern interest in communist China was Maoism and its solidarity with Third World countries that had or were under various degrees of colonial and Western domination. The Kurdish liberation movement, a major component of the Middle East struggle, was no different from the larger Middle East struggle, and so was naturally influenced by the same parameters. Recognizing that the Soviets had already sponsored the Iraqi Communist Party's (ICP) shift towards an Arab nationalist agenda in Iraq, and in light of Anglo-American misconceptions about the KDP's leftist and Marxist tendencies, some KDP politburo members thought that there was a critical need to find new allies with interests in the Middle East. Communist China hence became a natural choice.

It was at this time that Jalal Talabani – a member of the KDP's Politburo – raised the possibility of striking an alliance with Maoist China. In his 1955 visit to China, the young and energetic Marxist Talabani, a leading figure in the Kurdish revolution, was very impressed with Mao Zedong's "People's War," translated and reinterpreted as revolutionary warfare in the mountains against the dictatorship in Baghdad. The KDP's expectations and preparations for the Kurdish people's war as a result of the rise of pan-Arabism in Iraq was inevitable.[62] The KDP's relations with the ICP were generally tense. There were two major reasons for this. First, both political parties were highly competitive, with the ICP having a relatively large following among the Kurds, especially the educated middle class. Second, the ICP's emphasis on Iraqi nationalism and its rejection of Kurdish nationalism and separatism infuriated the KDP.

With the emergence of the Sino-Soviet split in the early 1960s, Sino-Soviet ideological polemics divided the leftist movement in Iraq. And when Jalal Talabani and some of his comrades split from the KDP on 7 July 1964 he led the left-wing splinter group (although still claiming to be KDP), which subscribed to Maoist ideology; from that date until the late 1980s they openly upheld Mao Zedong's philosophy and opposed the Soviet Union and the United States in their competition for influence in Iraq.[63] Talabani's Maoism was a Marxism-Leninism with an oriental agricultural outlook, different than the Marxism-Leninism based on the rise of Western industrialism later subscribed to by Ocalan's PKK (Kurdistan Workers' Party). Talabani was, essentially, a major advocate of Maoism in the 1960s, when the debate between Beijing and Moscow culminated in the ideological split of the international communist movement. Not only was he an early promoter of Maoism within the ranks of his faction of the KDP, but he also later played a leading role in setting up the PUK.

Founded in Damascus in June 1975, the PUK brought three Marxist groups together: Talabani's Maoist – "General Line," the Marxist – "Toilers League," chaired by Nawshirwan Mustafa, and the Socialist – "Revolutionaries," led by Fuad Masum. Essentially a Maoist group became one of the major components of the PUK and the generator that powered the 1976 armed resistance movement in Iraqi Kurdistan.[64] However, this perspective no longer holds sway in the Kurdistan Region due to several factors. Communism's decline at the international level following the collapse of the Soviet Union has left them with little political clout, so for the Kurds to pursue them as an ally of their liberation movement was impractical. And from a pragmatic point of view there was little to gain from Russia. The late Mullah Mustafa Barzani spent almost 12 years in exile in the Soviet Union (1947–1958); this legacy still remains part of the KDP psyche. Nevertheless, the "Red Mullah," as some in the West came to call the late Barzani, is something the KDP does not want to recall or associate with. Maoism was not popular among Iraqi communists as the communist model they were emulating was the one in Moscow not Beijing, and the prime reason the leftist faction within the KDP and later Talabani himself pursued Maoism was to find a new patron for the Kurdish cause. The Kurdish liberation movement was predominantly framed by pragmatism and concern for its higher cause, in other words the objectives of the Kurdish liberation movement and not ideological differences.

The outlawed Turkish Revolutionary Peoples Liberation Party – Front (DHKP/C) also subscribes to Maoism, but the party, although supporting Kurdish nationalist rights, is far too weak and small to have any influence on the Turkish political stage. The other outlawed pro-Kurdish Turkish communist party is the Marxist-Leninist Communist Party (MLKP). As for the legal Turkish Communist Party (Turkiye Komonist Parti), it is a hugely chauvinist and anti-Kurdish rights party. However, the Turkish leftist orientated Peoples' Democratic Party (HDP) is favorable towards Kurdish nationalist rights in Turkey and has good relations with the major political parties in the Kurdistan Region of Iraq.

After the toppling of Saddam Hussein, in August 2003 Jalal Talabani, now secretary general of the PUK and a member of the interim Iraqi Governing Council under the US-led occupation, visited China. He visited China again, as the first Iraqi Kurdish head of state, arriving in Beijing in June 2007, the very first visit to China by an Iraqi president since the two countries forged diplomatic ties in 1958.[65] President Talabani had always taken pride in his lifelong "special" history that linked him to the Chinese; as president, he took an even keener interest in the relationship with China. He successfully lobbied to appoint Dr. Mohammed Sabir Ismail, his brother-in-law, as the first post-invasion Iraqi Ambassador to China in June 2004.[66] Ambassador Ismail served as Iraq's ambassador to China from 2004 to 2010. Although there is no evidence to suggest Chairman Mao nor any of his successors had any particular interest in the Kurds, purely from a pragmatic point of view it made sense for the Kurds to have a good relationship with a permanent member of the UN Security Council and an ascending major power on the world stage. In 2006 President Masoud Barzani was invited to visit Beijing but due to the level of reception at the Chinese Communist

Politburo level, which was deemed too low for the president, the visit was cancelled.

The Kurdistan region has two major objectives in its attempts to enhance China-Kurdistan relations. The first is an economic objective. What is seen in terms of Kurdistan's energy policy as sidestepping Baghdad is an attempt at gaining economic independence; it is only with economic independence that a viable independent Kurdistan can survive. If Kurdistan produces enough oil, independence will be easier to achieve and sustain. According to the Kurdistan's Ministry of Natural Resources, the oil production forecast is 1 MBD by the end of 2015 and 2 MBD by 2019. When this happens, the Kurdish leadership anticipates that the international community will have an interest in a viable, stable, democratic and oil-producing Kurdistan. It is for these reasons that the KRG, despite all the obstacles created by Baghdad, is unwavering and determined to produce and export its own oil. In late 2014 the KRG produced a monthly income of 400 million USD; however, for the daily running of the entity 1 billion USD are needed per month. In the summer of 2014, the KRG connected Kurdistan's oil pipeline to the newly controlled oil fields of Kirkuk Province, which means that economic independence is plausible and increasingly likely. Kurdistan's oil production in early 2014 was 250,000 barrels per day (BPD) and by the end of the same year was 500,000 BPD. However, with the additional potential oil production capacity of Kirkuk at 370,000 BPD with the *de facto* integration of the major oil fields of Kirkuk and Bai Hassan in July 2014, the economic independence of the Kurdistan region is closer than ever.

Another Kurdish objective is to attract international investment. Doing so would give various regional and international powers a stake in the continuity and success of the Kurdistan region and eventually its independence. The KRG is pursuing a strategy of awarding highly lucrative production sharing agreements (PSA) to international oil companies – allowing 25–35% of the profit. This factor has attracted oil giants like Chevron, ExxonMobil, Total, and Gazprom. However, Arab Iraq only awards service contracts to international oil companies that leaves them only 15–18% of the profit. The KRG's liberal investment law of 2006 –one of the most foreign-investor friendly in the Middle East – has been a major contributing factor for foreign investment. According to the latest government figures, 2,955 foreign companies are registered in the region.[67]

The underlying reason for the Kurdistan region's pursuit of this highly controversial unilateral oil policy, in defiance of Baghdad, is to secure several political objectives. The KRG wants to ensure diplomatic recognition, independence from Baghdad, and ultimately gain political support for the Kurdish entity. The earliest of these attempts go back to 2004 when the first oil rig in Kurdistan was constructed by the Chinese Great Wall Oil Drilling Company. Moreover, the KRG signed a production sharing agreement with China's largest oil company, Sinopec, to develop the Taq Taq oil field, which has consequently been blacklisted by the Iraqi Oil Ministry in Baghdad. Demonstrating this interest, so far, the Chinese ambassador to Baghdad has visited the president of the Kurdistan region in the capital city of Erbil on four occasions – in 2005, 2012 and 2013, and in 2014 – to enhance Sino-Kurdish relations.[68]

As for trade relations, Kurdish interest in China started after a small number of Iraqi Kurdish businessmen started visiting China for business purposes in 2004 after the overthrow of Saddam's regime; this number dramatically increased by 2007 with increasing familiarity and confidence of these individuals with the Chinese commercial and cultural setting. Most of these businessmen settled and established their businesses primarily in the two cities of Wuyi in Zhejiang Province and Guangzhou in Guandong Province;[69] they started by purchasing small amounts at the bulk wholesale level, gradually increasing the quantity to container loads of goods for export to Arab Iraq and the Kurdistan region. A prime example would be the Kurdistan-based Al-Sard Group that sells 70% of its imported Chinese goods to Southern (Arab) Iraq and only 30% of its goods to Kurdistan. Even before the toppling of Saddam's regime, imported Chinese goods found their way to Kurdistan through Iran. Before 2012 Chinese businessmen dealt with all Iraqi businessmen in the same light; however, since 2012 they have been able to distinguish between the Kurdish and Arab Iraqis. They now appreciate that there is an Arab Iraq and the Kurdistan region, allowing greater attention and interest in the latter. There are now approximately 500 Kurdish shipping companies transporting goods to Iraq that sometimes ship goods worth 5 million USD per shipment. Most of the goods arrive through the Iraqi port of Um Qasir, and smaller quantities through the ports of Mersin (Turkey), Bandar Abbas (Iran) and Aqaba (Jordan). The KRG also purchases military uniforms for its military (the Peshmerga) from China in large quantities due to its affordable price. However, the Kurdistan region relies for most of its imports, especially home appliances, building materials, and furniture, on Turkey. This reliance is due to both the geographical proximity of Turkey and also for the political appeasement of the Turkish government. The Kurdish leadership is acutely conscious of Turkey's traditional animosity to the Kurdish liberation movement in

Iraq and for this reason treads carefully. Also, Turkey's traditional close ties with Europe, its membership in NATO and its perceived secularism, features that are visible and similar to Kurdistan's outlook and aspirations for the future, make Turkey the most logical regional partner at the practical level. Kurdistan also perceives Chinese goods as being of poor quality.[70]

Arab Iraq, however, largely depends on Chinese goods, requiring Société Générale de Surveillance (SGS), Bureau Veritas (BV) and Cotecna, which are all health and safety, environmental protection, and quality control certificate providers in addition to Iraqi attempts at enlisting the China Quality Certification Centre to ensure quality.[71] Due to the security situation, after 2004 American companies were replaced by Chinese companies, since Chinese workers were generally not perceived as targets by radical and violent groups in Iraq. Chinese globalized companies have a major presence in Iraq and play a major role that other international companies cannot, in providing desirable and culturally attuned products. Chinese telecommunication companies like Huawei and ZTE provide 80% of Kurdistan and Iraq's communications, through three major Iraqi mobile carriers, Asia Cell, Zain, and Korek. The Kurdistan region is also a heavy consumer of Chinese goods, although it also varies in its openness to trade with China. The Kurdish province of Sulaimani, with its geopolitical proximity to Iran and the alliance of the PUK, which largely administers the area with the Islamic republic, essentially falling into Iran's sphere of influence, has possibly given the province greater acceptance of Chinese goods. By comparison, Erbil's seemingly less flexible and less positive stance on Chinese products is a consequence of the KDP's strong alliance with Turkey, Erbil's closer geographical proximity to Turkey, and their perception of poor quality of Chinese products. After Saddam's overthrow, Kurdish-Turkish relations greatly soured, with the Turks seeing the Kurds as opportunists seeking secession. But gradually, after US mediation from 2008 onward, the tension gradually thawed with Turkey benefitting immensely from Kurdistan's booming economy and the KRG seeking an outlet for its oil production in its attempts to evade Baghdad.

There are two types of Chinese companies in Kurdistan. The first are sole agents (distributors) like the Al-Sard Group – these are in the majority. The second group (in the minority) are direct representatives of major Chinese companies. According to the official KRG government directory, 17 Chinese companies are currently operating in the Kurdistan Region, including DQE, an oil and gas services company, and the Beijing-based Sinopec. At the cultural level, the Chinese language (Mandarin) is being taught at various language centers in major cities around the Kurdistan region. A small number of Kurdish students are currently studying in China at universities in which the language of teaching is English. There are five postgraduate Kurdish students studying in China in total.[72] The reasons for this small number are the apprehension felt by many Kurdish students concerning the Chinese language, and a perception of Chinese culture as distant and mysterious.[73] This perception will, however, most likely change over time with the further opening of Kurdistan to the outside world and the new Chinese consulate in Erbil.

As for the nature of Sino-Kurdish relations, there has been no clear Chinese policy towards Kurdistan other than economic interest. Essentially there is no core difference between Kurdistan's and Arab Iraq's policy objectives towards China; Kurdistan wants Chinese support for its domestic, regional, and international issues as is the case with Arab Iraq. In an ideal world, the KRG would want its relations with China to be on a par with relations between China and other sovereign countries in the region, which it lacks as it is not yet an independent state. Chinese companies are investing in Kurdistan, but only in the oil sector, although they are also active in the telecommunications sector. Although there is no exact data on the volume of trade between China and Kurdistan. China certainly sees Kurdistan as a new source of energy.[74] The presence of around 800 Chinese workers and businessmen currently residing in Kurdistan suggests that the China-Kurdistan relationship is solid and inspires hope that the future will see it develop and grow, to the mutual benefit of both sides.

China's trade interactions with Erbil are more at the unofficial business level, whereas Baghdad's relations are more formal and official at the governmental level. But this stands to change. On 30 December 2014 the Chinese government opened its very first consulate in Erbil with Mr Tan Banglin as its first Consul General. The government of the People's Republic of China decided in 2012 to open its consulate general in the Kurdistan region's capital city, Erbil. Minor logistical issues were taken care of so that the office would be opened by the end of 2014.[75] China became the fifth and final permanent member of the UN Security Council to open an official representation in the Kurdistan Region. With both the Kurdistan Region Prime Minister Nechirvan Barzani and China's Vice Foreign Minister Zhang Ming attending (the highest Chinese official ever to visit the Kurdistan Region), both stressed the importance of such a relationship. The fact that the prime minister himself attended the inauguration with many other senior Kurdish figures, including Iraq's former first lady, wife of leading Kurdish nationalist figure Jalal

Talabani, and his son who is now the Kurdistan Region's deputy prime minster highlights the importance of this relationship to the Kurdish leadership. Prime Minister Barzani's highlighting of China's humanitarian assistance to the Kurdistan Region in wake of the Islamic State's incursions into Kurdish held territory in northern Iraq further proves this point. Moreover, hints by Wang Yi (China's foreign minister) at providing possible military support to Iraq during a meeting in New York in September 2014 with Iraq's foreign minister Ibrahim al-Jaafari is an indication of China's deep interest in the country.[76] China has declared numerous times that it supports all efforts to confront terrorism, which could see security and military treaties signed by both states. Testimony to this enhanced role is the current 1 million USD contract with the Chinese company Xin Shi Dai to purchase light weaponry for Iraq's Ministry of Interior, as well as the training of 19 Iraqi defense ministry officers in China on the removal of landmines.[77]

Notes

1. Michael Doran, Pan-Arabism Before Nasser: Egyptian Power Politics and the Palestine Question, (New York, Oxford University Press, 2002), p. 84.
2. Jason Langley. (2013). Politics and Religion in Iraq and Syria: What is the Ba'ath Party?. [Global Research] Available at: <URL: http://www.globalresearch.ca/the-baath-party-as-the-west-doesnt-want-you-to-know-it/5319120> Access Date: 7 March 2015.
3. Jack Kenny, Iraq War Paying Off – for China. [The New American]. Available at: <URL: http://www.thenewamerican.com/world-news/asia/item/15599-iraq-war-paying-off-for-china> Access Date: 22 February 2015.
4. Tim Arango and Clifford Krauss. 'China Is Reaping Biggest Benefits of Iraq Oil Boom', The New York Times, (2013, June 3). p. A1.
5. Shafeeq Choucair. (2013). *China's New Diplomacy towards the Middle East.* [Aljazeera Center for Studies] Available at: <URL: http://studies.aljazeera.net/en/reports/2013/04/201341611204179344.htm> Access Date: 18 August 2014.
6. *Ibid.*
7. *Ibid.*
8. Inside Story. (2014). *Oil and Gas: At What Price?.* [Aljazeera] Available at: <URL: http://www.aljazeera.com/programmes/insidestory/2014/03/oil-gas-at-what-price-2014320165719593411.html> Access Date: 15 February 2015.
9. Elly Rostoum. (2014).*Dissecting China's $1 Trillion in Investments Globally.* [Foreign Policy Association] Available at: <URL: http://foreignpolicyblogs.com/2014/07/14/dissecting-chinas-1-trillion-in-investments-globally/> Access Date: 5 February 2015.
10. Tim Arango and Clifford Krauss. 'China Is Reaping Biggest Benefits of Iraq Oil Boom', The New York Times, (2013, June 3). p. A1.
11. Ibid.

12. Choucair (2013), *op. cit.*
13. Christina Lin. (2013). *China's Strategic Shift Toward The Region of the Four Seas: The Middle Kingdom Arrives in the Middle East.* [Gloria Center: Global Research in International Affairs] Available at: <URL: http://www.gloria-center. org/2013/03/chinas-strategic-shift-toward-the-region-of-the-four-seas-the-middle-kingdom-arrives-in-the-middle-east/> Access Date: 19 August 2014.
14. *Ibid.*
15. *Ibid.*
16. *Ibid.*
17. Arango and Krauss (2013), *op. cit.*
18. *Ibid.*
19. U.S. Energy Information Administration. (2015). *Iraq was second-leading contributor to global oil supply growth during 2014.* Available at: <URL: http:// www.eia.gov/todayinenergy/detail.cfm?id=19911> Access Date: 9 March 2015.
20. Arango and Krauss (2013), *op. cit.*
21. *Ibid.*
22. Iraq Trade Link News Agency. (2015). *PetroChina opens its airport kin Missan.* Available at: <URL: http://www.iraqtradelinknews.com/2015/01/petrochina-opens-its-airport-kin-missan.html> Access Date: 5 March 2015.
23. Arango and Krauss (2013), op. cit.
24. *Ibid.*
25. Mahmoud Ghafouri. (2009).*China's Policy in the Middle East.* [Middle East Policy Council] Available at: <URL: http://www.mepc.org/journal/middle-east-policy-archives/chinas-policy-persian-gulf?print> Access Date: 3 March 2015.
26. Arango and Krauss (2013), op. cit.
27. *Ibid.*
28. Jawhar Hassan, E-mail Interview with Author, 12 July 2014.
29. Arango and Krauss (2013), op. cit.
30. Iraqi Embassy – Beijing, China. (2013). The People's Republic of China – Political Report 2014.
31. *Ibid.*
32. Jawhar Hassan, E-mail Interview with Author, 12 July 2014.
33. Peter Ford. (2014). *Why China Stays Quiet on Iraq Despite Being No. 1 Oil Investor.* [The Christian Science Monitor] Available at: <URL: http://www. csmonitor.com/World/Asia-Pacific/2014/0627/Why-China-stays-quiet-on-Iraq-despite-being-no.-1-oil-investor-video> Access Date: 6 March 2015.
34. Teddy Ng. (2014). *China* pledges to pump more funds into Iraq's oil sector infrastructure. [South China Morning Post] Available at: <URL: http://www. scmp.com/news/china/article/1434025/china-pledges-pump-more-funds-iraqs-oil-sector-infrastructure> Access Date: 19 August 2014.
35. U.S. Energy Information Administration. (2014). *Iraq.* Available at: <URL: http://www.eia.gov/countries/cab.cfm?fips=iz> Access Date: 20 February 2015.
36. Iraqi Embassy – Beijing, China. (2014). op cit.
37. Iraqi Embassy – Beijing, China. (2013). The People's Republic of China – Political Report 2013.
38. Jawhar Hassan, E-mail Interview with Author, 12 July 2014.

39. Iraqi Embassy – Beijing, China (2013), *op. cit.*
40. *Ibid.*
41. Kuangyi Yao, 'Development of Sino-Arab Relations and the Evolution of China's Middle East Policy in the New Era', Journal of Middle Eastern and Islamic Studies (in Asia) Vol. 1, No. 1 (2007): p. 4.
42. Arango and Krauss (2013), op. cit.
43. Yitzhak Shichor. (2006). *China's Kurdish Policy*. [The Jamestown Foundation] Available at: <URL: http://www.jamestown.org/programs/chinabrief/single/?tx_ttnews%5Btt_news%5D=3919&tx_ttnews%5BbackPid%5D=196&no_cache=1> Access Date: 20 July 2014.
44. *Ibid.*
45. Gulf Research Center and The Nixon Center. (2010). *China's Growing Role In the Middle East:Implications for the Region and Beyond*. Available at: <URL: http://www.cftni.org/full-monograph-chinas-growing-role-in-me.pdf> Access Date: 23 August 2014.
46. Mohammed Shareef. (2009). Kurdistan: Political Stability and Widespread Security. Article in the Italian language on the Kurdistan Region of Iraq and its emerging political influence in the Middle East. Published by Fondazione Eni Enrico Mattei in 'Equilibri' in cooperation with il Mulino, the premier Italian University Publisher, EQUILIBRI / a. XIII, n. 3, December 2009, p. 443.
47. Shichor (2006), op. cit.
48. *Ibid.*
49. *Ibid.*
50. US Consulate Kirkuk. (2005). China Woos Iraqi Kurds. [WikiLeaks] Available at: URL: https://www.wikileaks.org/plusd/cables/05KIRKUK300_a.html Access Date: 20 June 2014.
51. *Ibid.*
52. *Ibid.*
53. Jonathan Sanford. (2003). Iraq's Economy: Past, Present, Future (Order Code RL31944). Washington, D.C.: Congressional Research Service.
54. Xinhuanet. (2011). *China, Iraq pledge further reciprocal cooperation as PM visits*. Available at: <URL: http://news.xinhuanet.com/english2010/china/2011-07-/18/c_13993129.htm> Access Date: 20 August 2014.
55. Omar Al-Shaher. (2013). *Iraq Aims to Increase Oil Output*. [Al-Monitor] Available at: <URL: http://www.al-monitor.com/pulse/originals/2013/03/iraq-increase-oil-output.html#> Access Date: 20 July 2014.
56. Iraq Project. (2014). *Oil and Gas in Iraq*. Available at: <URL: http://iraqproject.com/investment-in-iraq/oil-and-gas/> Access Date: 20 July 2014.
57. Wayne Arnold. (2014). *Despite its Investments, China Won't Feel Big Energy Pinch from Iraq*. [The Wall Street Journal – Business] Available at: <URL: http://blogs.wsj.com/economics/2014/06/23/despite-its-investments-china-wont-feel-big-energy-pinch-from-iraq/> Access Date: 19 August 2014.
58. International Energy Agency. (2014). *Update on Overseas Investments by China's National Oil Fields: Achievements and Challenges since 2011*. Available at: <URL: http://www.iea.org/publications/freepublications/publication/PartnerCountrySeriesUpdateonOverseasInvestmentsbyChinasNationalOilCompanies.pdf> Access Date: 11 July 2014.
59. Jawhar Hassan, E-mail Interview with Author, 12 July 2014.

60. Iraqi Embassy – Beijing, China. (2013). op cit.
61. Iraqi Embassy – Beijing, China. (2014). op cit.
62. Saed Kakei, (2009). *Kurds in Iraq: Through the Lenses of International Relations*. (Unpublished master's thesis). Norwich University, Northfield, VT., p. 36.
63. Hafizullah Emadi, 'China and Iraq: Patterns of Interaction, 1960–1992', Economic and Political Weekly Vol. 29, No. 53 (1994): p. 3316.
64. Hishyar Abid. (2010). *Talabani: China's "Special Friend"*. [KurdishMedia] Available at: <URL: http://www.kurdmedia.com/article.aspx?id=16556> Access Date: 19 August 2014.
65. People's Daily Online. (2007). *Iraqi president kicks off first China visit*. Available at: <URL: http://english.people.com.cn/200706/21/eng20070621_386171. html> Access Date: 19 August 2014.
66. Hishyar Abid. (2010). *op. cit.*
67. Kurdistan Regional Government. (2014). *Foreign Companies Resume Regular Activity in Kurdistan*. Available at: <URL: http://cabinet.gov.krd/a/d. aspx?s=010000&l=12&a=52312> Access Date: 19 February 2015.
68. Kurdistan Region Presidency. (2013). *President Barzani Welcomes China's Ambassador to Iraq*. Available at: <URL: http://www.presidency.krd/english/ articledisplay.aspx?id=Xrmz/ZUCdbM=> Access Date: 25 February 2015.
69. Bahaldin Shikh Saaed, E-mail Interview with Author, 18 June 2014.
70. *Ibid.*
71. Iraqi Embassy – Beijing, China (2013), *op. cit.*
72. Jawhar Hassan, E-mail Interview with Author, 16 June 2014
73. *Ibid.*
74. Jawhar Hassan, E-mail Interview with Author, 16 June 2014.
75. Huzan Balay, E-mail Interview with Author, 12 July 2014.
76. Najmeh Bozorgmehr and Lucy Hornby. (2014). *China Offers to Help Sunni Extremists*. [Financial Times] Available at: <URL: http://www.ft.com/ cms/s/0/3f4dc794-8141-11e4-b956-00144feabdc0.html#axzz3TlAyIIdq> Access Date: 8 March 2015.
77. Iraqi Embassy – Beijing, China (2014), *op. cit.*

References

Abid, Hishyar. (2010). *Talabani: China's "Special Friend"*. [KurdishMedia] Available at: <URL: http://www.inarchive.com/page/2011-03-15/http://www.kurdmedia. com/article.aspx?id=16556 > Access Date: 19 August 2014.
Al-Shaher, Omar. (2013). *Iraq Aims to Increase Oil Output*. [Al-Monitor] Available at: <URL: http://www.al-monitor.com/pulse/originals/2013/03/iraq-increase-oil-output.html#> Access Date: 20 July 2014.
Arango, Tim and Clifford Krauss. 'China Is Reaping Biggest Benefits of Iraq Oil Boom', *The New York Times*, (2013, June 3). p. A1.
Arnold, Wayne. (2014). *Despite its Investments, China Won't Feel Big Energy Pinch from Iraq*. [The Wall Street Journal – Business] Available at: <URL: http://blogs. wsj.com/economics/2014/06/23/despite-its-investments-china-wont-feel-big-energy-pinch-from-iraq/> Access Date: 19 August 2014.
Balay, Huzan, E-mail Interview with Author (KRG Official – Department of Foreign Relations – Erbil), 12 July 2014.

Bozorgmehr, Najmeh and Lucy Hornby. (2014). *China Offers to Help Sunni Extremists.* [Financial Times] Available at: <URL: http://www.ft.com/cms/s/0/3f4dc794–8141–11e4-b956–00144feabdc0.html#axzz3TlAyIIdq> Access Date: 8 March 2015.

Choucair, Shafeeq. (2013). *China's New Diplomacy towards the Middle East.* [Aljazeera Center for Studies] Available at: <URL: http://studies.aljazeera.net/en/reports/2013/04/201341611204179344.htm> Access Date: 18 August 2014.

Doran, Michael, *Pan-Arabism Before Nasser: Egyptian Power Politics and the Palestine Question,* (New York, Oxford University Press, 2002).

Emadi, Hafizullah, 'China and Iraq: Patterns of Interaction, 1960–1992', *Economic and Political Weekly* Vol. 29, No. 53 (1994): pp. 3315–18.

Ford, Peter. (2014). *Why China Stays Quiet on Iraq Despite Being No. 1 Oil Investor.* [The Christian Science Monitor] Available at: <URL: http://www.csmonitor.com/World/Asia-Pacific/2014/0627/Why-China-stays-quiet-on-Iraq-despite-being-no.-1-oil-investor-video> Access Date: 6 March 2015.

Ghafouri, Mahmoud. (2009).*China's Policy in the Middle East.* [Middle East Policy Council] Available at: <URL: http://www.mepc.org/journal/middle-east-policy-archives/chinas-policy-persian-gulf?print> Access Date: 3 March 2015.

Gulf Research Center and The Nixon Center. (2010). *China's Growing Role In the Middle East: Implications for the Region and Beyond.* Available at: <URL: http://www.cftni.org/full-monograph-chinas-growing-role-in-me.pdf> Access Date: 23 August 2014.

Hassan, Jawhar, E-mail Interview with Author (Consul, Iraqi Embassy – Beijing), 12 July 2014.

Inside Story. (2014). *Oil and Gas: At What Price?.* [Aljazeera] Available at: <URL: http://www.aljazeera.com/programmes/insidestory/2014/03/oil-gas-at-what-price-2014320165719593411.html> Access Date: 18 February 2015.

International Energy Agency. (2014). *Update on Overseas Investments by China's National Oil Fields: Achievements and Challenges since 2011.* Available at: <URL: http://www.iea.org/publications/freepublications/publication/PartnerCountrySeriesUpdateonOverseasInvestmentsbyChinasNationalOilCompanies.pdf> Access Date: 11 July 2014.

Iraqi Embassy – Beijing, China. (2013). *The People's Republic of China – Political Report 2013.*

Iraqi Embassy – Beijing, China. (2014). *The People's Republic of China – Political Report 2014.*

Iraq Trade Link News Agency. (2015). *PetroChina opens its airport kin Missan.* Available at: <URL: http://www.iraqtradelinknews.com/2015/01/petrochina-opens-its-airport-kin-missan.html> Access Date: 5 March 2015.

Iraq Project. (2014). *Oil and Gas in Iraq.* Available at: <URL: http://iraqproject.com/investment-in-iraq/oil-and-gas/> Access Date: 20 July 2014.

Kakei S., (2009). *Kurds in Iraq: Through the Lenses of International Relations.* (Unpublished master's thesis). Norwich University, Northfield, VT.

Kenny, Jack, *Iraq War Paying Off – for China.* [The New American]. Available at: <URL: http://www.thenewamerican.com/world-news/asia/item/15599-iraq-war-paying-off-for-china> Access Date: 22 February 2015.

Kurdistan Regional Government. (2014). *Foreign Companies Resume Regular Activity in Kurdistan.* Available at: <URL: http://cabinet.gov.krd/a/d.aspx?s=010000&l=12&a=52312> Access Date: 19 February 2015.

Kurdistan Region Presidency. (2013). *President Barzani Welcomes China's Ambassador to Iraq.* Available at: <URL: http://www.presidency.krd/english/articledisplay.aspx?id=Xrmz/ZUCdbM=> Access Date: 25 February 2015.

Langley, Jason. (2013). *Politics and Religion in Iraq and Syria: What is the Ba'ath Party?.* [Global Research] Available at: <URL: http://www.globalresearch.ca/the-baath-party-as-the-west-doesnt-want-you-to-know-it/5319120> Access Date: 7 March 2015.

Lin, Christina. (2013). *China's Strategic Shift Toward The Region of the Four Seas: The Middle Kingdom Arrives in the Middle East.* [Gloria Center: Global Research in International Affairs] Available at: <URL: http://www.gloria-center.org/2013/03/chinas-strategic-shift-toward-the-region-of-the-four-seas-the-middle-kingdom-arrives-in-the-middle-east/> Access Date: 19 August 2014.

Ng, Teddy. (2014). *China pledges to pump more funds into Iraq's oil sector infrastructure.* [South China Morning Post] Available at: <URL: http://www.scmp.com/news/china/article/1434025/china-pledges-pump-more-funds-iraqs-oil-sector-infrastructure> Access Date: 19 August 2014.

People's Daily Online. (2007). *Iraqi president kicks off first China visit.* Available at: <URL: http://english.people.com.cn/200706/21/eng20070621_386171.html> Access Date: 19 August 2014.

Rostoum, Elly. (2014).*Dissecting China's $1 Trillion in Investments Globally.* [Foreign Policy Association] Available at: <URL: http://foreignpolicyblogs.com/2014/07/14/dissecting-chinas-1-trillion-in-investments-globally/> Access Date: 5 February 2015.

Sanford, Jonathan. (2003). *Iraq's Economy: Past, Present, Future* (Order Code RL31944). Washington, D.C.: Congressional Research Service.

Shareef, Mohammed. (2009). *Kurdistan: Political Stability and Widespread Security.* Article in the Italian language on the Kurdistan Region of Iraq and its emerging political influence in the Middle East. Published by Fondazione Eni Enrico Mattei in 'Equilibri' in cooperation with il Mulino, the premier Italian University Publisher, EQUILIBRI / a. XIII, n. 3, December 2009, pp. 440–444.

Shichor, Yitzhak. (2006). *China's Kurdish Policy.* [The Jamestown Foundation] Available at: <URL: http://www.jamestown.org/programs/chinabrief/single/?tx_ttnews%5Btt_news%5D=3919&tx_ttnews%5BbackPid%5D=196&no_cache=1> Access Date: 20 July 2014.

Shikh Saaed, Bahaldin, E-mail Interview with Author (Iraqi Kurdish Businessman Based in China), 18 June 2014.

US Consulate Kirkuk. (2005). *China Woos Iraqi Kurds.* [WikiLeaks] Available at: <URL: https://www.wikileaks.org/plusd/cables/05KIRKUK300_a.html> Access Date: 20 June 2014.

U.S. Energy Information Administration. (2015). *Iraq was second-leading contributor to global oil supply growth during 2014.* Available at: <URL: http://www.eia.gov/todayinenergy/detail.cfm?id=19911> Access Date: 9 March 2015.

Xinhuanet. (2011). *China, Iraq pledge further reciprocal cooperation as PM visits.* Available at: <URL: http://news.xinhuanet.com/english2010/china/2011–07-/18/c_13993129.htm> Access Date: 20 August 2014.

Yao, Kuangyi, 'Development of Sino-Arab Relations and the Evolution of China's Middle East Policy in the New Era', *Journal of Middle Eastern and Islamic Studies (in Asia)* Vol. 1, No. 1 (2007): pp. 3–19.

6

An Analysis of the Evolution of Sino-Egyptian Economic Relations

Yasser M. Gadallah

Egypt is one of only five countries in the African continent that have been chosen by the Chinese government to host a special economic zone (SEZ). China has signed 33 investment promotion and protection agreements and 11 double taxation agreements with African countries. Algeria, The Democratic Republic of Congo, Nigeria, Egypt, and Zambia (out of 31 countries) received Chinese FDI flows of more than $100 billion. For comparison purposes, between 2005 and 2010, Nigeria had the lion's share of Chinese investments, reaching approximately $15.35 billion. Comparatively, Algeria had $9.16 billion, Congo $5.89 billion, and Zambia $1.01 billion.

According to the Egyptian investment agency, 1,066 Chinese companies have invested in Egypt, with a collective registered capital of $320 million, and paid-in capital of $285 million. The growth rate in the Egyptian foreign direct investment (FDI) flows to China reached 53%, while the Chinese FDI flows to Egypt during 2005–2012 grew at a rate of 27% a growth rate. Egypt is focused on improving this trade imbalance to a more equitable position to help strengthen its economy.

In 2012, Sino-Egyptian trade volume reached $9.6 billion, of which China's exports to Egypt were $8.5 billion and imports from Egypt were $1.06 billion. Moreover, the growth rate of the deficit volume in the Egyptian trade balance reached 16.2% between 1995 and 2012. Egyptian exporters have yet to methodically study the Chinese market in terms of the required goods and services needed from the Egyptian side based on the competitive advantage (the price and the quality). Accordingly, it is very important for Egyptian producers to improve many industrial processes for the primary goods before exporting them to China in order to increase its value. Doing so could give exports a higher value and to offset the acceleration of imports from China, thus narrowing the deficit in the balance of payments.

Historical background

Egypt owns the Suez Canal, a key strategic shipping point for global commerce, upon which China relies heavily as it expands its trade ties with the Mediterranean region and Europe. Egypt was the first among the Arab and African countries to establish diplomatic relations with China on 30 May 1956. Since then, in China, President Gamal Abdel Nasser has become the symbol of national independence and solidarity with peace-loving people. Consequently, the bilateral cooperation has expanded, as can be seen in the different signed agreements and protocols between the two countries, especially in the economic and commercial spheres. In this chapter, I analyze the background between the two countries from the 1950s until 2014

Relations between the two countries started in 1953, when Egypt sent a commercial representative to offer the Chinese party its cotton. By the end of 1953, the trade volume was $11 million in terms of $10.4 million Egyptian exports versus $0.6 million Chinese exports. In 1955, the two governments had signed a commercial agreement in Beijing; starting from May 1956, there were several trade exchanges between the two countries. In 1964 in Beijing, they signed a technical and economic cooperation agreement, which has been used to renew the commercial agreement between the two countries every year. In 1972, the Chinese-Egyptian cooperation witnessed a new orientation in the age of President al-Sadat: the establishment of a brick factory in Egypt funded by China. Moreover, the two countries also established a joint Chinese-Egyptian committee in Cairo to enhance cooperation in technical and electrical projects. In 1987, meetings for the first phase of the technological and scientific cooperation between the two countries took place in Cairo. These meetings led to more than ten cooperation agreements in the pharmaceutical, medical equipment, and agricultural industries being signed. Consequently, the trade volume between the two countries grew to $135 million, of which $125 million were in exports to Egypt and $10 million were in exports to China. (State Information Service in Egypt, 2014)

The Chinese minister of economy and foreign trade visited Egypt in 1995 to study how to strengthen commercial and economic cooperation between the two countries. Accordingly, there was progress in the trade volume, which increased to $452.7 million ($439.6 million

Chinese exports versus $13.06 million Egyptian exports). In his 1997 visit to China, the Egyptian prime minister signed a memorandum of understanding (MOU) to name China as a major partner in the Suez Economic Zone North-west Gulf.[1] Moreover, a number of agreements had also been signed in the electricity and rural development areas. As a result of these efforts, by the end of 1997, trade volume jumped to $520.7 million ($464 million exports to Egypt and $56.7 million exports to China). (State Information Service in Egypt, 2014)

The year 1999 is considered a turning point in the bilateral relations between Egypt and China following the visit of President Hosni Mubarak. In that year, the two countries signed a strategic cooperation agreement that encompassed several dimensions, including politics, the economy, parliament, culture, tourism, and more. Consequently, the economic relations changed from the traditional form (exports and imports) to joint projects and investments, especially the cooperation in the Suez Economic Zone North-west Gulf, in addition to establishing the Egyptian companies' affiliates in China, including an oriental weaver carpet company. The SEZ, which was developed by Egypt and the Tianjin Economic-Technological Development Area (TEDA)[2], represents one of the main fruits of President Mubarak's 1999 visit to China, in addition to the China-Africa Development Fund. (State Information Service in Egypt, 2014)

The government of Tianjin in China has promised to provide a subsidy of 5% of the actual investment amount, pay the utility costs (rent, gas, water, and electricity), and provide full foreign investment insurance and overseas personal accident insurance for three years for service enterprises in the zone. A Suez Economic Zone (SEZ) provides Chinese companies with access to the world's principal maritime routes, leading to consumer markets for their merchandise – most notably the Mediterranean and transatlantic trade areas. Consequently, Chinese companies will have a relatively short distance to reach ports on both the northern, southern, and eastern Mediterranean borders, and they will have reduced the distance to North American consumer markets approximately by half.

An integral component of the Suez SEZ, construction of Sokhna port, began in April 1999. The build-to-order transfer (BOT) was signed by the Egyptian government and the Sokhna Port Development Company (SPDC) for the development of the super-structure, which is designed to control trade between the south and the north. The port has direct access to the Mediterranean and Indian oceans and is close to major international markets. Because of the high quality of the port's infrastructure (energy, communications, water, drainage, protection against torrential rains and means of transportation), the port is poised to become a leading global trade hub for just-in-time transit operations (General Authority for Foreign Investment and Free Zones (GAFI) in Egypt, 2009b and GAFI, 2009c). Some Chinese manufacturers in this zone are producing for the European market (e.g., garments); others are serving the Egyptian market (e.g., oil rig assembly, women's sanitary products); and yet others are exporting back to China (e.g., marble).

By the end of 2005, the Chinese had 35 projects in Egypt in the textile, chemical, engineering, food, and shoes industries, as well as construction materials, petroleum, maritime, metal, and infrastructure sectors. Based on the statistics from the Chinese Ministry of Commerce, in that year (2005) there were about 43 joint investment projects in Egypt focusing on the clothes industry, textiles, shoes, plastic products, and carpets. The contractual cost of these projects was $50 million. In 2011, the trade volume increased to $9 billion, and new Chinese investments within Egypt amounted $80 million. In 2012 – after President Mohamed Morsi's visit to China – the two countries signed a cooperation memo to strength the bilateral relations in the area of water resources. (State Information Service in Egypt, 2014) Moreover, they studied the possibility of constructing a high-speed rail line connecting Cairo and Alexandria. To pave the way for Chinese investors to construct a power station in Upper Egypt, they signed seven major agreements. And, to support small- and medium-sized enterprises, the China Development Bank (CDB) gave the National Bank of Egypt a soft loan of $200 million. Additionally, the Chinese government provides $70 million as charitable grants to establish joint ventures in infrastructure, electricity, and environmental focus areas in Egypt.

The volume of Chinese aid to Egypt increased by $14.16 million in 2012. Furthermore, TEDA will invest in establishing almost 150 factories ($1.5 billion) in the North-west Gulf of Suez area, which will create roughly 40,000 jobs. Overall, the value of the investment deals and joint ventures between Egyptian and Chinese companies is estimated to be $4.9 billion (China Brief Volume: 12 Issue: 18)

In 2014 an Egyptian business delegation visited China to study the new investment opportunities in support of the economic cooperation between Egypt and China. Representatives of the biggest multinational corporations in China showed that there are good investment opportunities in the Egyptian market, part of the larger Middle Eastern market. That year, Chinese investments in Egypt reached $500 million, and an agreement to extend cooperation between the two countries in projects covering infrastructure, railways, energy, natural gas, renewable energy, industry, modern agriculture, and satellite technology were reached. Moreover, the Chinese cooperation in the new Suez channel project is estimated to will create approximately 1,300 jobs initially and 6,000 jobs by the end of first phase of the project. (State Information Service in Egypt, 2014)

In December 2014, during his visit to China, Egyptian President al-Sisi signed a comprehensive strategic partnership agreement with that country, as a logical step towards supporting the relations between the two countries. The two countries plan on cooperation in the following areas: technology, economic development, new and renewable energy, and space exploration. In addition, they will establish a joint Chinese-Egyptian Laboratory for renewable energy. Trade volume between the China and Egypt reached $11 billion by the end of 2014. (State Information Service in Egypt, 2014)

Egypt is focused on developing linkages with countries that respect its sovereignty and who will consider it as an equal partner. Considering that China's pragmatism in international relations is based on respecting national sovereignty and peaceful and fair integration of international relations, China is an ideal partner for Egypt for developing bilateral economic and political relations. (Ahmed El-Sayed Al- Naggar, 2014)

This chapter will analyze the status quo of the economic and commercial relations from 1995 to 2012 between the two countries, based on available data. In addition, the chapter will attempt to predict developments during the 2015 to 2019 period. It focuses on analyses of investments flows between the two countries and the economic impacts, as well as clarifying the main obstacles and barriers facing Chinese investors in Egypt.

Investment flow and its economic impacts

As mentioned, Egypt is one of only five countries in Africa selected by the Chinese government to host an SEZ. In 2010, Egypt received a 2.6% share of the Chinese FDI in Africa. South Africa received 31.8%, and Nigeria 9.3%.[3] The most important sectors for Chinese investment are textiles, garments, petroleum equipment, chemical production, engineering, and construction materials. Smaller private manufacturing companies take the lion's share in the amount of investment, with several projects in the oil services sector. In 2009, Chinese companies signed new business contracts in telecommunications, a cement factory, and a sulphuric acid plant, with a total value of $1.1 billion. By the end of 2009, Chinese companies completed an estimated nearly $800 million worth of contracts. (Charles Robertson & Lucy Corkin, 2011)

In terms of employment, Egypt allows one foreign employee for every nine employed Egyptians. The first stage of the TEDA zone has more than 1,800 local employees and about 80 Chinese staff, which means that the Chinese employees' share falls below 5%. The general contractor for this zone is an Egyptian company, and some of the construction work was subcontracted to local Egyptian companies. According to the Egyptian regulations and laws, foreign companies may have a maximum of 10% of their payroll allocated to foreign employees. Consequently, 90% of the workforce in this zone will be Egyptian. Currently, there are 1,600 employees employed in the Chinese Suez SEZ (GAFI, 2009b).

As can be seen in Figure 6.1, there is a strong positive trend in the Chinese FDI flows to Egypt versus a slightly positive trend in the Egyptian FDI flows to China, which results in a positive impact on the Egyptian Economy. During the 2005 to 2012 period, there was a 53% growth rate in Egyptian FDI to China; the corresponding FDI growth rate, China to Egypt, was 27%.These results should be read with caution because, although the growth in the Egyptian FDI flow is accelerated, the net flow from China in favor of Egypt are in absolute figures. Chinese FDI to Egypt in 2009 was approximately $134 million. Compared with the 2005 to 2012 overall period, the amount appears high, yet can be justified in terms of the concentration of the Chinese investments in Suez SEZ that opened that year. Therefore, it was expected that these investments would be lower in 2010 ($52 million) and 2011 ($66 million), with an increase beginning in 2012 ($119 million) as a result of expansion of the Chinese investments in West Gulf Suez.

Egyptian investment in China are depicted in the Figure 6.1. As shown, investment was modest in 2005, totalling $1 million. However, it grew through seven years to reach $72 million by the end of 2012. The growth rate was 53%, which reflects a strengthening of the ties between the two countries and the success of Egyptian investors' access to the Chinese market (especially in carpets, tourism, and banking services). According to the Chinese Ministry of commerce, several Egyptian companies, with $20 million in capital, are represented in China, including a representative office for Egyptair in Beijing, a Star company office for tourism, and the National Bank of Egypt in Shanghai.

In terms of the development in Egypt, Chinese investments will attract Egyptian citizens to host and work in Suez area, which is apart from Cairo. Moreover, these investments will build new infrastructure and improve the existing infrastructure. Production in this zone is expected

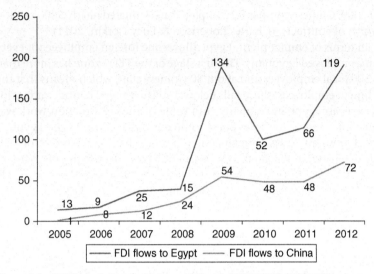

Figure 6.1   FDI flows between China and Egypt, 2005–2012 (US$ million)

Source: Figure based on data cited from: UNCTAD, FDI/ TNC database, based on data from the Central Bank of Egypt and the Ministry of Commerce (MOFCOM).

to increase as a result of Chinese investments, adding value to the gross domestic product by creating exports and attracting more foreign investments, all of which should lead to sustainable development in the area. Enhancing development in Egypt will deepen the strategic role of the Sino-Egyptian relationship, thus enabling a high level of economic and political stability in Egypt, as China is a strategic, high-level partner. The new bilateral approach toward between the two countries after President al-Sisi's visit encourages full partnership in all fields. As a result, Chinese investors visited Egypt to study how to invest in the projects around the new Suez channel project, especially around the southern gate of the channel. Likewise, Han Bing, the commercial counselor in the Chinese embassy in Egypt, reports that the new Suez channel will attract about $2 billion in investments, creating jobs and increasing the trade volume between Egypt and China.

Obstacles facing Chinese investors

In April 2014, 182 companies were listed on the Egyptian Exchange (EGX), Egypt's registered securities exchange, with a market capitalization of nearly 500 billion Egyptian pounds. Stock ownership is open to foreign and domestic individuals and entities. (US Department of State, 2014) Foreign investors must wait several weeks for legal transfers of foreign exchange in Egypt. While businesses do not face these restrictions, extensive documentation can be required. Labor rules prevent companies from hiring more than 10% non-Egyptians (25% in Free Zones), and foreigners, including Chinese, are not allowed to operate simple partnerships.

The World Bank's 2014 Ease of Doing Business Index ranked Egypt 128 out of 185 economies and 105 out of 189 for ease of registering property. For Chinese investors, the General Authority for Foreign Investment (GAFI) in Egypt has an administrative services center in the Suez SEZ, which was financed through a $20 million grant from the Chinese government. The goal of the center is to reduce the bureaucratic procedures and administrative costs that Chinese investors face and facilitate the process for doing business, including approval, registration, licensing, and certification for new projects. (*China Daily*, 14 November 2007). In addition, the Chinese government has agreed to provide up to $200 million in low interest loans to Egyptian manufacturers who want to import production lines and other equipment from China. (Farah Halime, 2012)

At the beginning of the TEDA participation, a gap existed between the expected and the offered services. After few years, the Egyptian government succeeded in achieving most of the promised services. However, the government still has not been able to guarantee a permanent supply of adequate water to the Suez Zone, for instance. (Deborah Brautigam and Xiaoyang Tang)

According to the Egyptian Labor Law, foreign investors cannot be granted work visas unless their Egyptian employees account for 90% of the staff (75% in cases of free zones). Also, although work visas are only granted for short periods, the procedures needed to secure them are complicated and time-consuming. These inconveniences negatively affect the normal operations of investment projects. (Foreign Market Access Report, Egypt, 2010)

In 2011, the Ministry of Manpower and Migration in Egypt imposed restrictions on access for foreigners to Egyptian employee visas. Visas for unskilled employees will be phased out. For most other jobs, employers may hire foreign employees on a temporary six-month basis, but should also hire two Egyptians to be trained to do the same job during that period. Only jobs where it is not possible for Egyptians to acquire the requisite skills will remain open to foreign employees. (US Department of State, 2014)

Trade between Egypt and China and its impacts

Sino-African trade volume increased from $12 million to $250 million between 1950 and 1965. In 2000, bilateral trade volume exceeded $10 billion for the first time, and in 2003 it reached a record $106.84 billion. Due to the global financial crisis, bilateral trade decreased in 2009 but increased in 2011 to $166.3 billion. The Sino-African relationship has had three phases of development. The first phase was from the early 1950s to the late 1970s and was focused on the political development through adoption of the open-up and reform policy. In the second phase in the 1980s, China was interested in strengthening the cooperation with Africa on principles of equality, mutual benefit, and diversification in the economic development patterns. After the end of the Cold War, China tended to government-sponsored assistance projects in order to acquire ground in the domestic markets. In the 21st century, China's policy aimed at encouraging friendship and political equality; mutual benefit, reciprocity, and common prosperity in the economic sphere; and mutual support and close coordination within the international Community. (Zhang Chun, 2012)

Based on recent statistics, Sino-Egyptian trade grew from about $870 million in 2000 to $9.6 billion in 2012, which reflects the surplus in trade balance in favor of China, making Egypt one of China's top trading partners in Africa. Accordingly, Egyptian officials have made many visits to China to study possible opportunities for opening Chinese access to Egyptian goods and services. In terms of technology transfer, China has provided technological assistance and support in agriculture and in developing a nuclear plant at al-Dabaa to improve energy supplies to Egypt. (Chris Alden and Faten Aggad-Clerx, 2012)

In 2012, Sino-Egyptian trade volume reached $9.6 billion, of which China's exports to Egypt were $8.5 billion and Chinese imports from Egypt were $1.06 billion. Comparatively, the total volume of Sino-Egyptian trade in 1995 was $363 million, of which the Chinese exports to Egypt were $355 million versus Chinese imports from Egypt $8 million (see Figure 6.2). Also shown in Figure 6.2 is the exponential growth in the volume of Egyptian imports from China with a correspondingly slight progress in Egyptian exports to China to the extent that its curve seems to be very near to the horizontal line.

From 1995 to 2012, trade volume between Egypt and China increased by 18.2%, from $363 million in 1995 to $9.6 billion in 2012. However, the balance of trade displays a rapidly increasing trade deficit with China, largely due to the significant increase of Egypt's imports from

Figure 6.2 Total Egyptian exports and imports to and from China, 1995–2012 (US$ million)

Source: Figure based on data cited from UNCTAD, The *United Nations Conference on Trade and Development* UNCTAD Statistics.

China, which are not met with an equivalent increase in the volume of exports (see Figure 6.3). Moreover, the growth rate in the deficit volume in the Egyptian trade balance reached 16.2% between 1995 and 2012. In terms of absolute figures, the deficit in 2012 was $–6.5 billion versus $–302.2 million in 1995. The main reason for the increase in the deficit in favor of the Chinese can be explained by the low value added of the Egyptian exports to China.

Using semi-log function, we made a regression to predict the volume of exports, imports, and deficit in the Egyptian balance of trade with China for the 2015–2019 period using the time series 1995–2012. The results reveal that the deficit will be increased to equal $–20.2 billion in 2019, and exports will be increased to $10.2 billion versus $30.4 billion in 2019 (see Table 6.1). Of course, many factors exist that could determine the value and trend of exports and imports in the future, which need to be discussed in future research work. Therefore, it seems crucial to study the Chinese market in terms of the required goods and services from Egypt based on the competitive advantages of price and quality.

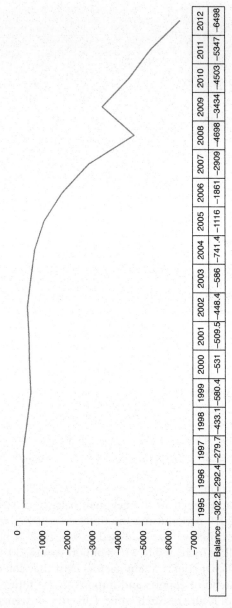

	1995	1996	1997	1998	1999	2000	2001	2002	2003	2004	2005	2006	2007	2008	2009	2010	2011	2012
Balance	-302.2	-292.4	-279.7	-433.1	-580.4	-531	-509.5	-448.4	-586	-741.4	-1116	-1861	-2909	-4698	-3434	-4503	-5347	-6498

Figure 6.3 Development of deficit in Egypt's balance of trade with China, 1995–2012

Source: Figure based on data cited from UNCTAD, UNCTAD Statistics.

Table 6.1   Prediction of the Egyptian exports and imports to and from China, 2014–2019 ($US millions)

Years	Exports	Imports	Balance
2015	3,091.48	13,267.3	–10,176
2016	4,166.39	16,322.4	–12,156
2017	5,615.03	20,081	–14,466
2018	7,567.37	24,705.1	–17,138
2019	10,198.5	30,393.9	–20,195

Source: Results of regression of logarithm per each exports, imports and balance on time. Estimated by the author.

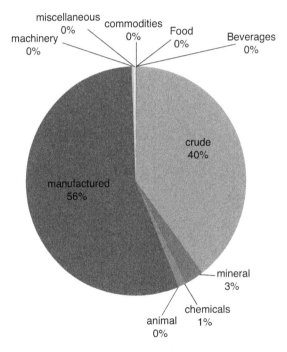

Figure 6.4   Egyptian exports to China by economic sector, 2002
Source: Figure based on data cited from UNCTAD, UNCTAD Statistics.

Figure 6.4 illustrates Egyptian exports, by economic sector, to China in 2002. As show, almost 96% out of total exports in 2002 was concentrated in manufactured goods (56%) and the crude materials sectors (40%). Comparing 2002 with 2012, there is significant reduction – to

7% in the manufactured goods, and the crude sector dropped to 10% (see Figure 6.5). On the other hand, 2012 exports show increases in the mineral sector, which takes the lion share (70% out of the total exports).

Regarding Egyptian imports from China by economic sector, there are four dominant sectors. The largest is miscellaneous manufactured articles, and this sector accounted for 29% of Chinese imports in 2002 versus 22% in 2012. The next largest sector is the machinery and transport equipment sector (28% in 2002 versus 34% in 2012), followed by manufactured goods (21% in 2002 versus 31% in 2012) and chemicals and related products (not elsewhere specified n.e.s. sector) with 11% in 2002 versus 10% in 2012. (See Figures 6.6 and Figure 6.7). These results refer to reasonable changes in the structure of imports, which reflect that the Egyptian economy depended extensively upon these types of imports during the 2002 to 2012 period. On the other hand, no

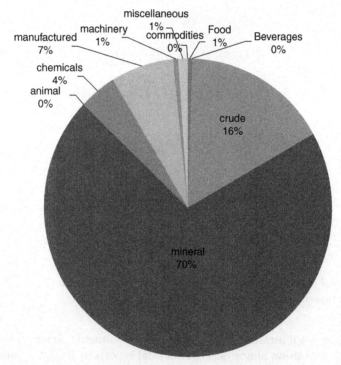

Figure 6.5 Egyptian exports to China by economic sector, 2012
Source: Figure based on data cited from UNCTAD, UNCTAD Statistics.

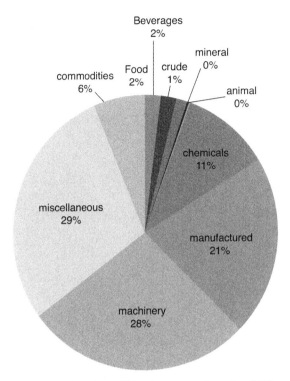

Figure 6.6 Egyptian imports from China by economic sector, 2002

Source: Figure based on data cited from UNCTAD, UNCTAD Statistics.

continuous growth is seen in Egyptian exports in any specific economic sector during the same period, which reflects a lack of clear polices to promote exports. Consequently, Egypt is facing deficit growth in its trade with China. At present Egypt has no precise procedures to effectively exploit the goods and services imported from China that can be re-exported to China or other countries or to slow the volume of imports from China.

As shown in Figure 6.8, for Egyptian exports to China, the mineral fuels and lubricants sector saw 23% growth from 2001 to 2012. In comparison, the chemicals and related products, n.e.s. sector, showed a 15% growth rate. The miscellaneous manufactured goods and food and live animals sectors each grew by 14% between 2002– 2012. With respect to the growth rate in the Egyptian imports from China by economic sector,

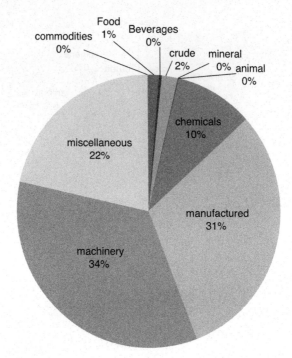

Figure 6.7   Egyptian imports from China by economic sector, 2012
Source: Figure based on data cited from UNCTAD, UNCTAD Statistics.

Figure 6.9 shows that all sectors witnessed growth increases, except the commodities and transactions, n.e.s. (–15%) and animal and vegetable oils, fats and waxes (–1%) sectors. The growth rate in the manufactured goods sector was 14%, while it was 13% in the machinery and transport equipment and crude materials sectors, glass and its products. (Ministry of Trade and Industry, 2009)

Likewise, Egypt is one of the largest exporters of high-quality marble, and 70% to 80% of its marble exports go to China. Other exports to China include oil, granite, raw cotton, industrial carpets, ceramic and sanitary wares, linen, crystal, and glass. The major Egyptian imports from China include chemicals, electric goods, footwear, textiles and apparel and beans. (Charles Robertson & Lucy Corkin, 2011)

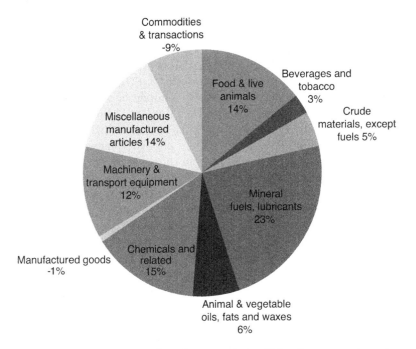

Figure 6.8 Growth rate in Egyptian exports to China by economic sector (2002–2012)

Source: Figure based on data cited from UNCTAD, UNCTAD Statistics.

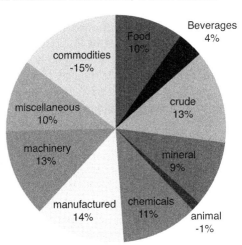

Figure 6.9 Growth rate in Egyptian imports from China by economic sector (2002–2012)

Source: Figure based on data cited from UNCTAD, UNCTAD Statistics.

Obstacles to trade from the Chinese perspective

Some of biggest obstacles Chinese exporters face are the transparency and consistency of Egyptian international trade policies. For example, in 2009 Egypt's Ministry of Trade and Industry (MFTI) issued a decree that imposed a temporary one-year duty on the import of cotton yarn, mixed yarn, cotton textiles, and sugar. However, these and additional fees were removed after only one month, in an effort to stabilize the economy. Despite Egypt's efforts to remove these protective measures, Chinese importers still feel a negative effect that those abrupt tax increases had on them. (Foreign Market Access Report, Egypt, 2010)

Another obstacle Chinese exporters face are the severe inspections and examinations by the Egyptian standards institutions. Egypt reports to the World Trade Organization (WTO) and justifies its strict import inspections as a means to ensure safety, hygiene, and environment protection. Imported goods are frequently declined by the government based on the non-conformity with the Egyptian standards in quality and specifications. Once the imported goods are considered as non-conforming, they are shut out by Customs. Nowadays, many trade disputes between China and Egypt are due to this sort of non-conformity to Egyptian standards. Consequently, importers or Chinese exporters are advised to be attentive to Egyptian standards to avoid unnecessary losses. (Foreign Market Access Report, Egypt, 2010)

As a reaction to the 2008 world financial crisis, in December 2009, MFTI in Egypt announced a 50% rise in export subsidies in favor of the domestic industries, which are funded by the Egyptian Exports Development Fund. China considers this increase in subsidies a violation of the Agreement on Subsidies and Countervailing Measures of the WTO since such subsidies are defined as prohibited subsides in that agreement. (Foreign Market Access Report, Egypt, 2010) By the end of 2009, Egypt had initiated 17 trade remedy investigations against China, concentrated largely in imported goods in the sectors of light industry, mechanics, and chemicals and minerals. Of the 17 investigations, 16 are anti-dumping cases and one concerns safeguard measures. (Foreign Market Access Report, Egypt, 2010)To address the concerns of investors, the Egyptian government in 2012 establish a Public-Private Partnerships (PPP) Supreme Committee. This committee oversees any PPP dispute, which may be resolved not only through Egyptian courts but also via commercial arbitration administered by the Cairo Regional Centre for International Commercial Arbitration under United Nations Commission on International Trade Law) procedures. (OECD, 2014)

The Egyptian government is working to establish an electronic system to register companies, which is designed to help streamline the bureaucratic processes. The first phase of on-line registration was launched in 2010, which gives investors the opportunity to submit their applications and follow their status via the Internet. However, paper applications will be continued beside the electronic system until the electronic system is fully functional.

In another effort to improve transparency for investors, Egypt's new (2014) constitution provides for the establishment of an Anti-Corruption Commission to emphasize dealing with conflicts of interests, standards of integrity, and government transparency.

Conclusion and policy implications

Sino-Egyptian economic relations are of long duration and relatively stable, reflecting the strong ties between the two countries. Chinese investments in the Suez zone in Egypt are strengthening the economic relations between China and Egypt. Both countries clearly are intent on maximizing their benefits when selecting trading partners. China uses Egypt's location to help disseminate its exports worldwide. The Suez Canal also helps reduce the costs of transportation.

Egypt, on the other hand, benefits from trade with China through an easing of its high unemployment, attraction of FDI, and the increase in production volume, which will help achieve economic stability.

However, the trade balance between China and Egypt is not at present equitably distributed, and Egypt's trade deficit with China is expected to be harmful to its economy.Egypt's goal is to encourage Chinese investors to do more business in Egypt, which it hopes will ease the high unemployment and improve the Egyptian resources exploitation industry. This goal requires Egypt to create precise and stable polices in international trade in order to achieve an equitable trade balance that offers mutual benefits to China. On the other hand, the Chinese government has not yet considered how to facilitate access for the Egyptian products into its market.

For its part, the Egyptian government has yet to effectively explore the Chinese market and to develop different scenarios for Egyptian exporters to access this market under preferential agreements with China. Changing the nature of Egyptian exports is required: diversifying the exports and increasing the value added by the Egyptian exporters should be considered in order to achieve high profit and improve the economic growth rate of the Egyptian economy.

Egypt's recognition of China dates to President Abdel-Nasser's era, which was followed by the signing of the first commercial agreements. President al-Sadat adopted the economic openness policy for foreign investments, with the first Chinese factory opening in Egypt during his presidency. President Mubarak, in addition to implementing commercial and economic agreements, opened the door for the establishment of the SEZ; as a result, China signed an agreement to establish an SEZ in the north west Suez economic zone. By the time of President Morsi's visit to China, he focused on building the sustainability of Egypt's relations with China. He renewed some previous agreements and signed additional new ones. Most recently, President al-Sisi stressed obtaining the full support of China in helping the Egyptian economy. His goal was to take a progressive step towards implementing many Chinese projects in Egypt through a comprehensive strategic partnership with China in all fields, thus raising the degree of cooperation between the two countries to that of true strategic partners. President al-Sisi established a special unit for China, administrated by the Ministry of International Cooperation under the umbrella of the Egyptian Cabinet. The main objective of this unit is to study the needs of Chinese investors and try to overcome the key difficulties and barriers facing them, as well as granting incentive packages to encourage them to invest in Egypt.

Notes

1. The Special Economic Zones (SEZ) Law 83 of 2002 in Egypt allows establishment of special zones for industrial, agricultural, or service activities designed specifically with the export market in mind. The law allows companies operating in these zones to import capital equipment, raw materials, and intermediate goods duty free. Companies established in the SEZs are also exempt from sales and indirect taxes and can operate under more flexible labor regulations.
2. It was formed in 1984 and considered a free market zone. TEDA is located in Tianjin, within the Tanggu District, along the northeastern coast of China. TEDA has been a major hub for foreign business and investment for more than ten years. TEDA is located less than an hour from downtown Tianjin, a quick ride away on the Binhai Mass Transit that was built in 2004. TEDA acts like its own city: It has its own schools, residential areas, transportation networks, and a port. Beginning in the late 1990s, MOFCOM (Ministry of Commerce of the People's Republic of China) began studying China's developmental zones and different indicators of economic and technological performance, and TEDA has always been at the top of the list. Visit: http://understand-china.com/tianjin-economic-technological-development-area-teda/
3. Chinese MOFA, China's African Policy, 2006, http://www.fmprc.gov.cn/eng/zxxx/t230615.htm

References

A New Egypt Looks to China for Balance and Leverage Publication: China Brief Volume: 12 Issue: 18.

Ahmed El-Sayed Al- Naggar, 2014, Egypt-China: Meeting of Civilization, Principles and Interests. Available at: http://english.ahram.org.eg/ NewsContentP/4/118926/Opinion/EgyptChina-Meeting-of-civilisations,- principles-an.aspx

Charles Robertson & Lucy Corkin, 2011, China in Africa, Country profile: Egypt's relations with China, Update Economics and Strategy Research, Renaissance Capital Available at: http://www.fastestbillion.com/res/Research/China_in_ Africa-210411.pdf

China Daily, 14 November 2007.

Chris Alden and Faten Aggad-Clerx, 2012, Chinese Investments and Employment Creation in Algeria and Egypt, Economic Grief, African Development Bank.

Davis, Marlyn, 2010, How China is Influencing Africa's Development, Background Paper for the perspectives on Global Development 2010 Shifting Wealth, OECD Development Centre.

Deborah Brautigam and Xiaoyang Tang, China's Investment in Special Economic Zones in Africa, Chapter 4. Available at: http://www.american.edu/sis/faculty/ upload/brautigam-chinese-investment-in.pdf.

Farah Halime, 2012, Chinese Firms Brave Uncertainty in Egypt to Gain a Foothold in Middle East Available at: http://www.nytimes.com/2012/08/30/world/ middleeast/chinese-firms-brave-uncertainty-in-egypt.html?_r=0]

Foreign Market Access Report, Egypt, 2010.

GAFI, 2009b, MDC Presentation, Arab Republic of Egypt, Ministry of Investment.

GAFI, 2009c, Ministerial Presentation, Arab Republic of Egypt, Ministry of Investment (in Arabic).

Han Bing, 2014, China-Egypt Economic Cooperation, Lecture Presented at the 4th Season of Chinese-Egyptian Research Center, Helwan University, Egypt, Unpublished.

Industrial Development Authority. The Industrial Development in Suez [Online]. Available at: http://www.ida.gov.eg/l[03 July 2013].

Ministry of Trade and Industry, 2009, Egypt-China Economic Relations Fact Sheet, Cairo, Arab Republic of Egypt, Ministry of Trade and Industry.

OECD, 2014, Business Climate Review of Egypt: Investment Policies and Public-Private Partnerships, Private Sector Development Project Insights.

State Information Service in Egypt, 2015, Economic and Commercial Relations between Egypt and China. Available at: http://www.sis.gov.eg/Ar/Templates/ Articles/tmpArticles.aspx?CatID=5374#.VNTV4eaUepc

US Department of State, 2014. Available at: http://www.state.gov/documents/ organization/227163.pdfUNCTAD, FDI/ TNC Database, Based on Data from the Central Bank of Egypt and the Ministry of Commerce (MOFCOM).

UNCTAD, UNCTAD Statistics

Zeng, Zhihua, 2010, How Do Special Economic Zones and Industrial Clusters Drive China's Rapid Development, in Zhihua Zeng, D (eds.). Building Engines for Growth and Competitiveness in China: Experience with Special Economic Zones and industrial Clusters, Washington DC: World Bank. Available at: http://documents.worldbank.org/curated/en/2010/01/12735386/building-engines-growth-competitiveness-china-experience-special-economic-zones-industrial-clusters

Zhang Chun, 2012, The Sino-African Relationship: Toward a New Strategic Partnership, Available at: http://www.lse.ac.uk/IDEAS/publications/reports/pdf/SR016/SR-016-Chun.pdf

7
Chinese and US Energy Policy in the Middle East

Gawdat Bahgat

The United States (US), the world's largest economy, seemed destined to continue its heavy reliance on imported fossil fuels. American oil production peaked in the early 1970s and the nation has become addicted to oil. With stagnant and declining production, foreign supplies increasingly met the gap between production and consumption. In the last several years however, technological innovation known as fracking has fundamentally changed the US energy outlook. This advance, along with changes in China and the Middle East, have substantially changed the energy landscape in the Middle East and, indeed, in the entire world. The US is now emerging as a major producer and exporter of natural gas, and to a lesser degree, petroleum. Feeling less vulnerable to interruptions in foreign energy supplies, some analysts and policymakers have predicted that the US will dis-engage from the Middle East.

For about two decades, the Chinese economy has been the world's fastest growing economy. This sustained economic growth was, and still needs to be, fueled by all sources of energy. Not surprisingly, China accounts for most of the increase in oil demand in coming years and decades. According to the latest BP Energy Outlook, China's import requirement is projected to more than double from today's levels – to almost 14 million barrels per day (b/d), a level and share of demand higher than the US at its peak. China is likely to surpass the US as the world's largest importer in 2014 and largest consumer by 2029.[1]

Finally, the Middle East, with its massive proven oil and natural gas reserves and low-cost production, will continue to lead global energy markets. According to the International Energy Agency (IEA), by the mid-2020 non-OPEC production starts to fall back and countries in the Middle East will provide most of the increase in global supply.[2] Given that global energy markets (oil more so than natural gas) are well-integrated, relations with the major oil and gas producers and exporters in the Middle East (and elsewhere) will continue to be a key factor in the international economic and strategic policies.

To sum up, in recent years Washington has become less dependent on foreign supplies from the Middle East and elsewhere while China is moving in the other direction. This chapter will examine the strategic implications of these emerging trends. I believe that the United States is not likely to withdraw from the Middle East and be replaced by China. Rather, I contend, the two global powers are likely to work together to promote and ensure economic and political stability. As the world's largest economy, economic prosperity and political stability in the Middle East are key US national security objectives. Furthermore, Washington has other key strategic national interests in the region (i.e., security of Israel, counter-terrorism, and nuclear non-proliferation). Rhetoric aside, American dis-engagement from the Middle East is not likely. On the other hand, Chinese economic and energy interests in the Middle East are flourishing. But it is also true that China depends on the United States to secure oil shipping lanes. There are no indications that China is willing or able to challenge US domination as the main security guarantor in the Middle East. Indeed it can be argued that China is satisfied with the current conditions under which it continues to receive oil and gas shipments from the Persian Gulf without paying a price. The US Fifth Fleet and the broader US presence in the region are providing security to the energy infrastructure and transportation.

United States energy policy in the Middle East

Very few relations can rival those between the United States on one side and Saudi Arabia and the other five Gulf monarchies on the other side, which have been built on long-standing traditions of friendship and informal alliance. Oil is at the heart of this close American-Saudi cooperation. Leaders on both sides perceive the substantial and uninterrupted oil supplies from the kingdom as one of the most important elements of global energy security and development of the world economy. Thus, for more than half a century, Saudi Arabia, in cooperation with the US government and American oil companies, has played a pivotal role in promoting moderation and stability in energy pricing and policies.

Unlike other major producers in the Persian Gulf and the Organization of Petroleum Exporting Countries (OPEC), oil explorations and developments in Saudi Arabia have been carried out almost entirely by American companies. In the early 1930s, US oil companies were looking for commercial opportunities overseas. Promising oil reservoirs had been discovered in Iran, Iraq, and Bahrain. This newly discovered hydro-carbon wealth was dominated by European companies, particularly from Great Britain. Meanwhile, indigenous leaders were interested in granting concessions to foreign companies in order to strengthen their rising economic and political power.

Thus, to great extent, oil was discovered and developed in most Middle Eastern countries by European oil companies. In 1945 the United States took a symbolic, but significant, step to challenge this European domi-nation. President Franklin Roosevelt met with King Abd Al-Aziz Ibn Saud, the founder of modern day Saudi Arabia, and cemented what is widely known as the oil for security deal. The essence of this deal is that the United States would guarantee the Saudi and Gulf security and in return the kingdom would meet the demand for oil supplies at reason-able prices. The Carter Doctrine in the late 1970s reinforced this deal by highlighting that any threat to the Gulf region would be considered a threat to core US national interests. In August 1990, when Saddam Hussein invaded and occupied Kuwait, the United States led an interna-tional coalition and liberated the Gulf state, proving itself as a reliable partner.

In the ensuing decades the two sides have kept their commitments to a great extent. The United States has supported Saudi Arabia (and other Gulf states) against external threats from Arab nationalism (Nasser of Egypt and Hussein of Iraq), from Iran, and from Al-Qaeda and other Islamist groups. Meanwhile, with the exception of the oil embargo (1973–1974), the kingdom has played a leading role in bringing stability and predictability to the global oil markets. The two nations also had been able to overcome several major disagreements and crises, most notably the September 2001 attacks on US in which several Saudi nationals were involved.

As has been widely argued, the partnership between Washington and Riyadh is better described as a marriage of convenience that is based on mutual interest rather than shared values. In recent years the founda-tions of this marriage have been challenged. Primarily, the United States is becoming less vulnerable to the changes in oil policies and prices.

Since the 1973–1974 Arab oil embargo, the United States has been preoccupied both with its own and its allies' dependence on imported energy sources, especially in relation to the stability and interdepend-ence of global energy markets. The United States and other major consuming countries (mostly members in the Organization for Economic Cooperation and Development [OECD]) created the IEA to improve their energy security and reduce their vulnerability to political and economic unrest in the global system and oil producing countries.

Since the early 2000s two major developments have contributed to the improvement in the overall US energy outlook. First, for decades several laws and regulations have been enacted and efforts made to contain consumption and boost a culture of energy efficiency. This policy has paid dividends. In recent years American oil consumption has been in decline. Despite economic and population growth, oil consumption fell from 19,761 thousand b/d in 2002 to 18,555 thousand in 2012.[3] This decline in consumption, or improved efficiency, is projected to continue in the foreseeable future. Population growth affects energy use through increases in housing, commercial floor space, transportation, and economic activity. However, the structure and efficiency of the US economy are changing in ways that can lower energy use. Changes in consumer behavior can also have an impact, such as changes in the rate of vehicle miles traveled per licensed driver. US population is forecast to increase by 0.7% per year from 2012 to 2040; the economy, as measured by gross domestic product (GDP), increases at an average annual rate of 2.4%; and total energy consumption increases by 0.4% per year. As a result, energy intensity measured both as energy use per person and as energy use per dollar of GDP, declines over the projection period.[4]

Equally important, the sustained investment in fracking and horizontal drilling has started paying off. The United States has always been a resource-abundant country and has successfully converted its ample energy, agriculture, water, mineral, and human capital resources to fuel its economic growth. Over the last several decades and until about 2010, the size of economically recoverable oil and gas resources available in the United States diminished, and the country relied increasingly on imported oil and natural gas. This growing import dependence and the reality of US vulnerability to the often-volatile global oil markets (and the widely shared expectation that these two conditions would only deepen over time) resulted in a national view that the United States was a relatively resource-constrained and energy-insecure country.

But in 2012, oil and gas exploration and production companies operating in the United States added 4.5 billion barrels of crude oil and lease condensate proven reserves, an increase of 15.4% from 2011 – the largest annual increase since 1970. US proven reserves of crude oil and lease condensate have also risen for four consecutive years. Proven reserves of oil exceeded 33.4 billion barrels for the first time since 1976.[5] Between 2005 and 2014, US crude oil production rose nearly 65% and natural gas production was up 34%. Both increases are a result of tight oil and shale gas development.[6]

Despite this significant improvement in the nation's energy outlook, the United States is highly unlikely to withdraw or disengage from the Middle East for at least three overlapping reasons:

- As a major global power, the United States simultaneously pursues several economic and strategic objectives. These objectives include steady oil supplies, Arab-Israeli peace, counter-terrorism and non-proliferation of weapons of mass destruction. For decades, American leaders and diplomats have invested substantial time, efforts, and political capital trying to reach a peaceful solution that would guarantee the security of Israel and the establishment of a Palestinian state. Since the September 11th attacks, counter-terrorism has become a major US national security objective. Similarly, containing the proliferation of chemical, biological, and nuclear weapons has been at the top of the American strategic agenda in the Middle East and elsewhere. For instance, American policy toward Iran and Iraq is better explained by strategic drives than by narrow oil interests.
- Global oil markets are well-integrated. It does not make much difference who sells and who buys a barrel of oil. Interruption of supplies or fluctuation in prices would directly affect Asian and European consumers more than the United States given their heavy dependence on foreign suppliers. However, the heavy and growing interdependence between the American economy on one side and Asian and European economies on the other means any energy-driven crisis would impact all parties.
- Despite Saudi and other Gulf states' efforts to build strategic and military relations with other global powers (Russia, China, France), the United States continues to be the major global power able to project substantial fire power to maintain and/or restore Middle East regional stability. Other global powers either lack the will or the means to project the needed military capability.

China's energy policy in the Middle East

China is the world's most populous country with a fast-growing economy. Since initiating market reforms in 1978, China has shifted from a centrally planned to a market-based economy and experienced rapid economic and social development. Gross development product (GDP) growth averaging about 10 percent a year has lifted more than

500 million people out of poverty. With a population of 1.3 billion, China recently became the second largest economy and is increasingly playing an important and influential role in the global economy.[7] This combination of a large population and fast-growing economy has led it to be the largest energy consumer and producer in the world. It is the world's second largest oil consumer behind the US and became the largest global energy consumer in 2010. China was a net oil exporter until the early 1990s. It became the world's second largest net importer of crude oil and petroleum products in 2009 and surpassed the United States in this role in 2014. The nation's oil consumption growth accounted for one-third of the world's oil consumption growth in 2013.[8]

This surge of China's energy consumption is largely driven by the last few decades of unprecedented and impressive economic development. The Chinese economy has been able to sustain one of the highest economic growth rates in the world since the early 1980s. This growth is fueled by all sources of energy. In recent years many analysts have highlighted Beijing's ambitious plans to utilize nuclear and renewable energy. China's broad energy strategy lists the following objectives:

- Ensure energy self-sufficiency;
- Secure sufficient and stable supplies of energy resources at reasonable prices;
- Invest in more energy-efficient technologies and increase the share of renewable energy sources in total energy consumption;
- Establish strategic reserves for use when resources are in short supply or during price hikes in the world market;
- Diversify imports of fossil fuels through trade and cooperation with more countries;
- Sign long-term supply contracts for energy import; and
- Sign more international contracts for resource exploration and development of new resource bases.[9]

Although nuclear generation is a small portion of the country's total power generation portfolio, China is actively promoting nuclear power as a clean, efficient, and reliable source of electricity generation. At the end of 2013, China had 31 reactors.[10] Most of the new nuclear reactors will be built in China, more than tripling China's current capacity. Following Japan's Fukushima nuclear accident in March 2011, China suspended government approvals for new nuclear plants until safety reviews of all facilities were completed and a safety framework was approved by the State Council. New plant approvals and construction resumed in October 2012.

China has a goal to produce at least 15% of its overall energy output by 2020 from renewable energy sources as the government aims to address environmental issues. China is taking the lead in solar and wind power. Because of its cost-effectiveness and sizeable resource potential, hydro-electricity has become the key source of renewable energy in China. These investments and utilization of green energy does not suggest a shift from fossil fuels. China is still heavily dependent on coal, oil, and natural gas and this heavy dependency is projected to continue in the coming decades.

In recent years the large and growing gap between oil production and consumption has been filled by imports, which reached record highs in 2013 (an average of 5.6 million barrels per day). The IEA expects China to import over 66% of its total oil by 2020 and 72% by 2040 as demand is expected to grow faster than domestic crude supply.[11] The Middle East remains China's main source of oil, supplying more than half of the country's imports, followed by Africa (particularly Angola). Beijing's oil imports from Iran have recently been restrained first by contract disputes and then by the international sanctions imposed on Tehran by global powers and the United Nations. Accordingly, Iran's share of China's imports has fallen since 2013. Although Beijing has been able to import extra oil supplies from other producers, these international sanctions underscore how strategic disputes can negatively impact China's energy needs.

Although natural gas production and consumption are rapidly increasing, this fuel makes up only a small proportion of the country's total energy mix. In order to diversify the energy mix and reduce pollution, the Chinese authorities have sought to boost domestic gas production and imports. Thus, the share of natural gas in the total energy consumption is projected to reach 8% by 2015 and 10% by 2020. China was a net gas exporter until 2007, when shrinking production could not keep up with rising consumption. Currently, imported gas meets about one-third of the demand. Like other countries, China depends on both pipelines and liquefied natural gas (LNG) to import gas from foreign suppliers. In May 2014, Russia and China agreed on an estimated $400 billion deal, under which Russia will export a large volume of natural gas to China. Qatar is another leading supplier (in the form of LNG).

Most of China's oil and gas imports, particularly from the Middle East, pass through the Strait of Malacca. The Strait is located between Indonesia, Malaysia, and Singapore and is the main shipping channel between the

Indian Ocean and the Pacific Ocean. The Strait is the shortest sea route between the Middle East producers and Asian consumers. About one quarter of all oil carried by sea passes through the Strait, mainly from Persian Gulf suppliers to Asian markets such as China, Japan, and South Korea. The Strait is considered the key chokepoint in Asia.[12]

In recent years, China has played a major role in establishing several forums to enhance and promote its national interest, including energy security. These forums include the Shanghai Cooperation Organization, a Eurasian political, economic, and military organization founded by the leaders of China, Kazakhstan, Kyrgyzstan, Russia, Tajikistan, and Uzbekistan. The goal is to counterbalance rising American influence and combat Islamic and separatist political movements. Along with Russia, India, Brazil, and South Africa, China is a member in the BRICS Group. The grouping was originally known as BRIC before the inclusion of South Africa in 2010. The BRICS members are all developing or newly industrialized countries, but they are distinguished by their large, fast-growing economies. In May 2014 President Xi Jinping expressed interest in boosting the Conference on Interaction and Confidence-building measures in Asia (CICA). The CICA is an inter-governmental forum for enhancing cooperation towards promoting peace, security, and stability in Asia. It is a forum based on the recognition that there is close link between peace, security, and stability in Asia and in the rest of the world. The Chinese President said that the CICA should become a security dialogue and cooperation platform and should establish a defense consultation mechanism. Some analysts see this proposal as the latest effort by Beijing to build up groups of Asian and developing governments to offset the influence of the United States and other Western nations in global affairs.[13]

Conclusion: The way forward

The rapidly changing energy landscape underscores two significant trends. First, the United States is becoming more self-sufficient and less vulnerable to fluctuations in oil and gas prices and interruption of supplies. Second, China is moving in the opposite direction, becoming more dependent on foreign supplies. Within this broad context, the analysis in this chapter suggests four conclusions. First, due to technological innovations, the United States' energy outlook has significantly improved in the last few years. These improvements in oil and gas production have led to expectations that the US might soon become a major oil and gas exporter (the latter as LNG), reducing the significance of Middle East producers. It is important to note that the IEA does not endorse these expectations. Rather, it asserts that meeting long-term growth in oil demand relies on the holders of the large remaining conventional resources, which are concentrated in the Middle East.[14] It projects that by the mid-2020, non-OPEC production starts to fall back and countries in the Middle East will provide most of the increase in global supply.[15] The IEA also suggests that the expectation of a surge in new LNG supplies totally transforming gas markets needs to be tempered due to the high capital cost of LNG infrastructure.

The deteriorating security conditions in Iraq and the escalation of sectarian and ethnic conflicts have raised doubts on that country's ability to increase and sustain its oil output. Over the last several years, Iraq's oil production has steadily increased. Moreover, Iraq was projected to provide most of the incremental OPEC supplies in the next several years. These projections are at the moment highly uncertain. This conclusion applies equally to another OPEC member – Libya. In short, political instability and lack of security in several major oil producers suggest that the relatively more stable OPEC members are likely to play an even more important role in supplying adequate and steady supplies to consuming countries. In other words, Saudi Arabia, the United Arab Emirates, Kuwait, and Qatar will continue to play a major role in meeting the world's demand for fossil fuels.

Second, the United States is likely to remain fully engaged in the Middle East. The region occupies the driver's seat in the global oil market. Oil is, and is projected to remain, the main fuel despite the growing share of natural gas and renewable energy. In a well-integrated global economy any interruption of supplies would affect all parties.

Third, deepening Chinese oil dependency on the Middle East is only part of broader growing commercial and economic ties. In the last two decades, China has emerged as a major trade partner to several Middle Eastern states, and Chinese oil companies are key investors in the Persian Gulf. What is missing is cultural interaction. Few Middle Easterners speak Chinese and there are no Chinatowns in any Middle Eastern country. The United States enjoys great advantage in the cultural arena with China.

Fourth, China's rise as a dominant buyer of Middle East oil presents a conundrum for it and the United States. For China, it means its economy depends in part on oil from a region dominated by the US military. When tankers depart Persian Gulf terminals for China they rely in significant part on the US Fifth Fleet policing the area. For Washington, China's oil thirst raises doubt on justifying military spending that benefits a country many Americans see as a strategic rival and that frequently doesn't side with the US on foreign policy.[16]

The bottom line is that China's ability to project power in the Middle East is constrained. It doesn't have the military firepower or expertise to actively police conflict zones or shipping lanes. In addition, one can argue, China might not have the will to invest in building military power to police the Gulf region. On the other hand, the United States has the political will and military means to continue playing the role of security guarantor of oil and gas supplies from the Middle East. The non-interruption of these supplies serves the United States', China's, and the world's broad economic and strategic interests.

Notes

1. British Petroleum, BP Energy Outlook 2035, available at http://www.bp.com. Accessed January 20, 2014.
2. International Energy Agency, World Energy Outlook, Paris, November 2013, p. 14.
3. British Petroleum, BP Statistical Review of World Energy, London, p. 9 2014
4. Energy Information Administration, Annual Energy Outlook, Washington, DC: 2014, p. 76.
5. Energy Information Administration, US Crude Oil and Natural Gas Proved Reserves, 2012, Washington DC, April 2014, p. 1.
6. Sarah O. Ladislaw, Maren Leed and Molly A. Walton, New Energy, New Geopolitics, Center for Strategic & International Studies, Washington DC, available at http://www.csis.org. Accessed 30 May 2014.
7. World Bank, China overview, available at http://www.worldbank.org/en/country/china/overview. Accessed 30 June 2014.
8. Energy Information Administration, Country brief: China, available at http://www.eia.gov. Accessed 4 February 2014.
9. State Council of the People's Republic of China, China's energy conditions and policies, available at http://www.china.org.cn/english/whitepaper/energy/23708.htm. Accessed 1 July 2014
10. Ole Odgaard and Jorgen Delman, "China's energy security and its challenges towards 2035," Energy Policy, Vol.71, No.8, August 2014, pp. 107–117.
11. Energy Information Administration, Country brief: China, available at http://www.eia.gov. Accessed 4 February 2014.
12. Energy Information Administration, World Oil Transit Chokepoints, available at http://www.eia.gov. Accessed 24 May 2014.
13. Louise Watt, China Calls for New Asian Security Structure, Associated Press, available at http://abcnews.go.com/international/wirestory/china-calls-asian-security-structure-23805975. Accessed 24 May 2014.
14. International Energy Agency, World Energy Investment Outlook, Paris, 2014, p. 67.
15. International Energy Agency, World Energy Outlook, Paris, 2013, p. 4.
16. Brian Spegele and Matt Bradley, Middle East Oil Fuels Fresh China-US Tensions, Wall Street Journal, 17 April 2014 http://www.wsj.com/articles/SB10001424127887324755104570732839485177714.

8
Does Likud Have a "Look East" Option?

Niv Horesh

Introduction

January 2015 saw a rare visit to Israel by a Japanese Prime Minster. In light of Jerusalem's increasingly troubled relations with many of its traditional Western allies, Shinzo Abe's visit was something to celebrate. In the Prime Minister's entourage were no fewer than 100 government officials and business people, as if to demonstrate just how qualitatively different bilateral relations have become compared with the 1970s, when most of Japanese industry observed the Arab boycott of Israel. Asia as a whole has already edged out the US as Israel's second biggest trading bloc.[1]

Abe's previous stop on his Middle Eastern trip was Cairo, where he had pledged $200 million in non-military Japanese assistance for Arab countries battling the Islamic State of Iraq and a-Sham (ISIS). In Jerusalem, while Abe stressed the economic significance of his visit, because of ISIS' announcement that it would execute two Japanese hostages, he was inevitably drawn in to Benjamin's Netanyahu bleak Middle Eastern narrative. In a chilling video, ISIS demanded ransom for the two because Japan 'has proudly donated $100 million to kill our women and children and destroy the home of Muslims.' Previously, there have even been unconfirmed reports about ISIS operatives recruiting in Japan.[2]

Coming soon after the *Charlie Hebdo* and kosher supermarket terror attacks in Paris, there appeared at that moment no greater threat to world peace and prosperity than Islamist terrorism, at least through Israeli eyes. This belief held despite tentative signs that the US had been trying to wean itself off its reliance on Middle Eastern oil. In fact, oil prices had been dropping since late 2014 in the face of ISIS' takeover of a few oil fields across Iraq.

Needless to say, Netanyahu's pessimism about the Arab Spring over the past few years has on balance proven justified, compared with President Obama's optimism in his first term in the oval office. Talk of democratization of the Arab world had been at the time misguided and naïve, as many in Washington would now concede.[3] The region still harbors medieval-like animus against the West and is rife with religious fanaticism.

Yet, by definition all crises also carry opportunity, which perennial pessimism can shut out all too easily. More conciliatory rhetoric by Israel toward Palestinian President Mahmoud Abbas at that point in time could have, for example, opened doors for Israel in Europe and around the Middle East, where many leaders are equally concerned about the rise of ISIS. Indeed, there could have been much more global understanding for Israel's unique predicament in the eye of the storm, whether in Gaza or facing Hezbollah, had Netanyahu not rushed to cash in on ISIS' rise to bolster his 'no peace partner, no hope' narrative in the ears of foreign dignitaries, while mollycoddling the West Bank Settlement Lobby at the same time.[4]

Netanyahu was quoted as telling Abe his visit came at the right time because 'we aim to reduce our dependence on some markets in Western Europe. Western Europe is experiencing a wave of Islamization, anti-Semitism, and anti-Zionism so we need to ensure we have diverse markets around the world for years to come'.[5] To his credit, Netanyahu did mention to Abe that his "Look East" pitch was not confined to Japan: It took Netanyahu to Beijing a year and a half earlier, and saw him meeting his Indian counterpart at the last UN General Assembly. Getting Tokyo on its side was certainly encouraging for Israel. It also may have been gratifying because Abe's government – though angering China on numerous occasions – was at that point in almost complete unison with Beijing when it came to ISIS. For example, Ibrahim Jafari, Iraq's foreign minister, revealed in December 2014 that his Chinese counterpart, Wang Yi, had offered his country assistance including airstrikes in the fight against Sunni extremists.[6]

The purpose of this chapter is threefold. First, it argues that viewing Israel's relations with China, Japan, or India mainly through the prism of ISIS is simplistic and short-sighted. So is the presumption that East and South Asia, or China more specifically, can serve as a rough-and-ready substitute market in place of the EU and US. Secondly, this chapter offers an analysis of the rationale that underlies Netanyahu's right-wing Likud Party's Look East pitch as a hedging strategy versus the Obama administration, starting with Netanyahu's former party patron and defense minister Moshe Arens. Lastly, this chapter will consider the current pulses shaping the Sino-Israeli relationship against the backdrop of the great civil unrest sweeping across the Arab world.

Several historic policy narratives have carried over from the Cold War era and continue to impact political mind-sets in Jerusalem and Beijing. The main argument put forward in the following passages is that, while historic factors might help explain elements of tactical continuity in Chinese rhetoric vis-à-vis the Middle East across different periods, Chinese approaches to Israel have been re-configured since the early 1990s by virtue of external factors. These factors include the end of the Cold War and China's increasingly acute energy dependency in the 21st century – Chinese rapprochement with the US in the early 1970s took two more decades to translate into *major* Middle East policy shifts. The chapter concludes with a look into the next decade and Israel's strategic choices with regard to a globally resurgent China. Particular focus is placed on how China's rise is seen by Israelis, and the ways and means by which China might wish to position itself vis-à-vis Iran on the one hand and Saudi Arabia on the other.

The balance of power

Barack Obama's attempts to defuse visceral anti-Americanism in the Arab world was accompanied by assurances that the US would speed up its pull-out from Iraq and Afghanistan. The Obama administration initially presented a less belligerent approach to Iran's nuclear program than George W. Bush's administration; this was followed by a cautious reaction to the Egyptian and Libyan uprisings. President Obama's first term in office gave rise to speculations about a possible scaling down of US immersion in the Middle East in favor of focusing on domestic issues and on better managing China's rise in the Asia-Pacific region. On the other hand, Israeli and Saudi anxiety over Iran and their pessimistic appraisal of the budding post-Mubarak order in Egypt pitted both countries against Washington's cautious espousal of propagating democracy in the developing world; these differences, in turn, triggered speculations that other powers might wish to fill any void left in the region.

The popular unrest across the Arab world sparked a fresh debate over the scope of multinational intervention in 21st-century emergent humanitarian crises and the perimeters of promoting democratization in the developing world. This unrest also prompted a reassessment of America's ability to maintain its system of longstanding regional alliances in the face of economic recession at home, and amid President

Obama's apparent disowning of his predecessor's ebullient pre-emptive posture. Israel, Saudi Arabia, the Republic of China on Taiwan (ROC), and Australia –allies historically vulnerable to regional isolation – closely observed the Obama Administration's reactions to the demonstrations rocking the Arab world (and Iran). Analysts in these counties often wondered about the significance of Obama's professed non-belligerence to their own national-security interests. A few on the periphery of their countries' security establishments were even propelled to speculate openly that America might ultimately disengage from their arena in order to focus on domestic issues.[7]

Arguments linking the Mideast's malcontents with the proposition that the United States is swept up with isolationist sentiment and may no longer be able to afford an overdrawn military presence overseas and, consequently, might soon be forced to accommodate a more globally assertive China, are not uncommon. To that end, it is worth examining new perceptions of China's global rise that have become evident in one of America's staunchest regional allies, Israel.

Geo-political predictions are, of course, a risky business, particularly one might humoristically add when applied to the future. Anyone seriously contemplating a partial American disengagement from the Middle East or the Asia-Pacific region in the near future, followed by a dramatic projection of Chinese hard power, must surely recall Professor Kenneth Waltz's punt that Japan and Germany would likely start competing with US strategically once the Soviet Union had stopped posing a threat to stability in Europe and East Asia.[8] In the event, far from challenging the US, Japan has proven increasingly reliant on the US to contain China and shore up the Korean peninsula.

Once considered naturally poised to re-emerge as the regional hegemon, Japan's confidence fell flat in the early 1990s on the heels of an equity-price meltdown and skyrocketing public indebtedness, and it has not fully recovered. Against this backdrop, the question many ask is whether China's ability to eventually catapult itself into a serious competitor for global supremacy – military, economic, or cultural – may not be overstated. A decade ago, sceptics seem to have decisively won the argument. Note, for example, Professor Lucian Pye's 1998 scathing remarks about East Asian countries' chronic memory-blockage and the consequent identity malaise muting any East Asian claims to global leadership. At the height of the Asian Financial Crisis and merely a decade after the fall of the Berlin Wall, Pye deemed neither China nor Japan capable of rising above their own parochialisms and cultural self-absorption to find an appropriate global idiom with which to envision an alternative East Asian world order. Pye was not even sure China, despite its economic promise, fitted at all into the dominant nation-state world order, being as it was a "civilisation pretending to be a nation state." [9]

Over the next decade, the Chinese nation-building project steam-rolled ahead, and it would seem more than apposite to re-evaluate erst-while strategic mind-sets. Indeed, until recently, high-profile figures have been claiming that much of the China boom was oversupply in disguise and that China's implosion was imminent. Further, these figures also claimed that China's 'economic miracle' was predicated on state-run banks diverting capital to resuscitate moribund state-owned behemoths, and that China did not embrace the 'free-market' and 'de-regulate' its economy quickly enough.[10] These attributes might have stemmed from a Beijing-centric outlook rather than from a well-informed survey of the last three decades of complex and often contra-dictory economic reform thrusts in their entirety. As it turns out, the lingering economic crisis in the US is a constant reminder that leading Western banks do not seem to have allocated capital much more ration-ally than their state-controlled counterparts in the People's Republic of China (PRC).[11]

In contrast to Pye, Warren Cohen suggested that the question was not *whether* China would eventually contend with the US but precisely how soon this might happen. Nonetheless, Cohen had little doubt that China would eventually act just as aggressively on the world stage as those late 19th-century European powers. Thus, Cohen did not accord much faith to the rhetoric emanating from Beijing since the 1980s, which has been stressing the PRC's intent on a 'Peaceful Rise' (*heping jueqi*) and consider-ably softened Mao-era references to 'Western imperialism,' 'Soviet revi-sionism,' or 'world class warfare.'[12]

Yet Beijing insiders attest to a genuine division playing out in the Chinese Communist Party (CCP) Politburo between those who want to continue clinging to the late Deng Xiaoping's legacy of keeping a low profile on the world stage (*taoguang yanghui*), and those who are hankering after Mao-style retaliatory tactics.[13] The outcome of this debate during Xi Jinping's tenure might tilt perceptions of China's rise across much of the rest of the world. Notably, modernization efforts by the Chinese People's Liberation Army (PLA) have been progressing by leaps and bounds. As yet, however, it seems that the Obama Administration is slowly moving away from any hint of containment, in anticipation of PRC militarization or a government-orchestrated chauvinistic upsurge, to more extensive engagement: surely that must say something about the intelligence that Washington possesses concerning the nature of the

PLA's build-up, the CCP's popular support base or, indeed, the limited options for the US in confronting either.[14]

We propose here to conceptually take a step backward from the high-profile debate in the US over the implications of China's rise in order to draw attention to what may be new, important developments in the perception of China as seen through US allies' eyes. How seriously do such allies take China's transformation, the realignment opportunities and threats it might pose? Do such allies identify a new potent development model or any new policy prescripts afforded by the Chinese nation-building project, or is it the case that the discourse over China's rise is, for now at least, still confined to hackneyed 'war-and-peace' considerations or vast export-market clichés? In order to avoid sweeping generalizations, and in view of the vast global scope and rawness of this conceptual framework, here we offer the Israeli case study; we will provisionally focus on China's emerging 'hard' and 'soft' power as seen through Israeli eyes, as well as on the subtleties and evolution of the discourse on China's rise there.[15]

China's rise in the Israeli public eye: Arens as "seer"

Before the overthrow of Hosni Mubarak any public debate over the implications of the rise of China on Israel's longstanding alliance with the US had been all but consigned to backroom chatter. Arguably, the only prominent Israeli public figure calling for closer ties with Beijing irrespective of the US global desiderata has been aeronautical-engineering professor Moshe Arens, a former Defence Minister, one-time key Likud Party power-broker, and erstwhile mentor to the incumbent Prime Minister, Benjamin Netanyahu.

Arens has perhaps been the most consistent proponent of forging a Sino-Israeli pact, presumably as a safeguard against an imminent rupture between Jerusalem and Washington over the future of Jewish settlement construction in the West Bank.[16] Deeply embittered about what he saw as attempts by the (George H.W.) Bush administration to destabilize the hard-line Yitzhak Shamir Likud government (1986–1992) following the First Gulf War, Arens has long held that no inalienable, sentimental bond between Washington and Jerusalem existed.[17]

Indeed, Arens' suspicion of White House foreign policy motives turned into outrage when Israel was accused by the Pentagon of transferring Patriot Missile Shield technology to China. US Patriot batteries had first been deployed across Israel to fend off Saddam Hussein's Scud missile attacks during the First Gulf War. Though they did not prove exceedingly efficient, the batteries were subsequently commissioned by the Israeli Air Force on a long-term basis. Both Beijing and Jerusalem strongly denied any Patriot technology transfer, but US pressure to curb Israeli arms sales to China mounted in the following years. On 2 January 2003, State Department spokesman Richard Boucher formally stated that Israeli military exports to China were of concern to the United States. Immediately afterwards, Israel announced that it would comply with US demands, and halt all negotiations over the export of arms and security equipment to China. A spokesperson for the Israeli Defense Ministry announced on 8 January that, 'Defense relations between Israel and China require from time to time consideration of specific issues. The revision was concluded vis-à-vis China and on concrete issues also vis-à-vis the US, bearing in mind American sensitivity.' Israeli officials later indicated that Israel would continue to sell China military equipment that was available on the global arms market. China issued a communiqué in response to the Israeli announcement, insisting that 'the development of normal military trade cooperation with Israel is a matter between the two countries concerned.'[18]

The wider context of Boucher's pronouncement was, of course, the abrogation of the Phalcon reconnaissance aircraft deal between China and Israel, which nipped in the bud a dramatic strategic breakthrough between the two countries, and gave rise to years of recriminations between the Israeli defense establishment and the Pentagon. In 2001, under intense American pressure, Israel on short notice cancelled two key contracts with the Chinese PLA for the supply of the Phalcon. In 2004, Israel also cancelled the upgrading of Harpy drones for the PLA, inviting retaliatory measures from Beijing that, some say, persist to this day and constrain bilateral relations.[19]

The Patriot, Phalcon, and Harpy controversies culminated in 2005 in the resignation of Gen. Amos Yaron, the Director-General of Israel's Defense Ministry, thereby sending into deep freeze almost three decades of clandestine Sino-Israeli military collaboration. Notably, Chinese purchases of Israeli military hardware long predate the establishment of diplomatic relations between the two countries in 1992. As early as 1975, PRC officials had visited the Israeli pavilion at the Paris Air Salon. Similarly, in 1979, PLA envoys secretly expressed interest in Israel's capacity to upgrade Soviet materiel captured from Arab armies.[20]

Straddled with much the same obsolete materiel carried over from the era of Sino-Soviet cooperation, the PLA realised just how backward its firepower had become in the wake of the border war with Vietnam in 1979. Thus, during the 1980s, Israel ended up supplying weapons to both China and Taiwan. Interestingly, Taiwan's dependence on the US had not caused it to solicit Israeli weapons earlier, because it competed with the PRC for legitimacy in the Third World and entertained a rather pro-Arab posture until the early 1990s.[21]

From an Israeli perspective, therefore, there was no antagonism between PRC and ROC arms sales because neither market had held out the promise of a major foreign relations breakthrough for a very long time. If anything, despite the vast scale of PLA needs, PRC sales came across as more risky because of the greater likelihood that Israeli technology might end up being re-exported to Arab countries or Iran. [22]

Wider right-wing disillusionment with Washington

Though secular, Arens' views are shared by many religious right-wingers in Israel, who have so far had no reason to weigh into the debate on China's rise. In these quarters, visceral resentment of the US for foreign policy moves designed to placate Arab public opinion are prominent, however symbolic such moves may be. It is not uncommon to hear hardline West Bank settler leaders, many of whom have immigrated to Israel from the US themselves, historically casting American peace envoys to the region as imperial 'High Commissioners' dispatched to cozen Judea into ceding sacred land. Not surprisingly, President Obama's notorious bowing before King Faisal of Saudi Arabia is seized upon as proof of his clandestine pro-Palestinian bias and coddling of Arab tyrants.[23]

Arens' argument is, nonetheless, more grounded in *realpolitik* than in emotive symbolism. Implicit in his interpretation of American foreign policy imperatives is the belief that any condemnation of Israel's grip on the West Bank betrays growing concern in Washington, which needs access to Arab oil reserves. European Union foreign policy is seen, moreover, as hypocritically ingratiating with Arab tyrants and shedding false tears for the plight of Palestinians, so as to upstage Washington. The corollary might then be a cynical zero-sum game between dominant, re-emergent, and upstart global powers over Mideast hegemony. In this scenario, America is seen as using Israel no less than Israel benefits from American military and financial aid; and in which Europe offers countervailing blandishments to Arab incumbent leaders as well as to their domestic opposition, so as to in part, repress the vexed legacy of European colonialism. Further backstage, Russia is seen as intent on resuscitating Soviet-era pacts in the region, with China featuring as a new contender. Right-wing and centrist parties shrug off, by and large, the human rights dimension of Israel's grip on the West Bank as an artificially instigated discourse designed to infuse foreign powers' contests over energy supplies with a semblance of statesmanlike respectability. Ironically enough, this standpoint is not dissimilar to how Europe's far-left portrays the motives behind American policy in the region. In these terms, putative threats by the US to abandon Israel are seen as ones that can be fairly effectively countered with implicit Israeli rapprochement with Russia and, more subtly, a warming toward China.[24]

However, it is important to note that the changing demographics of Israel's mainstream secular population, following the large waves of immigration from the former Soviet Union in the early 1990s, might of themselves warrant better ties with the Russian Federation in the future because of the familial, cultural, and often religious ties that these immigrants retain with their country of origin.[25] China is a very different case, more culturally distant and much less understood in Israeli popular discourse.

Complementary economies?

China is portrayed in the Israeli media as desirous of access to Israel's high technology industry, particularly telecommunications equipment. But the extent that such interest can make up for the suspension of military technology transfers or strategically offset China's preoccupation with energy security and its historic ties with non-aligned and Arab countries is seldom broached.[26]

To be sure, Israeli IT firms have accounted for a large share of Israeli exports to China following the suspension of advanced arms sales. Still, Israel suffers from an acute trade deficit with China, and circumstantial evidence points to difficulties that Israeli start-ups have in penetrating the Chinese market. Moreover, the Chinese market – notwithstanding its fast growth rate – is still only Israel's fourth largest export destination. This standing is a stark contrast with arch-enemy Iran, whose trade links with China have become paramount in its national accounts, or even South Korea, which like Israel is a staunch US ally that established diplomatic relations with the PRC as late as 1992, but has since seen an explosion of bilateral investment and trade flows.[27]

Tellingly, the Sino-Israeli business deal touted as the 'most significant' in recent years was the sale of Makhteshim Agan, a manufacturer of generic pesticides, to ChemChina, a PRC state-owned firm. In contrast to the strident opposition that state-owned Chinese firms often face when bidding for a stake in foreign energy or mineral firms, the ChemChina deal was mostly welcome in Israel precisely because it had likely been approved by the Politburo, and interpreted as a sign of Chinese confidence in Israel's future.[28] However, Makhteshim's research and development has been lagging for years; it certainly does not share the high tech 'start up' aura that Israeli politicians like. Rather than signalling a new high tech trade vista, the deal might ultimately reflect Chinese leaders' confidence in their 'go abroad' (*zouchu qu*) strategy. It might be a mistake to think of the Makhteshim deal as ushering in a new dynamic that can make up for the suspension of military technology dimension in Sino-Israeli relations.

More recently, iconic Israeli dairy-product manufacturer, Tnuva, was sold to the Chinese state-owned enterprise Bright Foods. Bright Foods, now a global operator, paid $2.5 billion for a 56% stake, purchasing the shares from the Apax Group and other Israeli investors in May 2014.[29] This deal attracted more popular criticism than was the case with ChemChina, due, in part to Tnuva's storied position within the Israeli economy. Tnuva had been established long before the state of Israel came into existence, playing a crucial role in the coalescence of the Jewish settlement of then Palestine. In fact, former Mossad chief Efraim Halevy went as far as labelling the deal a risk to national security, yet his voice remained a lone one in the public fray, as other forms of opposition to the sale eventually died down.[30]

PLA modernization was, of course, one of the four drivers of Deng's reformist thrust and is still a very important priority for Beijing. Some levels of military collaboration are said to have survived the Phalcon crisis. However, while Chinese diplomats might, strictly off the record, express support for the tacit strategic understandings (*moqi*) between the two countries since, it is doubtful whether anyone in Beijing still views Israel as an *indispensible* outlet to PLA modernization. It thus makes for a purely hypothetical exercise to speculate if China would have sacrificed in any meaningful way its distinctly pro-Arab posture for the prospect of easier access to more advanced US military technology via Israel. Even without the US slamming the door on Sino-Israeli military collaboration, it is highly questionable whether Beijing would have compromised its immediate energy interests and hard-won reputation in the Arab world and Iran in return for such collaboration.

America-centrism and the Lieberman factor

That Arens seems to prize China over Russia as a potential ally should be seen as not so much a viable strategic option but as a peculiar idiosyncrasy of his own career path. Long before the ill-fated Phalcon deal,

Arens had been intimately involved in the development of Israel's second-generation fighter jet, the Lavi. The Pentagon initially supported the development of this jet, but later came to view it as encroaching on US export markets. In 1987, due to American pressure and exorbitant production costs that could not be borne by Israel's then-fragile economy, the Lavi project was aborted by the Israeli government; however, Lavi prototypes are rumored to have been sold to China in violation of US restrictions.[31]

The Phalcon fiasco demonstrated the limits of the Israeli lobby in Washington, whose power is often wildly exaggerated. For example, political scientist Nancy Tucker suggested rather controversially that "...weak players like Israel and Taiwan have penetrated the American government in their own version of 'divide and rule' while at the same time rallying interest groups and US public opinion on their behalf". However, even Tucker is quick to suggest that "weak, small allies are in the end at the mercy of their strong protectors," as America's 1979 formal recognition of the PRC as *the* "one China" clearly shows.[32] That momentous recognition begs the question whether Israel can – beyond bluff deterrence – avert a US recognition of a Palestinian state across much of the West Bank in the long run by warming to other global powers.

Israel's center-right – indeed, the very establishment as embodied by MIT-educated Prime Minister Benjamin Netanyahu – is still firmly married to the notion of America's indispensability to Israel's existence. This attitude is not just a corollary of the unparalleled foreign aid Israel has been receiving from the US since the 1970s, but is also a result of decades of intimate engagement between Jerusalem and Washington that both sides ascribe to "shared values".[33] Equally important in this context is the fact that Netanyahu spent much of his adulthood in the US, and that many of his mentors and campaign donors affiliate with the conservative wing of American Jewry. Thus, beyond recently suggesting that Mandarin ought to be taught at primary school level in Israel alongside English and Arabic,[34] Netanyahu has not officially said much about the more ponderous implications of China's rise. In order to offset Obama's overtures to the Muslim world, Netanyahu, therefore, has been accused of playing his support base in Congress and in the conservative US media against the White House.[35]

Notwithstanding the hitherto limited pull of China's rise on Israeli public discourse, a few on the right take a diametrically opposed view to that of Arens. The greed for oil is still seen as the driver of superpower interests in the region, but for Arens' critics, the instability in

Egypt – once a key US and Israeli ally and lynchpin of Mideast order – affords an opportunity to rehabilitate relations with the Obama administration. This school of thought suggests US-Israeli differences can be smoothed over through the concerns both countries share about the export of nuclear know-how from North Korea to the Middle East. China's checkered patronage of the Kim regime is anathema to American neo-conservatives and their Israeli cohort, and thus has the potential of resurrecting Cold War alignments. In return for unconditional Israeli support, should the Korean crisis get out of control, right-wing analysts in Israel expect Obama to relinquish his efforts to win over the hearts and minds of Muslims.[36]

Pitting China as a threat might be an easy sell to Israeli mainstream public opinion, which is averse to PRC's current voting pattern in the UN Security Council and to ongoing North Korean or putative Chinese assistance to Iran's and Syria's respective nuclear programmes.[37]

Hard-line Moldova-born former Foreign Minister Avigdor Lieberman, who had until recently been widely touted as a future prime minister despite criminal indictments, may ably harp on such sentiments if the Korean arena heats up uncontrollably.[38] Lieberman is close to Putin and Medvedev, and may lobby to bring Israel somewhat closer to Moscow's orbit if re-elected; he has gained notoriety around the world for being flippant with the West and at what little is left of the stalled Israeli-Palestinian peace process. Yet it is far less well known, amongst observers of Israeli foreign policy, that Lieberman's in-your-face conduct concerned the PRC on at least one occasion. In October 2009 he remained conspicuously absent from a reception organized by the PRC embassy in Tel Aviv in protest over China's vote at the UN endorsing the Goldstone probe into human rights violations during the Israeli-Hamas confrontation earlier that year.[39]

The weight of history? Changing mutual perceptions

China's rise in Israeli popular discourse cannot be adequately understood outside of the historic context of Zionism, Chinese nationalism, and their changing mutual perceptions. This section aims to highlight in broad strokes past bilateral narratives that, to some extent, still shape foreign policy mind-sets in Jerusalem and Beijing.

For regionally isolated allies such as Israel, security dependence on the US has been so strong in the latter part of the 20th century that considerable psychological impediments to any serious discussion of Washington's indispensability must exist. However, in Israel's case, history suggests the allegiance to Washington should not be taken for granted despite assurances from mainstream politicians in both countries. Though the US supported the UN resolution in favor of the partition of Palestine and the creation of the state of Israel in 1948, it was reluctant at first to sell weaponry to the beleaguered Jewish state. Israel's War of Independence was fought with ammunition supplied by then non-allied countries, including the former Czechoslovakia. Even after Ben-Gurion, one of Israel's Founding Fathers and its first Prime Minister, had decided to side with the West during the Korea War, it was mainly France that supplied Israel with advanced weaponry until 1967. Nasser's progressive leaning toward the USSR after the 1967 Six-Day War radically re-drew regional axes. For instance, post-colonial France increasingly distanced itself from Israel to pursue a third-power strategy, while the US became a more explicit advocate of Zionism, in part due to the social-economic mobility of American Jewry. But, ultimately, Israel still owes much of its seminal nuclear and aeronautical know-how to Paris, not to Washington.[40] In fact, Ben-Gurion had envisioned the current rise of India and China as early as the 1950s. The deterioration of Israel's relations with much of Asia in the intervening years – in the face of Ben-Gurion's prescience and his well-known intellectual fascination with Buddhism – had a profound impact on Israel's self-perception of its strategic position on the Asian continent.[41]

Notably, although Sun Yat-sen was strongly anti-colonialist, he was nevertheless known to have been generally sympathetic to the Zionist cause in the early 1920s. Long after his death, however, the ROC abstained from the UN vote on the partition of Palestine in 1948.[42] The decline of European colonialism in the immediate post-war era then changed the nature of anti-Americanism, while the demise of Maoism as state doctrine also earned China new friends and foes. Upon its establishment, Israel had been non-aligned and despite much closer ties with the West in the late 1950s, it was led by the Mapai-Mapam socialist coalition from 1955 to 1977.

Once the PRC had been established, the centrist Mapai bloc moved to grant recognition of Beijing the following year. Mapam – being more leftist and in opposition to Mapai until 1955– was pushing for better ties with Communist countries. Yet this early recognition proved to be 'unrequited love' as, in contrast to Moscow, Beijing would refrain from establishing diplomatic relations with the Jewish state. Desperate to secure legitimacy among the newly established Arab members of the UN, Taipei also distanced itself from Israel until the late 1970s.[43]

Today, however, Mapam's reincarnation of sorts – the Meretz Party – has evolved into a marginal left-wing opposition party. Israel's tectonic drift to the right following the formation of the first Likud government under Menachem Begin in 1977 firmly placed Jerusalem as an implacable enemy of the Communist bloc, as well as eliciting growing hostility from Western Europe's social-democratic movement. Israel's increasingly marginal left-wing parties are now the ones calling for a more proactive American leadership vis-à-vis the stalled Israeli-Palestinian peace process, not for less US intervention. Long gone, of course, are the early-1950s pronouncements of Mapam solidarity with Stalin and Mao.[44]

Rarely critical of America's campaigns in Iraq or Afghanistan, Meretz has on the other hand evolved into the party most vocally critical of Beijing's human rights record. Its former leader, Yossi Sarid – while far from enamoured of US neo-conservatives –even called for the boycotting of the Beijing Olympics because of China's political repression. Similarly, Israeli libertarians such as Avraham Burg, while serving as Knesset Speaker, met with and endorsed the Dalai Lama's non-violent doctrines. The only distinctly pro-Beijing voice in Israeli radical-left discourse is that of Hebrew University academic Yuri Pines, the most prominent amongst Israel's third-generation China specialists, as well as a renowned conscientious objector and peace activist.[45]

Depictions of Israel in the Chinese press

On its part, Chinese state media has been much more critical of Israel than unmediated Sino-Israeli encounters might suggest. Chinese media has traditionally projected Israel as a trigger-happy entity, but its tenor has softened somewhat in recent years. Among the Chinese intelligentsia, a genuine streak of admiration for the achievements of Jewish scientists, statesmen and thinkers has carried over from the pre-war era, and quite often flows onto popular impressions of Israel, in defiance of editorialised content. Private sphere perceptions of Israel may thus no longer be entirely coloured by old Cold War rhetoric.[46]

While for the most part avoiding the acrimony of Soviet-style anti-Semitism prevalent in that era, the earliest PRC book on Israel dates back to 1956 and is predictably replete with condemnation of Zionism as a manifestation of imperialism and thus in collusion with Hitler and Mussolini.[47] Beyond largely negative newspaper articles, there have been surprisingly few books since that time that are dedicated to Israel in the PRC. One of the most recent ones reflects quite negatively on the labor conditions of thousands of PRC construction workers contracted to work in Israel in lieu of Palestinians.[48]

That the first PRC book on Israel was published in 1956 is no accident. Indeed, the Bandung Conference (1955) was a critical turning point after which the PRC's pro-Arab stance emerged openly, and whose legacy is in a sense still casting a shadow on Sino-Israeli relations. Then, China's Great Leap Forward and its Cultural Revolution saw yet a greater intensification of anti-Israeli pronouncements, including by Mao himself. Even after the Cold War had ended, the legacy of Bandung could be detected in China's abstention in the UN vote over whether or not to revoke the equation of Zionism with racism.[49]

Although diplomatic relations between Moscow and Jerusalem were cut off in 1967, attempts were constantly made to engage the PRC in the last decade of Israeli diplomatic presence. In 1956, the same year in which the first anti-Israeli book was published, Israel's ambassador to the USSR was allowed to visit Beijing but was told that the time was not right to broach diplomatic relations. The only Israelis who could meet Mao in person at that period were Communist Party leaders. Before the Sino-Soviet split had come to light, Shmuel Mikunis, for example, visited Mao on recommendation from his European communist counterparts, Maurice Thorez and Palmiro Toglatti. Mikunis even asked Mao to intercede with Khrushchev, so that restriction on Jewish cultural life in the USSR could be lifted. Beijing, however, never formally acknowledged Israel's persistent UN vote in favor of accepting the PRC as a member state in the face of ROC protests. The last sign of recognition, albeit mute, on the PRC's part before it was swayed by the extremities of the Cultural Revolution was the 1960 exhibition "China Today" in Tel Aviv, with photos donated by the PRC Committee on Foreign Affairs (*Zhongguo duiwai guanxi weiyuanhui*). [50]

In 1965 Mao was quoted in the Egyptian newspaper *Al-Anwar* as stating "Imperialism fear Chinese and Arabs. Israel and Taiwan are Imperialism's bases in Asia." Upon its establishment in 1959 the Palestinian Fatah movement received immediate recognition from Beijing, and some Palestinian Liberation Organisation (PLO) activists were later said to have trained with the PLA.[51] PRC contacts with Israel over the purchase of advanced weapons did not at first impact its sponsorship of the PLO. It was only in 1988 that Beijing admitted publicly that contacts with Israel had been made, but at the same time it upgraded the PLO office there to the level of a full-fledged embassy so as to mollify Palestinian concerns.[52]

The "unrequited love" motif

Despite the longstanding PRC ties with the PLO, and perhaps to America's chagrin, Israel continued to vote in favor of accepting Beijing as a UN member, except for a brief intercession in the late 1960s. US opposition to PRC contacts ceased being an issue for Israel only when Nixon struck his deal with Mao in Beijing in 1972.[53] Unfortunately for Israel, however, the Sino-Soviet split only militated the PRC to compete with the Soviet Union over influence in the Arab World, and thereby hardened its stance toward Israel. In that sense, Israel's "unrequited love" for China was equalled by the PRC's 'unrequited love' for Gamal Abd En-Nasser's Egypt, who nonetheless remained fairly suspicious of Beijing. Indeed, Nasser was aghast at the Great Leap Forward even though he was far from enamoured of the alternative Soviet-style communism. China, for its part, denounced Nasser only when he outlawed the Syrian communist party as part of the move to establish a United Arab Republic.[54]

When the Sino-Soviet split came to the boil in 1960, France was still Israel's main strategic ally, with Washington struggling to remain on the sidelines of the Israeli-Arab conflict. Only after De Gaulle had pulled out of Algeria in 1962, and cooled relations with the "stubborn" Jewish state did Washington come more forcefully to Israel's defense. The concrete, formal origin of the US-Israeli alliance, therefore, does not long predate the 1973 Yom Kippur war, in which Nixon famously helped save Israel from a humiliating defeat with an unprecedented airlift of military supplies.[55]

Nixon's visit eventually paved the way for China to first express a desire to play a role in Israeli-Arab peace negotiations in the late 1980s, and in turn to establish diplomatic relations with Israel in 1992. After decades of "unrequited love," the Israeli establishment as a whole went out of its way to foster budding open bilateral contacts. Yitzhak Rabin's Labor government, which had taken over from Shamir's Likud in 1992, undertook to maintain Israel's official silence on the 1989 Tiananmen crackdown so as to pave the way for PRC formal recognition of Israel later that year.

But the problem of modifying the PRC's historic allegiances in the Arab world became evident when Shimon Peres – who became Prime Minister after Rabin's assassination – visited Beijing for the first time in 1994. As part of a tightly packed schedule, Peres was, according to some anonymous sources, supposed to inaugurate a Center for Israel Studies at Peking University, and name it after Ben-Gurion. The Center had been approved in advance by the PRC's Foreign Ministry, the *Waijiaobu*.

However, the university cancelled the inauguration ceremony a mere two hours before it was set to begin due to Arab sensitivities. In retaliation, Israel is said to have withdrawn the funding for the Center.[56]

Conclusions: who needs shared values?

If arguably ahead of their time, Arens' views are atypical of mainstream analyses in a country such as Israel, long accustomed to bipartisan, extensive engagement with Washington, and whose largest diaspora community resides in the US. China's rise has otherwise made only a very superficial imprint on academic discourse beyond generic calls for more attention to be paid to South and East Asia. In that sense, the "rising China" debate is predictably more evident in countries with larger comparative trade volumes with the PRC. The growth of Israel's trade with China since the botched Phalcon deal has lagged far behind other countries in the region: China is only Israel's third-largest trading partner, well behind Europe and the US. Beyond trade, China still wields relatively little soft power in Israel, reflecting perhaps the most acute area of deficiency in its foreign policy.

In the wake of Mubarak's ouster, renowned political scientist Minxin Pei was one of many who suggested that unrest in the Middle East might sooner or later ignite the fury of China's disenfranchised, and that the CCP was bracing itself – alarmingly – for protest with a crackdown on human rights activists. Other reports even suggested that the ripples sent by the Mideast malcontents were also being uncomfortably felt in Moscow. Yet circumstantial evidence suggests that so far the turmoil in the Middle East has not led to widespread riots elsewhere in Asia or Eastern Europe.[57]

This chapter pointed to another, much less-discussed but equally important consequence of the turmoil in the Arab world; namely, the subterranean anxiety, which many regional US allies feel as they watch President Obama's rebuke for longstanding pro-American figures such as Mubarak, and his initially cool response to events in Tunisia and Libya. This anxiety seems to be spanning pro-US democracies such as Taiwan, Israel, and Australia – as well pro-US monarchies including Saudi Arabia and Jordan. All of these US allies seem to be ultimately concerned about gradual American disengagement from their region.

Drawing on domestic politics, popular perceptions, and business press reports, the foregoing passages examined how the relatively peripheral "rising China" debate has evolved in Israel. Among right-wing circles, Obama's perceived pro-Palestinian bias, his slow response to the Arab uprisings, and abandonment of Mubarak have instigated some unprecedented voices of skepticism of Israel's alliance with the US. Some see signs of looming American disengagement therein, particularly in view of the by-now open rift between Obama and Netanyahu following the latter's recent speech before the Israeli lobby in Washington (American Israel Public Affairs Committee [AIPAC]).

Others in Israel, however, see an opportunity to eventually re-bond with Washington on the back of Israel's perceived stability as compared with neighboring countries; still others, like Arens and Lieberman, conjure up a warming to Beijing or Moscow in a bid to defuse US pressure for territorial compromise with the Palestinians. Whether these latter premonitions coalesce into a mainstream serious re-think of Sino-Israeli relations depends on how Washington reacts to Israel's growing fear of strategic abandonment. Such fear is based on the US abandonment of Mubarak and the impending thaw in US-Iran relations following the 2015 Vienna Nuclear Accord.

Eager to maintain AIPAC support in the lead-up to the 2012 presidential elections, Obama promised to convince Europe to oppose a unilateral Palestinian declaration of statehood. Yet Obama remains acutely at loggerheads with Netanyahu, and did not shy away from insisting to AIPAC that Israel must accept 1967 lines as its future border with a viable and contiguous Palestinian state a part of negotiated settlement; that is, a state sprawling over much of the West Bank.[58] In the interim, an Israeli pre-emptive strike on Iran's nuclear programme would only accentuate its isolation if launched without consultation with Washington. The intermediate-term prospects for a dramatic breakthrough in Sino-Israeli bilateral relations as a way of averting such isolation seem, at any rate, quite tenuous.

The notion that Israel can stand its ground in its febrile part of the world simply by pitching beyond Europe and constantly hedging against the Obama administration is precarious. Israel cannot afford to write Europe off. In that sense, Netanyahu should learn from Erdogan's mistakes following Turkey's membership rebuff from the EU. The Turkish PM has already tried to steer Turkey away from Europe with, among other things, upbeat rhetoric on Asia. He has gained little of substance from it so far.

Notes

1. http://www.haaretz.com/news/diplomacy-defense/.premium-1.638581 (Accessed 10 February 2015).

2. http://www.dailymail.co.uk/news/article-2917804/Video-Islamic-State-group-threatens-kill-Japan-hostages.html (Accessed 10 February 2015).
3. http://www.foreignaffairs.com/articles/67862/larry-diamond/a-fourth-wave-or-false-start (Accessed 10 February 2015).
4. http://www.foxnews.com/politics/2014/10/06/netanyahu-us-criticism-israeli-settlements-against-american-values/ (Accessed 10 February 2015).
5. http://www.independent.co.uk/news/world/middle-east/israeli-pm-netanyahu-warns-of-wave-of-islamisation-sweeping-across-europe-9987035.html (Accessed 10 February 2015).
6. http://www.ft.com/cms/s/0/3f4dc794–8141–11e4-b956–00144feabdc0.html#axzz3RMNofYHg (Accessed 10 February 2015).
7. Speculations about a possible US disengagement from Asia seem to have emerged afresh toward the end of George W. Bush's tenure. See e.g. Robert Stutter, "China's Regional Strategy and Why It May Not Be Good for America," in David L. Shambaugh ed., *Power Shift: China and Asia's New Dynamics*, (Berkeley, CA: University of California Press, 2006), p. 300: "[T]he United States should carefully manage the U.S.-China relationship from an overall position of U.S. confidence and strength. Alternatively, the United States may over time move away from its insistence on maintaining the dominant strategic position in Asian and world affairs. This could set the stage for a different kind of Sino-American accommodation, with the United States pulling back strategically from Asia as China rises to regional leadership." For more recent Taiwanese anxiety over Obama's China policy and a possible spurning by Washington, see e.g. William Lowther, "China Talks about Early Unification Policy", *Taipei Times*, 10 April 2011, http://www.taipeitimes.com/News/taiwan/archives/2011/04/10/2003500382 (Accessed 27 April 2011); for a recent Australian perspective on the possibility US disengagement from the Pacific, see e.g. Hugh White, "Power Shift: Australia's Future Between Washington and Beijing", *Quarterly Essay*, No 39 (2010), p. 36; on Saudi concerns, see e.g. Robert Dreyfuss, "Saudi Arabia's Fear of Egypt", *The Nation*, February 13, 2011, http://www.thenation.com/blog/158523/saudi-arabias-fear-egypt (Accessed 27 April 2011); on Israeli concerns, see e.g. anon., "Israel concerned over U.S.' Abandonment' of Mubarak", *Catholic Online*, 2 February 2011, http://catholic.org/international/international_story.php?id=40181 (Accessed 27 April 2011).
8. Kenneth N. Waltz, "The Emerging Structure of International Politics", *International Security*, Vol. 18, No 2 (1993), pp. 44–79.
9. Lucian Pye, "International Relations in Asia: Culture Nation and State," in *The Second Gaston Sigur Annual Lecture* (Washington, DC: George Washington University. Sigur Center for Asian Studies, 1998).
10. See e.g. Gordon Chang, *The Coming Collapse of China* (New York: Random House, 2001).
11. Until recently, an extensive banking reform was viewed by some as an urgent requisite for sustained PRC growth. See Nicholas R. Lardy, *China's Unfinished Economic Revolution* (Washington D.C.: Brookings Institution Press, 1998). For a more optimistic appraisal, see Barry Naughton, *Growing Out of the Plan: Chinese Economic Reform, 1978–1993* (New York: Cambridge University Press, 1996).
12. Warren I. Cohen, 2009. "China's Rise in Historical Perspectives," in Zhao and Liu eds., *Managing the China Challenge: Global Perspectives (*New York: Routledge,

2009), pp. 23–40. On the strategy behind China's 'Peaceful Rise,' see also Yan Xuetong and Sun Xuefeng, *Zhongguo jueqi ji qi zhanlue (China's Rise and Its Strategy)* (Beijing: Beijing University Press, 2006).

13. Willie Wo-lap Lam. *Chinese Politics in the Hu Jintao Era: New Leaders, New Challenges* (London: ME Sharpe, 2006), p. 174.

14. For an overview of the PLA build-up, see e.g. Robert S. Ross, *Chinese Security Policy: Structure, Power and Politics* (London: Taylor & Francis, 2009).

15. For a thought-provoking re-interpretation of how China's 'hard' and 'soft' power' might interplay in practical terms over the next few decades, see Yan Xuetong, *Ancient Chinese Thought, Modern Chinese Power* (Princeton N.J.: Princeton University Press, 2011).

16. Arens views are summed up retrospectively in this op-ed, "Kach hechmatznu et Sin" ("This is how we missed China"), *Harretz*, 22 September 2009, http://www.haaretz.co.il/hasite/spages/1116043.html (Accessed 27 April 2010).

17. Moshe Arens, Broken Covenant: *American Foreign Policy and the Crisis between the U.S. and Israel* (New York: Simon & Schuster, 1995).

18. For an overview of Sino-Chinese military collaboration, see e.g. Michael E. Brown (2000), *The Rise of China* (MIT Press, 2000), pp. 13–16, 96–98; on the Patriot accusations, Gill Bates and Taeho Kim, *China's Arms Acquisition from Abroad: A Quest for 'Superb and Secret Weapons'* (New York: Oxford University Press, 1995), pp. 81–86; see also the following reports (All Accessed 27 April 2011): anon., "China's Missile Imports and Assistance From Israel", *Nuclear Threat Initiative* (online version), 28 March 2003, http://www.nti.org/db/china/imisr.htm; Clyde R. Mark, "Israeli-United States Relations", *CRS Issue Brief for Congress*, 21 December 2001, http://fpc.state.gov/documents/organization/7933.pdf; Patrick E. Tyler, "No Evidence Found of Patriot Sales by Israel to China", *New York Times* (online version), 3 April 1992, http://www.nytimes.com/1992/04/03/world/no-evidence-found-of-patriot-sales-by-israel-to-china.html.

19. See Du Xianju, *Zhongguo he Yiselie guanxishi (History of Sino-Israeli Relations)* (Hong Kong: Wenhua chuanxun, 2009), p. 120; see also survey by Yossi Melman, "Kulam rotzim kesher im Sin hutz mimisrad habitachon" ("All intent on closer ties with China except the Ministry of Defense"), *Haaretz* undated, http://www.haaretz.co.il/hasite/pages/ShArt.jhtml?more=1&itemN o=1013920&contrassID=2&subContrassID=2&sbSubContrassID=0 (Accessed 27 April 2011).

20. Jonathan Goldstein, "Introduction," in idem. ed., *China and Israel 1948–1998: A Fifty Year Retrospective* (Westport, Conn.: Praeger, 1999), p. xiv; Yitzhak Shichor, "Israel's Military Transfers to China and Taiwan", *Survival*, Vol. 40, No 1, pp. 68–91.

21. The Taipei Economic and Cultural Office in Tel Aviv was established in 1993, namely, only a year after the PRC established its embassy there.

22. Yitzhak Shichor, *East Wind Over Arabia: Origins and Implications of the Sino-Saudi Missile Deal* (Berkeley: University of California Working Paper, 1989); Bates Gill, "Chinese Arms Exports to Iran", *Middle East Review of International Affairs* Vol. 2, No 2 (1998), pp. 55–70.

23. Richard T. Antoun, *Understanding Fundamentalism: Christian, Islamic and Jewish Movements* (Lanham, Maryland: Rowman and Littlefield, 2001), pp. 101–105; see also Yossi Blum-Halevi, "Biden, Atta lo hanatziv haelyon shelanu" ("Biden,

You are not our High-Commissioner"), *Arutz Sheva*, 10 March 2010, http://www.
inn.co.il/Articles/Article.aspx/8698 (Accessed 27 April 2011); Carolyn Gluck,
"Hanatziv haelyon shel Obama" ("Obama's High Commissioner"), *Latma*, 29
June 2009, http://www.latma.co.il/article.aspx?artild=4826 (Accessed 27 April
2011); *Haaretz Service*, "Did Barack Obama bow to Saudi King Abdullah?", 9
April 2009, http://www.haaretz.com/news/watch-did-barack-obama-bow-to-
saudi-king-abdullah-1.273824 (Accessed 27 April 2011)

24. Shmuel Tal, "Lieberman: Leshadreg hayahasim im Russya" ("Lieberman: Israel
Needs to Upgrade Its Ties with Russia"), *Reshet Bet News* (online version), 8
November 2010, http://www.iba.org.il/bet/?type=1&entity=688188&topic=3
07 (Accessed 27 April 2011)

25. On the Russian immigration to Israel, see e.g. Guy Ben-Porat, *Israel since 1980*
(New York: Cambridge University Press, 2008), pp. 54–56.

26. On Iranian and Middle Eastern oil exports as determinant of Chinese foreign
policy, see e.g. Manochehr Dorraj and Carrie L. Currier, "Lubricated With Oil:
Iran-China Relations in a Changing World", *Middle East Policy* (2008), No 15,
pp. 66–80.

27. For the latest trade statistics and analyses, see the following sources (All
accessed 24 May 2011): Anon. "Israel Economy and the Israeli Export", *The
Israel Export and International Cooperation Institute*, February 2011, http://www.
export.gov.il/NewsHTML/economy/Israel%27sEconomicReviewFebruary201
1.pdf; Najmeh Bozorgmehr and Geoff Dyer, "China Overtakes EU as Iran's
Top Trading Partner", *Financial Times*, 8 February 2010, http://www.ft.com/
intl/cms/s/0/f220dfac-14d4–11df-8f1d-00144feab49a,dwp_uuid=be75219e-
940a-11da-82ea-0000779e2340.html#axzz1NEwF2Qvr;

Adam Gonn, "Sino-Israel trade boosted for mutually benefits" [*sic*] 4
April 2011, http://news.xinhuanet.com/english2010/china/2011–04-
/04/c_13812028.htm; The US-China Business Council, "US-China Trade
Statistics and China's World Trade Statistics", http://www.uschina.org/
statistics/tradetable.html

28. *The Marker* (online version), "Nesi Hatechniyon leshe'avar: mechirat
Machteshim laSinim – yom atzuv lata'asiya" ("Former Techion President:
Makhteshim's Sale to the Chinese is a Sad Day for the Industry"), 30
December 2010, http://www.themarker.com/markets/1.587410 (Accessed 27
April 2011).

29. http://www.timesofisrael.com/chinese-state-company-buys-controlling-
stake-in-tnuva/

30. http://www.jpost.com/Opinion/Editorials/Selling-Tnuva-351231

31. Robert Hewson, "Chinese J-10 'benefited from the Lavi project'", *IHS Jane's:
Defense & Security Intelligence & Analysis*, 19 May 2008, http://www.janes.
com/products/janes/defence-security-eport.aspx?ID=1065926403&pu=1&rd
=janes_com# (Accessed 27 April 2011).

32. Nancy B. Tucker, "Introduction: Aid and Influence," in idem. ed., *Taiwan,
Hong Kong and the United States, 1945–1992: Uncertain Friendships* (New York:
Twayne, 1994), pp. 1–8.

33. Michael Oren," 'The Ultimate Ally': The 'Realists' Are Wrong – America Need
Israel Now More Than Ever" *Foreign Policy*, May 2011, http://www.foreign-
policy.com/articles/2011/04/25/the_ultimate_ally (online version, Accessed
24 May 2011).

34. See e.g. Boaz Wallinitz, "Netanyahu: kol yaldei Israel tzrihim lilmod Sinit" ("Netanyahu: Every Child in Israel Ought to Learn Mandarin"), *Wallah News*, 31 May 2011, http://news.walla.co.il/?w=/21/1828389 (Accessed 7 June 2011).

35. See e.g. Helene Cooper, "Invitation to Israeli Leader Puts Obama on the Spot", *New York Times*, 20 April 2011, http://www.nytimes.com/2011/04/21/world/middleeast/21prexy.html (Accessed 27 April 2011).

36. See e.g. Alon Marom, "HaSinim Ba'im, HaSinim Ba'im" ("The Chinese are Coming, the Chinese are Coming"), *Maariv*, 20 February 2011, http://www.nrg.co.il/online/1/ART2/213/844.html (Accessed 27 April 2011).

37. Gawdat Bahgat, "Nuclear proliferation: The Islamic Republic of Iran", *Iranian Studies* Vol. 39, No 3 (2006), p. 311; Christina Y. Lin, "China, Iran, and North Korea: A Triangular Strategic Alliance", *Middle East Review of International Affairs* Vol. 14, No 1 (2010), pp. 50–67.

38. On Lieberman, see Arian et al (2006), pp. 145–148 ; Reich (2008) pp. 281–283; *Israelis of Russian Descent* (2010), p. 116

39. Roni Sofer, "Sarim: Nahrim et hagigot yom ha'atzmaut shel Turkya" (Ministers: We Shall Boycott the Turkish Independence Day Banquet", *Yedioth Ahronot*, 18 October 2009, http://www.ynet.co.il/articles/0,7340,L-3791792,00.html (Accessed 27 April 2011).

40. Avner Cohen, *Israel and the Bomb* (New York: Columbia University Press, 1998).

41. Meron Medzini, "Reflections on Israel's Asian Policy," in Michael Curtis and Susan Gietelson eds., *Israel in the Third World* (New Brunswick, NJ: Transactions, 1976), pp. 200–211.

42. Zhou Xun, *Chinese Perceptions of the 'Jews' and Judaism* (London: Routledge, 2011), pp. 121–124.

43. On the Mapai era in Israeli history see Peter Y. Medding, *Mapai in Israel: Political Organisation and Government in New Society* (Cambridge: Cambridge University Press, 1972).

44. Thomas G. Mitchell, *Indispensable Traitors: Liberal Parties in Settler Conflicts.* (New York: Greenwood, 2002), pp. 42–48.

45. Yossi Sarid, "Stop the Dream, I want to Get Off", *Haaretz*, 8 August 2008, http://www.haaretz.com/print-edition/opinion/stop-the-dream-i-want-to-get-off-1.251368 (Accessed 27 April 2011); Yuri Pines, "Giant Lies about China", *Haaretz*, 24 July 2007, http://www.haaretz.com/print-edition/opinion/giant-lies-about-china-1.228081 (Accessed 27 April 2011).

46. Zhou Xun, *Chinese Perceptions of the 'Jews'*, (New York: Routledge, 2013), pp. 158–169.

47. Yitzhak Shichor, *The Middle East in China's Foreign Policy, 1949–1977* (London: Cambridge University Press, 1979), pp. 57–58.

48. Cao Xin, *Chu yiselie ji: yi ge zhongguo nu jizhe de zhenshi zaoyu* (Exodus from Israel: An Account of a Chinese Female Reporters' Ordeal) (Beijing: Zhongguo chengshi chubanshe, 2005).

49. Yitzhak Shichor, *The Middle East in China's Foreign Policy, 1949–1977* (London: Cambridge University Press, 1979), pp. 9–74; Hashim S.H. Behbehani, *China's Foreign Policy in the Arab World, 1955–75: Three Case Studies.* (London: Kegan Paul International, 1981), pp. 1–20.

50. Du Xianju, *Zhongguo he Yiselie guanxishi* (*History of Sino-Israeli Relations*) (Hong Kong: Wenhua chuanxun, 2009),, pp. 42–42; on Israeli Communist

Party ties with China, see Aron Shai, "The Israeli Communist Party's Policy toward the People's Republic of China, 1949–1998," in Jonathan Goldstein. ed. *China and Israel 1948–1998: A Fifty Year Retrospective* (Westport, Conn: Praeger, 1999), pp. 83–94.

51. Hashim S.H. Behbehani, *China's Foreign Policy in the Arab World, 1955–75: Three Case Studies*. (London: Kegan Paul International, 1981), pp. 20–73.
52. Du Xianju, *Zhongguo he Yiselie guanxishi (History of Sino-Israeli Relations)* (Hong Kong: Wenhua chuanxun, 2009),, p. 160.
53. Yitzhak Shichor, *The Middle East in China's Foreign Policy, 1949–1977* (London: Cambridge University Press, 1979), p. 115.
54. Joseph E. Khalili, "Communist China and the United Arab Republic", *Asian Survey* Vol. 10, No. 4, pp. 309–19. April 1970
55. Raymond Aron, *De Gaulle, Israel and the Jews.* (London: Transactions, 2004).
56. Du Xianju, *Zhongguo he Yiselie guanxishi (History of Sino-Israeli Relations)* (Hong Kong: Wenhua chuanxun, 2009), pp. 189–90.
57. Pei Minxin, "The Message for China from Tahrir Square," *Financial Times*, 12 February 2011, http://www.ft.com/intl/cms/s/0/233f88aa-361b-11e0-9-b3b-00144feabdc0.html#axzz1QdsCQDhy (Accessed 28 April 2011); Andrew Jacobs, "Where 'Jasmine' Means Tea, Not a Revolt", *New York Times*, 2 April 2011 (Accessed 28 April 2011), http://www.nytimes.com/2011/04/03/weekinreview/03jacobs.html; Dmitri Trenin, "Russia and Egypt: An Old Relationship", *Aspenia Online* (rep. Carnegie Moscow Center),11 February 2011, http://carnegie.ru/publications/?fa=42598 (Accessed 28 April 2011).
58. Helene Cooper, "Obama Presses Israel to Make 'Hard Choices'", *New York Times*, 22 May 2011, http://www.nytimes.com/2011/05/23/world/middleeast/23aipac.html (Accessed 7 June 2011).

9

China and the Gulf Co-operation Council: The Rebound Relationship

Neil Quilliam

Introduction

The relationship between the six states of the Gulf Co-operation Council[1] (GCC) and China is advancing quickly. There is plenty of evidence to demonstrate that both China and the GCC states recognise the growing value of partnership and have invested time, money, and effort to lift relations to a new level. In many ways, the relationship should be a natural fit: China is growing quickly (GDP was estimated at $13.39 trillion in 2013)[2], despite cyclical downturns, and is, therefore, energy hungry. Its growing population (estimated 1.4 billion in 2014)[3] requires staggering amounts of energy; with an expanding middle class, oil demand is set to grow by 8 million barrels per day (MBD) to reach 18 MBD by 2035.[4] The Gulf Arab states that make up the GCC hold approximately 33% of the world's oil reserves,[5] and Qatar operates the largest non-associated gas field and is the number one exporter of liquefied natural gas (LNG).[6] Moreover, as energy demand amongst the Organization for Economic Cooperation and Development (OECD) countries stagnates and, in some cases, even declines, the GCC-China relationship looks set to strengthen.

The question that this chapter attempts to answer is whether the relationship, which is built primarily on energy, at present, will develop beyond a transactional association and lead to a closer strategic partnership. I argue that while the relationship will continue to be driven by energy interdependency, there are very few signs to suggest that it will develop into a strong and durable alliance. In other words, although the economic dimension of the relationship will continue to grow, it is unlikely that political and diplomatic co-operation will undergo any significant change. Moreover, China will not replace the US (Western) alliance, which has proven so durable since the end of the Second World War, with the GCC states, at least in the medium term.

This chapter comprises five sections: warming relations; demanding China, obliging GCC; investing together for the future; the exit strategy; and the conclusion.

For the purposes of this chapter, the author will use the terms GCC and Gulf Arab states interchangeably. While there is insufficient space to draw out all the distinctions amongst the six member states, differences on key issues will be highlighted.

Warming relations

On paper, the GCC-China relationship looks set to strengthen and should form the basis of a strategic alliance. However, I argue that it will remain largely transactional in nature as it remains an immature relationship characterized by low levels of trust and comfort. At present, neither China nor the Gulf Arab states share sufficiently close ties either at senior government levels (political and military) nor through state bureaucratic processes to work together as strategic partners, though trade deals and memoranda of understandings (MOUs) are commonplace. Of course, the strength of the GCC-US relationship, which has come under considerable strain since 2010 (see below) has given GCC leaders pause for thought and an occasion to review their key partnerships.

It is unsurprising therefore that increasing trade and investment links have been accompanied by a number of high-profile visits. There has been a discernible increase in diplomatic traffic between China and the GCC, notably, high-level visits over the past five years, including Prime Minister of Kuwait Sheikh Jaber Mubarak Al-Hamad Al-Sabah (June 2014);[7] Saudi Crown Prince Salman (March 2014);[8] UAE Minister of State, Sultan Al Jaber, (January 2014);[9] King Hamad Bin Isa Al Khalifa of Bahrain, September 2013;[10] and Kuwaiti Emir Sheikh Sabah al-Ahmad al-Jaber al-Sabah (May 2009).[11]

The uptick in senior level visits to Beijing has likely been driven by two factors: first, a desire to strengthen economic relations and encourage cross investment, especially in the energy sector, which we discuss below; second, rising discontent with US policy towards the Middle East region, especially since the start of the Arab Spring in 2010, and the intention to signal this displeasure.[12] As such, the broader GCC-China relationship, while evolving organically and as a corollary to growing energy interdependency, has also benefited from a downturn in US-GCC relations.

Two major US-related events in the past five years have given GCC-China relations a significant boost. The first event is the US shale gas revolution, which promises the superpower self-sufficiency by the end of the decade. The second is the withdrawal of US military from Iraq and Afghanistan, coupled with US President Obama administration's resistance to re-engage militarily in Iraq and Syria. Both events have led many policy-makers in the Gulf region to assume that Washington's interest in the Gulf is in danger of diminishing and, as a result, the US will further examine ties with China.

Although the US re-engaged militarily in September 2014 and led a new coalition of states, including Saudi Arabia, Qatar, and the UAE in a series of airstrikes against ISIS in Iraq (US) and Syria (Saudi Arabia, Qatar, and UAE), policy-makers in the Gulf are fearful that they can no longer depend upon Washington to provide an effective security umbrella. Gulf leaders, notably King Abdullah of Saudi Arabia and Crown Prince of Abu Dhabi Muhammed bin Zayed, have also expressed concern that the Obama administration abandoned long-time Egyptian ally President Hosni Mubarak during the Arab Spring and have, therefore, called into question US commitment to support Gulf Arab ruling families in times of trouble. The prospect of the US achieving energy self-sufficiency has only exacerbated these fears, as it appears to Gulf policymakers that the oil-for-security deal agreed by former US President Franklin D Roosevelt and Saudi King Abdulaziz bin Saud in 1945 is no longer required.

The combination of China's growing energy demand, the advent of US shale gas and oil, pensive US policy towards the Gulf, and an increase in GCC energy exports and services to China has led some analysts to argue that the GCC-China relationship will undergo a major transformation. There is little doubt that the relationship will intensify, as energy draws the two parties together and their economic interests align further. However, it will require cultivating a deeper relationship built on strong personal, cultural, educational, political, and diplomatic ties before it can move away from being a transaction-based partnership. This chapter highlights the growth areas in China and the GCC's energy relationship, but also draws out the limitations in the overall partnership.

Demanding China, obliging GCC

China is the world's largest oil importer and according to the 2013 *World Economic Outlook*[13] will become the largest consumer, at approximately 18 MBD in 2040. China will account for 40% of world energy demand growth from 2014 to 2025. Furthermore, China's energy demand per capita is set to increase by 40%, reaching 2.8 tonnes of oil equivalent per capita, which will near European Union (EU) levels by 2035.

China's overall energy demand presents its government with a major challenge. Not only does the government and its state-owned energy companies have to secure sufficient and diverse energy resources to meet its energy security needs, but it has also set itself the task of building a strategic petroleum reserve (SPR) with a 100 days cover. At current rates of imports, that would mean at least 600 million barrels of crude oil.. Analyst estimates of how much China has managed to fill so far vary, ranging between 120 million and 260 million barrels.[14] Consequently, China is seeking to boost its energy security through a number of means, including not only warming relations with producer countries, but also by seeking strategic investments in the GCC region. In doing so, China has to compete for resources and price with its Asian neighbours, which also hold strong relationships with the GCC states.

China's demand for petroleum reached over 9.6 MBD in 2012. It imported 5.4 MBD of crude oil on average in 2012, rising 7% from 5.1 MBD in 2011, according to China's customs data and facts global energy. In 2013, import growth slowed to about 4.4% from 2012 levels, and crude oil imports averaged 5.6 MBD. However, it overtook the US as the world's largest net importer of crude in September 2013.

Crude imports now outweigh domestic supply, and they made up over half of total oil consumption in 2013. The government's current five-year plan targets oil imports reaching no more than 61% of its demand by the end of 2015. However, the EIA expects China to import over 66% of its total oil by 2020 and 72% by 2040 as demand is expected to grow faster than domestic crude supply.[15] This situation presents China with an energy security vulnerability. China is dependent upon producer countries to continue investing in upstream activities to arrest decline rates and maintain volumes at market rates, but to achieve security of supply, China's energy companies have invested in both upstream and downstream ventures in the GCC and the wider Middle East and North Africa (MENA) region.

According to an HSBC report, the MENA region supplied over 50% of China's overall crude imports in 2013. Out of the approximately 13 MBD produced by the GCC, about two-thirds are exported to the Asia-Pacific region. In 2012, two-thirds of GCC oil exports were delivered directly to Asia; China imported 36% of its crude oil from the GCC, and 20% directly from Saudi Arabia. In the meantime, oil exported from Saudi Arabia to India constituted 19% of total imports. At the same time, South Korea and Japan are heavily dependent on crude imports and receive 60% and 70% of their oil imports, respectively, from the Gulf Arab states.[16] While the GCC may view its relationship with China as strategic in the long-term, the relationships between GCC member states and other Asian partners are also important. Japan's dependence upon oil and LNG imports, for example, makes it a key partner for the UAE and Qatar.

Investing together for the future

China's competitive posture in the GCC's energy sector came to the fore in April 2014, when the China National Petroleum Corp (CNPC) announced that it had concluded a deal with the Abu Dhabi government to produce and export crude oil from onshore and offshore fields. The deal, which established a joint venture between CNPC and Abu Dhabi National Oil Company (ADNOC) and Al Yasat Company for Petroleum Operations, followed an earlier initiative in January 2012 to establish a strategic partnership to work on upstream projects in the UAE.[17] It marked the first entry of an Asian company into Abu Dhabi's upstream sector and gave an indication of how Abu Dhabi's leadership views its partnership with China and the emirate's future. At the same time, Western international oil companies (IOCs) competing with other Asian energy companies to renew the now expired 75-year concession have been kept waiting, indefinitely.

The UAE has followed a strategy of positioning itself as a reliable energy partner to China. Notably, though the UAE's direct exports to China at present remain limited, it chose a Chinese company to construct a pipeline that bypasses the Strait of Hormuz from its key oil fields to Fujairah. Not only has Abu Dhabi invited inward Chinese investment into its energy sector, but it has also made a number of strategic investments in China. For example, Borouge, the joint venture between ADNOC and Austria's Borealis, which manufactures polyoleofins, is planning a second factory in China. This follows the commissioning of a $60 million plant near Shanghai, which aims to produce 50,000 tonnes of polypropylene compounds a year.[18]

There is growing collaboration between Saudi Arabia and China. In its effort to transform Saudi Aramco from being a national champion into a global strategic energy company, the Saudi leadership has encouraged the company's senior management to not only develop its capabilities within Saudi Arabia, but also to secure long term market access to key energy partners through downstream joint ventures. In doing so,

Saudi Arabia moves up the energy chain by increasing its production of petroleum products and, at the same time, secures market share for its crude streams in targeted countries. It is not surprising, therefore, that Saudi Aramco, China Petroleum & Chemical Corporation (Sinopec), and ExxonMobil concluded an agreement in 2007 to construct a petrochemical complex and refinery in Fujian province to refine Saudi heavy crude.[19] This agreement, in which Saudi Aramco guaranteed market access to the refinery, allows both Aramco and Sinopec the ability to draw on ExxonMobil's technical expertise. Additionally, Sinopec acquired piecemeal security of supply. There are now proposals for a second refinery. Saudi also formed a joint venture with China's PetroChina for the construction of a 200,000 barrels per day (bpd) refinery in the southwestern Chinese province of Yunnan.

Following Chinese premier Wen Jiabao's visit to Saudi Arabia in January 2012, which formed part of a wider Gulf tour, Saudi Aramco announced the formation of another joint venture with Sinopec to build an $8.5 billion refinery complex at Yanbu on the Red Sea. The complex, designed to be one of the largest of its kind ever built, will process 400,000 bpd of heavy crude oil. Test runs began in September 2014. Saudi Aramco holds 62.5% share, with Sinopec holding the remaining 37.5% of the business.[20] The joint venture provides another example of the deepening energy relationship between China and the GCC. Although the product will be sold competitively, it provides both Saudi Arabia and China with the means to simultaneously shore-up security of supply and security of demand.

Saudi Arabia's primary petrochemical business, Sabic, and Sinopec established US$32 billion oil-processing joint venture in Tianjin in northern China, which went into operation in 2010 and produces 3.2 million tons of ethylene derivatives per year.[21]

There are a number of other such projects, which highlight further the growing trend of deepening energy relations between China and the GCC states. For example, the Aluminium Corporation of China (Chinalco) plans to establish a primary smelter in Saudi Arabia's Jizan Economic City;[22] Sinopec and Kuwait Petroleum Corporation signed a memorandum of understanding in 2009 to jointly build a 300,000 bpd refinery and petrochemical complex in Guangdong province, although a final decision has not yet been made. The project would secure Kuwait, the world's seventh-largest crude exporter, a stable outlet for its oil as it aims to more than double its crude exports to China to 500,000 bpd.[23] Qatar Petroleum's joint venture with Shell and CNPC to build a petrochemical plant in Taizhou that would have refined 20 million ton of crude and produced 1.2m tonnes of ethylene a year fell through in September 2013.[24]

China's strategic reserve

China's plan to build strategic petroleum reserves (SPR) and commercial crude oil reserves is part of its need to secure energy in light of its growing reliance on oil imports. As mentioned above, the government intends to build strategic crude oil storage capacity of approximately 600 million barrels by 2020. Currently, China has over 160 million barrels of total storage capacity for the SPR, and several sites are under construction. Phase 1 was completed in 2009 and has a total storage capacity of 103 million barrels at four sites. Phase 2 is expected to add at least 169 million barrels storage capacity to the SPR by 2015.[25] Similarly to the US, it is believed that the SPR will be used as a buffer against geopolitical events that disrupt global oil supply.

Although China's strategic reserve is shrouded in mystery, the International Energy Agency (IEA) calculated that the schedule drew upon oil roughly equivalent to 12% of Chinese imports during the second quarter of 2014.[26] China imports and produces more crude oil than its refineries can process into diesel or gasoline, which has led analysts at the IEA to believe that the remainder flows into storage. Although the price of crude dropped to $85 per barrel in October 2014, it had been uncharacteristically stable for the previous three years, in spite of market disruptions attributable to further conflict in Libya and Syria, US and EU energy sanctions against Iran, and the declaration by ISIS of a caliphate in parts of Syria and Iraq. Although few analysts knew with any certainty, it was believed by some, notably, Amrita Sen of Energy Aspects that China would buy and store crude whenever the price dipped below $100 per barrel. With the market well-supplied, at the time of writing, China's growth forecast slipping, the price reaching $85, Saudi Arabia refusing to cut production, and the prospect that OPEC will agree to a production cut at its November 2014 meeting, one can assume that the Chinese government is stockpiling, as long as sufficient storage has been constructed. To that end, the Saudi decision to live with a lower oil price and refusal to cut production, which was supported by Kuwait and the UAE, can only serve to strengthen relations between China and the GCC states. Furthermore, Saudi Arabia is the only country with significant spare capacity, so it is the one country that can play the role of swing producer. However, stockpiling China's SPR while serving as ballast against future geopolitical risk does not intrinsically serve the interests of the GCC states. Nonetheless, it would inadvertently support China in its quest for energy security.

The discussion so far has focused exclusively on China's quest to secure energy resources, namely, crude and refined products in a global market. China's reliance upon the Gulf Arab states is clear in that it is dependent upon crude oil imports from the sub-region, but one should not be left with the impression that China has not undertaken measures to access resources elsewhere in the region and further afield. Chinese companies, including CPNC and Sinopec, have made upstream investments in southern and northern Iraq, essentially through joint ventures with BP and Shell. China continues to enjoy a positive relationship with Iran, and although it has divested its interests in most upstream projects, it continues to import crude roughly in accordance with US Presidential waivers, which are aimed at limiting Iranian exports. Elsewhere, China has invested in the US, Canada and in a number of states in Africa, notably, Sudan. As with most oil-consuming states, China has developed a policy of diversity in its quest to achieve energy security.

The exit strategy

The chapter has so far focused on oil. The GCC states are generally gas poor and either flare associated gas or re-inject it, where possible. Oman is a net importer of gas, though is committed to supplying liquefied natural gas (LNG) to Japan through a long-term contract. Qatar is the only significant gas producer and major exporter amongst the six GCC states. It sits astride the world's largest unassociated gas field, which it shares with Iran and which is estimated to hold approximately 900 trillion cubic feet (tcf). It produces 77 million tons per annum and is currently the world's largest LNG exporter.[27] Qatar's original plan to export directly to the gas-dependent US was transformed almost overnight, once the US shale gas revolution became a reality. Nevertheless, Qatar's two gas companies, Qatargas and Rasgas, were able to switch markets and find entry points into Europe and Asia. To a large extent, it captured LNG market share by making strategic decisions where best to invest in regasification terminals and local infrastructure, such as the UK and Italy, as well as Japan, South Korea, and China.

According to the IEA, China consumes 6% of global LNG trade and is the world's third largest LNG importer. Qatar is currently China's largest supplier of LNG and meets 30% of China's demand through long-term contracts. As China's consumption of natural gas consumption grows, which is forecast to increase from 4% total energy consumption in 2011, 8% in 2015, and 10% in 2020, Qatar should expect to strengthen its energy ties. In real terms, China's natural gas consumption will equate to 4.6 tcf in 2011, 7.8 tcf in 2020, and 17 tcf in 2040.[28] The prospect of serving a near unquenchable Chinese thirst for natural gas should give Qatar's leadership reason to lift its current moratorium on its North Field.

Despite Qatar's success in developing and exporting natural gas, other newcomers, such as Australia, will soon challenge Qatar's primacy. Moreover, the development of unconventional gas resources, if repeated outside the US, will further challenge not only Qatar's position, but also its ability to shape long-term contracts that lock-in high prices and diversion clauses. Although still a projection, the World Energy Outlook in 2013 forecast in its New Policies Scenario (the most optimistic scenario) that because of the size of China's unconventional resource base (estimated 1,115 tcf), it would experience the largest growth in gas production and overtake Qatar by 2025.[29] The forecast was based on successful exploration and development of unconventional resources in the Ordos and Sichuan Basin by the numerous IOCs partnering with Sinopec and CNOOC, including Total, Shell, Chevron, BG, BP, Eni, and Anardarko.

Although Qatar lost its US market, it continues to hold a close relationship with China. By supplying China, and other Asian markets, Qatar is able to maintain a high price for delivering LNG eastwards. While the natural gas market remains regional, China and its neighbors can expect to pay a higher price for LNG. However, that will not prevent the Chinese leadership from trying to diversify sources.

China's deal to secure gas from Russia marks a step in its efforts to diversify energy resources. China secured a $400 billion deal between Gazprom and CNPC that would deliver pipeline gas at $10 mmbtu as part of a 30-year long-term contract.[30] The rate will give China greater leverage over other suppliers, notably Qatar, as the price $10 represents a 35% discount on existing LNG long-term contracts.

Conclusion

In June 2014, Beijing hosted the 10th China-Arab States Co-operation Forum. China's president Xi Jinping remarked at the opening ceremony: "The next decade will be a critical period for both China and Arab states, which calls on us to carry forward the Silk Road spirit and rejuvenate our countries." [31] The focus on the meeting was on ways to improve trade and energy co-operation. It is not surprising, given that China now imports more Middle East oil than the US, and the region accounts for more than 60% of all Chinese oil imports in 2012 – and yet, China's dependence, which brings with it vulnerability, will likely lessen in time as other sources of oil and gas are exploited.

The long-term decline in US energy imports from the Gulf means that figures are likely to show China surpassing the US as the largest trading partner for every Arab country. Trade could get a further boost if China and the GCC succeed in establishing a trade agreement, though such an agreement would likely take several years to conclude. It is difficult to envisage the relationship between China and its Gulf Arab state partners moving beyond the transactional. China shares common interests with the GCC states and, in some ways, is dependent upon them. China's growth could not continue apace without Gulf oil and gas. Nevertheless, China has gone to considerable lengths to diversity its sources of oil and gas, which it has done with some success. For example, China's oil production in overseas equity share and acquisitions amounts to 2 MBD. In the meantime, its consumption of home-grown coal, while an environmental hazard, accounts for 69% of total energy consumption.[32]

Without doubt, China is concerned about instability in the Gulf and MENA region, as it has the potential to disrupt the production and transport of crude and LNG through the Strait of Hormuz. However, as noted above, oil prices have been uncharacteristically stable since 2011, despite the Libyan and Egyptian revolutions, conflict in Syria, and the ISIS surge in Iraq. China appears to have made little effort to secure its interests in the Gulf beyond an arms deal with Saudi Arabia and active diplomacy at the United Nations Security Council aimed at deterring further military interventions by the US. As Mark Katz said: "...the utility of China for Riyadh is that it is an important petroleum buyer, and to some extent, a supplier of certain arms that Riyadh cannot always get from Washington. But since China prefers that America bear the main cost of underwriting Saudi security, Chinese and American interests in are convergent, not divergent."[33]

China's relationship with the GCC is unlikely to ever translate into a security for oil partnership. The perception that Western leaders are becoming fair-weather friends is likely to push GCC leaders closer to Asia, though it remains doubtful that China's leaders would be willing to greet them with open arms.

Notes

1. Saudi Arabia, Oman, Qatar, Bahrain, Kuwait and the United Arab Emirates (UAE).
2. https://www.cia.gov/library/publications/the-world-factbook/geos/ch.html
3. https://www.cia.gov/library/publications/the-world-factbook/geos/ch.html

4. *BP Energy Outlook 2035*, (January 2014), available at: http://www.bp.com/content/dam/bp/pdf/Energy-economics/Energy-Outlook/Energy_Outlook_2035_booklet.pdf
5. Calculated from Energy Information Administration (EIA), www.eia.gov
6. http://www.eia.gov/countries/cab.cfm?fips=qa
7. "Kuwait, China Ink Deals," *Arab Times*, 3 June 2014, available at: http://www.arabtimesonline.com/NewsDetails/tabid/96/smid/414/ArticleID/206579/reftab/96/t/Kuwait-China-ink-deals/Default.aspx
8. Youssef, Fatah Al-Rahman, "Saudi Crown Prince's Visit to China Set to Bolster Investment," *Asharq Al-Awsat*, 14 March 2014, available at: http://www.aawsat.net/2014/03/article55330027
9. "UAE Seeks to Strengthen Economic Ties with China," *Gulfnews.com*, 30 May 2014, available at: http://gulfnews.com/business/economy/uae-seeks-to-strengthen-economic-ties-with-china-1.1341102
10. "HM King Hamad's Historic Visit to China Hailed," *Bahrain News Agency*, 13 October 2013, available at: http://www.bna.bh/portal/en/news/584135
11. "China, Kuwait Sign Agreements to Step Up Ties," *China View*, 10 May 2009, available at: http://news.xinhuanet.com/english/2009-05/10/content_11348536.htm
12. Chatham House Roundtable, Riyadh, January 2014
13. http://www.iea.org/publications/freepublications/publication/weio2014.pdf
14. Singh, Mandip, "China's Strategic Petroleum Reserves: A Reality Check," Institute for Defense and Analysis, 21 May 2012, available at: http://www.idsa.in/issuebrief/ChinasStrategicPetroleumReserves_MandipSingh_210512
15. http://www.eia.gov/countries/cab.cfm?fips=ch
16. Körner, Kevin, and Oliver Masetti, *The GCC Going East: Economic Ties with developing Asia on the Rise*, Deutsch Bank Research, 18 February 2014, available at: http://www.dbresearch.com/PROD/DBR_INTERNET_EN-PROD/PROD0000000000329687/The+GCC+going+East%3A+Economic+ties+with+developing+Asia+on+the+rise.pdf
17. Fineren, Daniel and Chen Aizhu, "China Secures Abu Dhabi Oil Field Deal," *Reuters*, 29 April 2014, available at: http://www.reuters.com/article/2014/04/29/emirates-china-idUSL6N0NL27L20140429
18. http://www.borouge.com/MediaCentre/Lists/News/DispformCustom.aspx?id=140
19. http://www.oilprimer.com/exxon-news-2007.html
20. Bailey, Robert, "China And GCC: Growing Ties," *Gulf Business*, 16 April 2013, available at: http://gulfbusiness.com/2013/04/china-and-gcc-growing-ties/#.VEZusueUxLQ
21. "Shifting Sands: Saudi Arabia's Oil Moves East to China," 16 March 2011, available at: http://knowledge.wharton.upenn.edu/article/shifting-sands-saudi-arabias-oil-moves-east-to-china/
22. Bailey, Robert, "China And GCC: Growing Ties," *Gulf Business*, 16 April 2013, available at: http://gulfbusiness.com/2013/04/china-and-gcc-growing-ties/#.VEZusueUxLQ
23. "Sinopec Undecided on Kuwait Role in its Zhanjiang Refinery," Arab Times, 16 October 2014, available at: http://www.arabtimesonline.com/NewsDetails/tabid/96/smid/414/ArticleID/189017/reftab/69/t/Sinopec-undecided-on-Kuwait-role-in-its-Zhanjiang-refinery/Default.aspx

24. Moore, Malcolm, "Shell 'Shuts Down £8.3bn Project in China'," *The Telegraph*, 10 September 2013, available at: http://www.telegraph.co.uk/finance/news-bysector/energy/oilandgas/10300263/Shell-shuts-down-8.3bn-project-in-China.html

25. http://www.eia.gov/countries/cab.cfm?fips=ch

26. Bhattacharya, Abheek, "China's Petroleum Reserve Builds Shaky Floor for Oil", *Wall Street Journal*, 3 September 2014, available at: http://online.wsj.com/articles/chinas-petroleum-reserve-builds-shaky-floor-for-oil-heard-on-the-street-1409755068

27. http://www.eia.gov/countries/cab.cfm?fips=qa

28. http://www.eia.gov/countries/cab.cfm?fips=ch

29. 'Global energy trends to 2035: Finding our way in a new energy world', *World Energy Outlook*, International Energy Agency, 2013, pp. 67.

30. "Russia Signs 30-year Gas Deal with China," *BBC*, available at: http://www.bbc.com/news/business-27503017

31. Wildau, Gabriael, "New Silk Road Raises Hopes for Increased China-Arab Trade," *Financial Times*, 29 June 2014, available at: http://www.ft.com/cms/s/0/11190312-f874–11e3–815f-00144feabdc0.html

32. http://www.eia.gov/countries/cab.cfm?fips=ch

33. Sloan, Alastair, "China's Complex Relations with the Gulf States," *Middle East Monitor*, 8 June 2014, available at: https://www.middleeastmonitor.com/articles/middle-east/11953-chinas-complex-relations-with-the-gulf-states

References

http://www.borouge.com/MediaCentre/Lists/News/DispformCustom.aspx?id=140

http://www.eia.gov/countries/cab.cfm?fips=ch

http://www.eia.gov/countries/cab.cfm?fips=qa

http://www.iea.org/publications/freepublications/publication/weio2014.pdf

http://www.oilprimer.com/exxon-news-2007.html

Al Asoomi, Mohammad, "GCC Scripts Closer Strategic Equation with China," *Gulfnews.com*, 11 June 2014, available at: http://gulfnews.com/business/opinion/gcc-scripts-closer-strategic-equation-with-china-1.1345351

BP Energy Outlook 2030, (January 2013), available at: http://www.bp.com/content/dam/bp/pdf/statistical-review/BP_World_Energy_Outlook_booklet_2013.pdf

BP Energy Outlook 2035, (January 2014), available at: http://www.bp.com/content/dam/bp/pdf/Energy-economics/Energy-Outlook/Energy_Outlook_2035_booklet.pdf

Bailey, Robert, "China And GCC: Growing Ties," *Gulf Business*, 16 April 2013, available at: http://gulfbusiness.com/2013/04/china-and-gcc-growing-ties/#.VEZusueUxLQ

Bhattacharya, Abheek, "China's Petroleum Reserve Builds Shaky Floor for Oil", *Wall Street Journal*, 3 September 2014, available at: http://online.wsj.com/articles/chinas-petroleum-reserve-builds-shaky-floor-for-oil-heard-on-the-street-1409755068

CIA Factbook, https://www.cia.gov/library/publications/the-world-factbook/geos/ch.html

Chen, Mo, "Exploring Economic Relations between China and the GCC States," *Journal of Middle Eastern and Islamic Studies (Asia)*, Vol. 5, No. 4, 2011, available at: http://www.mesi.shisu.edu.cn/_upload/article/50/18/39a9b6b84c809216af d21f68549b/7f293490-776d-4ee0-831e-49ca5cd00849.pdf.

"China, Kuwait Sign Agreements to Step Up Ties," China View, 10 May 2009, available at: http://news.xinhuanet.com/english/2009-05/10/content_11348536.htm

Ditchley Park Conference, "The Shale Energy Revolution and Geopolitics," May 2014.

Economy, Elizabeth, and Michael Levi, *By All Means Necessary: How China's Resource Quest Is Changing the World*, (Oxford: Oxford University Press, 2014).

Fineren, Daniel and Chen Aizhu, "China Secures Abu Dhabi Oil Field Deal," *Reuters*, 29 April 2014, available at: http://www.reuters.com/article/2014/04/29/ emirates-china-idUSL6N0NL27L20140429

"GCC-China Trade Ties Grow Steadily," *Saudi Gazette*, 8 June 2014, available at: http://www.saudigazette.com.sa/index.cfm?method=home.regcon& contentid=20140609207814

'Global energy trends to 2035: Finding our way in a new energy world', *World Energy Outlook*, International Energy Agency, 2013.

"HM King Hamad's Historic Visit to China Hailed," *Bahrain News Agency*, 13 October 2013, available at: http://www.bna.bh/portal/en/news/584135

Kellner, Thierry, *The GCC States of the Persian Gulf and Asia Energy Relations*, The Institut français des relations internationales (Ifri), (September 2012).

Körner, Kevin, and Oliver Masetti, *The GCC Going East: Economic Ties with developing Asia on the Rise*, Deutsch Bank Research, 18 February 2014, available at: http://www.dbresearch.com/PROD/DBR_INTERNET_EN-PROD/ PROD0000000000329687/The+GCC+going+East%3A+Economic+ties+with+d eveloping+Asia+on+the+rise.pdf

Kostiner, J., "GCC Perceptions of Collective Security in the Post-Saddam, Era", in M. Kamrava (ed.), *International Politics of the Persian Gulf*, (Syracuse: New York, 2011).

KPMG, *An Emerging Strategic Energy Relationship*, 2014, available at: https:// www.kpmg.com/ID/en/IssuesAndInsights/ArticlesPublications/Documents/ Advisory-ENR-An-emerging-strategic-energy-relationship.pdf

"Kuwait, China Ink Deals," *Arab Times*, 3 June 2014, available at: http://www. arabtimesonline.com/NewsDetails/tabid/96/smid/414/ArticleID/206579/ reftab/96/t/Kuwait-China-ink-deals/Default.aspx

Moore, Malcolm, "Shell 'Shuts Down £8.3bn Project in China'," *The Telegraph*, 10 September 2013, available at: http://www.telegraph.co.uk/finance/newsbysector/ energy/oilandgas/10300263/Shell-shuts-down-8.3bn-project-in-China.html

"New Dynamics in GCC-UK Relations and the Prospects and Challenges for the GCC Union Workshop," Chatham House in partnership with the Gulf Research Centre, London, June 2014.

Ng, Teddy, "Beijing Eyes Broader role in Middle East," *South China Morning Post*, 10 January 2014, available at: http://www.scmp.com/news/china/article/1401774/ beijing-eyes-broader-role-middle-east

Oil and Gas Security: Emergency Response of IEA Countries, (IEA: 2012), available at: http://www.iea.org/publications/freepublications/publication/china_2012.pdf

Al-Rashid, Abdulrahman, "China and the Future Alliance with Saudi Arabia," *Al Arabiya News*, 16 March 2014, available at: http://english.alarabiya.net/

en/views/news/world/2014/03/16/China-and-the-future-alliance-with-Saudi-Arabia.html

Rof, Jordi, and Mahmoud, "China Reduces Its Exposure to GCC Imports, *Khaleej Times,* 22 July 2014, available at: http://www.khaleejtimes.com/biz/inside.asp?xfile=/data/opinionanalysis/2014/July/opinionanalysis_July36.xml&section=opinionanalysis

"Russia Signs 30-year Gas Deal with China," *BBC,* available at: http://www.bbc.com/news/business-27503017

Russell, Clyde, "Worst time for Saudi Arabia's Giant New Oil Refinery," *Mail Online,* 10 September 2014, available at: http://www.dailymail.co.uk/wires/reuters/article-2750241/Worst-time-Saudi-Arabias-giant-new-oil-refinery-Russell.html

"Saudi-British Relations Workshop," Chatham House in partnership with the Institute of Diplomatic Studies, Riyadh, April 2014.

"Saudi Oil Giant Aramco inks $8.5 bn Deal with Sinopec to Set Up Refinery at Red Sea Port," *ANI News,* 16 January 2012, available at: http://www.aninews.in/newsdetail3/story31849/saudi-oil-giant-aramco-inks-8–5-bn-deal-with-sinopec-to-set-up-refinery-at-red-sea-port.html

"Shifting Sands: Saudi Arabia's Oil Moves East to China," 16 March 2011, available at: http://knowledge.wharton.upenn.edu/article/shifting-sands-saudi-arabias-oil-moves-east-to-china/

Singh, Mandip, "China's Strategic Petroleum Reserves: A Reality Check," Institute for Defense and Analysis, 21 May 2012, available at: http://www.idsa.in/issuebrief/ChinasStrategicPetroleumReserves_MandipSingh_210512

"Sinopec Undecided on Kuwait Role in its Zhanjiang Refinery," *Arab Times,* 16 October 2014, available at: http://www.arabtimesonline.com/NewsDetails/tabid/96/smid/414/ArticleID/189017/reftab/69/t/Sinopec-undecided-on-Kuwait-role-in-its-Zhanjiang-refinery/Default.aspx

Sloan, Alastair, "China's Complex Relations with the Gulf States," *Middle East Monitor,* 8 June 2014, available at: https://www.middleeastmonitor.com/articles/middle-east/11953-chinas-complex-relations-with-the-gulf-states

Al-Tamimi, Naser, "Asia-GCC Relations: Growing Interdependence," *Al Arabiya News,* 18 June 2013, available at: http://english.alarabiya.net/en/special-reports/bridging-the-gulf/2013/06/18/Asia-GCC-relations-Growing-interdependence.html

Al-Tamimi, Nasser, "Asia-GCC Relations: Growing Interdependence," *ISPI,* Analysis No. 179, June 2013, available on http://www.ispionline.it/sites/default/files/pubblicazioni/analysis_179_2013.pdf

"UAE Seeks to Strengthen Economic Ties with China," *Gulfnews.com,* 30 May 2014, available at: http://gulfnews.com/business/economy/uae-seeks-to-strengthen-economic-ties-with-china-1.1341102

UN Comtrade International Trade Statistics Database, http://comtrade.un.org

US Department of Defense, *Quadrennial Defense Review,* 5 March 2014.

Wildau, Gabriael, "New Silk Road Raises Hopes for Increased China-Arab Trade," *Financial Times,* 29 June 2014, available at: http://www.ft.com/cms/s/0/11190312-f874–11e3–815f-00144feabdc0.html

Youssef, Fatah Al-Rahman, "Saudi Crown Prince's Visit to China Set to Bolster Investment," *Asharq Al-Awsat,* 14 March 2014, available at: http://www.aawsat.net/2014/03/article55330027

10

Chinese Policy in the Middle East in the Wake of the Arab Uprisings

Michael Singh

Introduction

China's role in the Middle East tends to be viewed one dimensionally by both Western and Chinese analysts – with the focus on either China's increasing need for energy imports or its rise as a strategic rival to the United States (US). Yet the reality of Chinese interests and policy in the Middle East is far more complex.

Interactions between China and the states of the Middle East date back 2,000 years. China and the peoples of the Middle East share a common, albeit painful, narrative as civilizations whose ancient histories are glorious yet whose modern history has been marked by the fitful and often bitter experience of decolonization. This shared history has made each wary of the West, even as they benefit from integration with it. Despite these commonalities; however, China and Middle Eastern states do not approach their relations today as peers. Beijing is finding its way as an emerging great power newly capable of exercising influence around the world; whereas the states of the Middle East are mired in the chaos that has followed the Arab uprisings of 2011 onward.

Those uprisings and Beijing's response to them illustrate the complicated, changing nature of Chinese policy in the Middle East. The events of the past several years have presented both challenges and opportunities to China, giving rise to the sort of policy dilemmas that Beijing has long sought to avoid. These dilemmas in the Middle East have proven as difficult for China to navigate as they have for the United States. They have also tested Beijing's longstanding strategy for advancing its interests in the region.

Dr. Pan Guang, a prominent Chinese scholar of the Middle East, described China's modern relations as being divided into four eras, the last of which began in 1977 with the premiership of Deng Xiaoping.[1] Today, China is embarking on a fifth period in its relations with the region. The policies that characterize this new era – and whether they are successful – will depend not only on how Beijing chooses to address its policy dilemmas, but on exogenous factors such as the involvement of other rising Asian powers in the region and China's own fortunes domestically and in East Asia. But perhaps more than anything else, they will depend on the future trajectory of US policy in the Middle East, and US-China relations broadly.

Chinese and American interests in the Middle East

Superficially, Chinese and American interests in the Middle East overlap significantly. However, the way in which the US and China pursue these interests tends to differ widely, so this overlap may more likely lead to increased tension than to cooperation.

Energy. The United States and China are the world's two largest energy consumers, as well as the two largest importers of crude oil.[2] Thus, each has a natural interest in the Middle East, which is home to many of the world's top oil exporters and accounts for more than half of inter-regional net oil exports globally, something that is forecast to remain relatively steady through 2035.[3]

Yet in other respects the two countries are moving in opposite directions. American oil consumption is forecast to rise slowly in the coming decades even as US domestic production increases rapidly, decreasing its dependence on foreign supplies of oil.[4] While this has led to hopeful talk of "energy independence," in fact the US and its allies will remain vulnerable to increases in energy prices, which are determined on the global market. In addition, many of those allies – such as South Korea and Taiwan – are highly dependent on oil imports and will remain so for the foreseeable future.[5] Thus the US will retain a strong interest in secure energy trade globally and incentives to resolve or mitigate the effects of crises that threaten either to raise energy prices or diminish supply.

Chinese demand, in contrast, is forecast to rise rapidly along with China's economic growth and urbanization[6]; more broadly, the vast bulk of growth in global oil demand is forecast to come from non-Organization for Economic Cooperation and Development (OECD) countries.[7] Chinese production will be woefully insufficient to meet the increase in domestic demand[8], sharply increasing China's dependence on foreign supplies – and thus on Middle Eastern energy sources.

Despite a certain convergence between American and Chinese energy interests in the Middle East, significant obstacles confront bilateral cooperation in this area. Foremost among these is China's emphasis on upstream involvement in energy projects as opposed to reliance on the market to meet its supply requirements. Given Beijing's demonstrated willingness to use control of resources for leverage in diplomatic disputes (for example by cutting off rare earth exports to Japan[9] or banana imports from the Philippines[10]), increasing Chinese involvement upstream in Middle East energy projects would be a point of concern for US allies that depend on Middle East supplies themselves, and thus for the United States as well. Conversely, Chinese strategists may also view the situation with some concern, as American vulnerability to an interruption of Middle Eastern energy supplies is diminishing as China's increases, but Washington's military and diplomatic influence in the Gulf far outstrips Beijing's.

Flow of commerce. The Middle East region is not a major trading partner for either the US or China, although it has served as a source of foreign investment in China, and China's own investments in the region play a strategic role in ensuring its energy security.[11] However, both the Chinese and American economies are highly dependent on global seaborne trade flows, a large portion of which flow through the sea lanes of the Middle East. Eight percent of seaborne trade and 4% of globally traded oil passes through the Suez Canal[12], and 20% of globally traded oil passes through the Strait of Hormuz[13]; much of the trade passing through both chokepoints is bound to or from China via the Arabian Sea and Indian Ocean.

Both the United States and China have taken direct action to safeguard these sea lanes. The United States maintains a robust naval presence throughout the region's seas, and bases its Fifth Fleet in Manama. China, beginning in 2008, has dispatched naval vessels on counter-piracy missions in the Arabian Sea, and those vessels have paid port calls in both Iran and the United Arab Emirates (UAE). Both countries have issued strong warnings to Iran against any attempt to close the Strait of Hormuz; former US Secretary of Defense Leon Panetta publicly warned in 2012 that such an attempt would constitute a red line for the United States[14], while China publicly rebuked Iran in late 2011 for its threat to close the Strait.[15]

As in the case of energy, the prospect for cooperation in this area is complicated by Chinese behavior elsewhere. Policymakers in Washington – and likely in the Middle East itself – would view increasing Chinese naval activity in the region with concern, given the People's

Liberation Army Navy's expansive view of its maritime prerogatives as demonstrated in the disputes in the South China Sea. While Beijing might argue that the two cases are different given its territorial claims in the South China Sea, this selective approach to respecting international maritime law and arbitration is likely to engender mistrust elsewhere.

Nonproliferation of WMD. Both China and the United States have asserted that they have an interest in nonproliferation in the Middle East. Indeed, the two countries have cooperated to an extent in the recent effort to dismantle Syria's chemical weapons[16] and jointly supported a number of UN Security Council resolutions and cooperated to negotiate the July 2015 Iran nuclear agreement or "Joint Comprehensive Plan of Action".[17] Nevertheless, China has also played a role in promoting proliferation in the region, for example by providing Iran in the 1990s with vital components of its nuclear program,[18] cooperation which reportedly has continued despite Beijing's membership in the P5+1 and ostensible support for international sanctions.[19]

Counter-terrorism. Both the United States and China have expressed grave concern regarding the spread of terrorism and extremist ideology from the Middle East. After the 9/11 attacks on the United States, China supported American-led military action in Afghanistan,[20] at least partly out of concern about the presence there of Al-Qaeda and the spread of Islamism to Central Asia.[21] More recently, both the United States and China have expressed serious concerns about the movement of foreign fighters to and from Syria and Iraq and the prospect that they would become involved in terrorist attacks on American and Chinese soil.[22],[23] Nevertheless, US-China cooperation on counter-terrorism has been limited by American concerns regarding Chinese authorities' tendency to conflate political dissent with violent extremism; Chinese support for US counter-terrorism efforts has in turn likely been hampered due to Beijing's suspicion that such efforts serve to project the power of the United States and its allies in ways that China typically opposes.[24]

Thus, despite the apparent overlap in American and Chinese interests in the Middle East, major obstacles exist to Sino-American cooperation in the region, due in part to the different manner in how Washington and Beijing pursue each of these interests individually. Furthermore, each country has other powerful interests not shared by the other – for example, the United States in safeguarding Israel, and China in securing an overseas market for its labor force. Difficulties in cooperation also arise from the starkly different regional strategies the United States and China have developed, which reflect the widely disparate capabilities and global roles of each, as well as the fact that the Middle East has long been a much higher priority in the United States' foreign policy than it has in China's.

While the United States and China have both sought to promote regional stability in order to advance their interests in the region, the United States has done so through a robust military presence, generous military and economic aid to allies, the promotion of political and economic development, and diplomatic and occasionally military intervention. China, on the other hand, has sought to cultivate cordial relations with all governments in the region (even those with ideologies Beijing finds concerning, such as Hamas when it won Palestinian elections in 2006 and the Muslim Brotherhood when it gained power in Egypt in 2012), and has focused on promoting trade and investment ties while largely eschewing the provision of aid or any significant diplomatic or direct military involvement in the region. While China has vociferously opposed external intervention in the region, it has not developed a policy to prevent it, and has thus far implicitly accepted and benefited from America's role in promoting regional stability.

More fundamentally, however, any possible cooperation to advance shared interests is constrained by the broader rivalry between the United States and China, which for Beijing often appear to trump considerations of its regional interests in the Middle East. For example, the United States has an interest in maintaining its freedom of navigation and action in the Middle East and elsewhere, whereas China's advocacy of non-interference reflects in large part a desire to constrain the United States. Certain Chinese policies in the region appear directly aimed at limiting US power, such as its cultivation of a strategic alliance with Iran,[25] which has included the transfer of Chinese weapons that have found their way into the hands of Iraqi, Lebanese, and Afghan militants fighting against the United States and its regional allies[26] as well as Chinese assistance in Iran's development of anti-access and area denial capabilities.[27] These policies reflect the same sort of zero-sum mentality that Beijing appears to apply to the American role in East Asia and challenges prospects for US-China cooperation in the region.

Post-2011 changes in the Middle East

In the past several years, changes in the Middle East, as well as in the United States and China, have altered the strategic landscape in the region, with implications for both Beijing and Washington.

The most significant change in the region has been the collapse of the post-Cold War security architecture built and upheld for two decades by the United States. Even before the 2011 Arab uprisings, American attitudes toward the region and toward foreign policy more broadly had shifted significantly.[28] As a result the Iraq and Afghanistan wars – which were long and costly yet yielded scant gains – the American public was wary of overseas intervention, especially in the Middle East.

President Obama was propelled to office in part by such sentiments, and accordingly he set about winding down American involvement in both wars and sought – rhetorically, if not practically – to rebalance US foreign policy away from the region and toward East Asia, to the alarm of Beijing and dismay of American allies in the Middle East. Beyond this, President Obama also seemed to bring to the White House skepticism of traditional US allies such as Israel and the Gulf Arab states, and a desire to instead reach out directly to citizens of Middle Eastern states and to take a more neutral or accommodating approach to resolving the Israeli-Palestinian and Iran nuclear crises. The financial crisis of 2008 led to sharp cuts to the American defense budget and increasing oil and gas production reinforced American disengagement from the Middle East.

It was in this environment that the Arab uprisings took place, serving to accelerate the US disengagement from the region. If that disengagement represented the weakening of the "hub" in the American hub-and-spoke security architecture in the Middle East, the Arab uprisings caused the abrupt separation of several spokes, including relatively pro-Western regimes in Tunisia, Egypt, and Yemen. The United States was confronted with a conflict between supporting traditional allies and supporting seemingly democratic revolutions; rather than facing this conflict decisively, the resulting American policies were hesitant and inconsistent, leading to increased frictions with remaining allies in the region, especially Saudi Arabia and Egypt.

The steady disengagement of the United States and the growing distance between Washington and its allies left a leadership vacuum in the region. This vacuum, however, has gone unfilled. Neither regional nor international institutions or coalitions have proven capable of responding effectively to Middle Eastern crises, and no other external powers, including China, have been capable or willing to do so either, despite efforts by states such as Egypt, Turkey, and Iran to substitute these powers in whole or part for the United States. A stark example of this unwillingness or incapacity is demonstrated by the extent of Chinese aid to the region; it provided $16 million in aid to Syrian refugees,[29] in contrast to the hundreds of millions of dollars donated by the United States, and a mere $10 million to the Palestinian Authority,[30] significantly less either than the United States or even regional powers with much smaller economies than China's.

In the absence of any external stabilizer and amid the chaos that has shaken up the region's longstanding relationships, regional powers have instead vied among themselves for pre-eminence, forming a number of ad hoc blocs and utilizing sectarian proxies and other tools to advance their interests. This arrangement has only deepened the region's instability, giving rise to serious implications for both American and Chinese interests.

Challenges and opportunities for China

For China, this new (and still changing) regional dynamic, together with Beijing's own shifting interests and evolving foreign policy strategy, has resulted in both challenges and opportunities.

Challenges

Fall of authoritarian allies. Until 1956, China lacked diplomatic relations with any Middle Eastern states, viewing them as anti-revolutionary. Eventually China established diplomatic ties with every regional state, and still seeks to maintain friendly – and lucrative – relations not only with all of the region's governments, but many substate actors such as Hamas and Hezbollah, despite the vast ideological chasms that separate it from these groups. To this end, China has sought to avoid taking clear sides in regional disputes and instead promulgated innocuous-sounding proposals to guide its regional relations, such as the economically-focused "1+2+3 Framework" articulated by Chinese President Xi Jinping at the 2014 China-Arab Cooperation Forum ministerial, or the four principles announced by former President Hu Jintao during his 2004 visit to the region.[31] Nevertheless, after China had spent decades cultivating its allies in the Middle East, many of them were swept away in the Arab uprisings. This development presented Beijing, just like Washington, with the challenge of rebuilding ties, often hamstrung by its past support for the former regimes.

Rise of political Islam and foreign fighters. As China's authoritarian allies fell, in many instances they were replaced by – or their departure created space for – Islamist parties or militias. This was true in Tunisia, Libya, and Egypt (and of course had long been the case in Iran); in addition, other substate or transnational Islamist groups either vied for power, as in the case of various Syrian Islamist militias, or seized territory, as in the case of the Islamic State in Iraq and al-Sham (ISIS). Beijing views Islamist ideology as a threat, and worries about its spread from the Middle East to China via Central Asia; it also worries about the prospect of Chinese foreign fighters traveling to fight with groups such as ISIS and then returning to China to commit acts of terrorism. Nevertheless, Beijing's discomfort with these ideologies did not prevent it from continuing its longstanding approach of seeking to cultivate cordial relations with governments of all stripes, such as Mohammad Morsi's Muslim Brotherhood government in Cairo.

Economic risks. The conflicts in the Middle East not only put China's political relationships at risk, but also threatened its economic interests. In addition to purchasing vast amounts of oil from the region, China has expanded its non-oil trade with the region, and sees the Gulf Arab states as a potential source of direct investment in China.[32] In addition, there are a large number of Chinese workers across the Middle East, not only in the Gulf, but also in places like Egypt and Libya (at least before the 2011 revolutions).[33] Indeed, China was forced to engage the PLAN in a rare expeditionary operation at short notice to evacuate Chinese citizens from Libya, leaving behind assets and abandoning once-lucrative contracts, an experience repeated in Yemen in 2014–2015.[34] Instability in the Middle East also risks sharp increases in energy prices, to which China is vulnerable.

Changing role of the United States. China has long been conflicted about the American role in the Middle East. On one hand, China has benefited from US efforts to provide regional stability and safeguard shipping lanes; on the other, it has disapproved of American intervention and sought to constrain US influence more broadly, and its willingness to work with any and all governments has clashed with the American approach. Illustrating this conflict, China strongly opposed US intervention in Iraq in 2003, but then supported the continued presence of American troops in Iraq as a stabilizing force.[35] The Arab uprisings posed similar dilemmas – on one hand the United States and its allies intervened in Libya, but on the other the uprisings further dampened Washington's enthusiasm for engagement in the region, and even led to calls by influential former officials to remove the Fifth Fleet headquarters from Bahrain.[36]

Opportunities

Changing US role. Even as American disengagement from the Middle East poses challenges for Beijing, it also offers opportunity for a would-be superpower. The United States has been less inclined to intervene militarily in the region after Iraq and Libya, as demonstrated by President

Obama's hesitation to enforce his red line on Syria and the strict limitations he imposed on American involvement in the campaign against the so-called Islamic State group. This stance not only comports with China's longstanding interest in deterring American intervention overseas, but diminished the possibility of a US-Iran military confrontation centering on the Gulf, thus reducing the pressure on China to accommodate American extraterritorial sanctions on Iranian oil and banking.

Increasing American disengagement also opens up a political and security vacuum in a region that has often attracted the involvement of great powers. But filling that vacuum will not come comfortably to China, which has had its own difficult experience with Western imperialism and does not yet appear reconciled to the idea – nor yet capable – of throwing its weight around outside of its immediate neighborhood.

China would nonetheless begin any such endeavor with certain advantages. It now has a long history of diplomatic relations with the states of the Middle East. For many of those states, the "China model" – described by one analyst in the region as "balancing economic development, state modernization, and political control…for countries that want to carefully manage their economic and political transformation"[37] – holds an undeniable appeal, especially in the wake of the Arab uprisings. China's stated interest in energy partnerships also sounds more attractive to the region's energy producers than Washington's talk of energy independence, a concept that is reassuring to American audiences but threatening to oil producers, some of whose economies are highly dependent on the energy trade with the United States. Indeed, in 2009 an advisor to the Saudi oil minister referred to Western talk of energy independence as a "wave of hostility."[38]

Nevertheless, one should not assume such convergences would lead to easy substitution of China for the United States as an ally for regional states, regardless of whether Beijing would be willing to play such a role. Middle Eastern officials have longstanding relationships in Western capitals – especially Washington – that would not be as easily built with Chinese officials, whose system is more opaque to outsiders and whose diplomats have a relatively limited understanding of Middle Eastern politics. Partnership with China also cannot for now provide the same diplomatic, military, or technological benefits as can the United States. Finally, China's assertive behavior toward neighbors in East Asia is likely to give states of the Middle East pause when considering the costs and benefits of inviting deeper Chinese involvement in their own region.

Economic opportunities. As it is widely recognized that stagnant economies were one of the root causes of the Arab uprisings, governments in the region have or likely will in the future embark on programs of economic reform and liberalization.[39] Such action, in turn, may open further opportunities for trade and investment for China, though perhaps not for Chinese labor given regional governments' imperative to create jobs for their own populations.[40] Further economic opportunities may be created by the economic opening of Iran and as a result of other regional governments' desire – whether out of pique at American policies or a more straightforward desire to balance their dependency on the United States – to diversify their defense relationships.

Again, however, what China can offer to the region is primarily transactional in nature; just as China is seeking to make its own difficult transition to a more market-oriented economy, many Middle Eastern governments need to shrink their public sectors, reduce their spending, bolster their social safety nets, and encourage private-sector–led growth. China is not the ideal partner for such a transition, given its own similar challenges. Nor will China find its path to greater economic opportunity in the Middle East an effortless or uncontested one. Beijing's One Belt, One Road initiative has gained little traction in the region; even in Egypt, which has been most receptive, recently awarded major infrastructure projects for the planned New Suez Canal to non-Chinese firms.[41]

What didn't happen (yet). While not precisely an opportunity arising from the Arab uprisings, Beijing will undoubtedly be heartened by what didn't happen in the region in recent years. As noted above, the United States, after intervening in Libya, did not intervene against the Syrian regime, or undertake a military strike on Iran despite repeated threats to do so. Political Islam, seemingly ascendant from 2011–2012, was dealt setbacks in Tunisia, Egypt, and elsewhere, and until the alarming advance of ISIS across northwestern Iraq, seemed to be receding as a political force if not as a military and terrorist threat. Some of China's closest allies – the Gulf Arab states and Iran, in particular – proved resilient in the face of the region's chaos, despite some analysts' predictions to the contrary. And – perhaps most important from Beijing's perspective – the "Arab Spring" did not ultimately spill over into China itself despite Chinese officials' obvious worries that it might do so.[42]

China's Middle East policy dilemmas

The United States has long faced policy dilemmas in the Middle East arising from conflicts between its various interests, or between its interests and its values. As its interests in the Middle East increase and as the United States pulls back from the region, Beijing will face similar dilemmas that will test Chinese analysts' oft-repeated refrain that it faces no "fundamental conflict of interests" in the region.

One of the clearest examples of such a policy dilemma has been Libya. There, China was faced with an immediate crisis directly affecting its security – the safety of its 36,000 nationals in the country. But it was also faced with a difficult choice regarding whether to support Libyan rebels. It could on the one hand uphold the principle of non-interference by opposing the ouster of Muammar Qadhafi, thereby running the risk of angering not only a future Libyan government – as it had soured relations with the Morsi government through its strong support for ousted Egyptian president Hosni Mubarak – but also China's other allies in the region, who as members of the Arab League were advocating action against Qadhafi. On the other hand, it could support the sort of Western-led intervention that China had so long opposed.

China sought to split the difference by supporting UN Security Council resolution 1970, which imposed sanctions on Libya, and abstaining from – i.e., not blocking – resolution 1973, which authorized international intervention. As American analyst of Chinese policy in the Mideast Jon Alterman details, Beijing hedged its bets by simultaneously continuing to cultivate close ties with Qadhafi;[43] it also later supported Moscow's assertion that Russia and China had been tricked into withholding their vetoes and did not anticipate that the resolution would result in Qadhafi's overthrow.[44] In effect, however, China not only supported an American intervention against an erstwhile ally, but conducted a small military expedition of its own to evacuate its nationals.

Increasingly, the Israeli-Palestinian conflict also poses a conflict for Beijing, between the Chinese policy of the past and modern-day Chinese policy. The late PLO chairman Yasser Arafat was characterized by one Chinese analyst as China's "only true friend" in the Middle East for many years[45]. China, in turn, was a strong supporter of the Palestinians, recognizing a Palestinian state when one was unilaterally declared by the PLO in 1988. Israel, on the other hand, was not recognized by China until 1992, despite an abortive flirtation between the two countries in the 1950s. China has continued to pay a certain amount of lip service to the Palestinian cause – for example, by recognizing the Hamas government resulting from the 2006 Palestinian Legislative Council elections and welcoming subsequent Hamas-Fatah unity governments that were shunned by the US and others.

However, the real story has been the burgeoning relationship between China and Israel, which has tracked with the diminishing importance of "revolutionary" ideology in Chinese foreign relations. China-Israel trade has increased two hundred-fold in the last two decades, to $10.8 billion in 2013.[46] Even more important than the quantity of the trade, from Beijing's perspective, has been its quality – China is enormously interested in Israeli expertise in high technology.[47] Chinese policy toward the Israeli-Palestinian conflict has at the same time moved toward the international middle ground, such that the four points[48] on the issue are nearly indistinguishable from US and European policy. To the extent China's diplomatic position is somewhat more favorable to the Palestinians than to Israel, it takes little action to advance it.

China also faces dilemmas with respect to Syria and Iran. Beijing has exercised its UN Security Council veto four times in the past three years to thwart resolutions on Syria – a remarkable number, given that China had previously used its veto power only five times over the previous four decades. Its decision to do so was not, it would seem, by any particular affinity for Syrian President Bashar al-Assad, who is not one of China's closer allies in the region. Rather, the decision was likely informed not only by its experience with Libya, but also by a desire to demonstrate solidarity with Moscow and uphold the principle of non-interference, especially given the simultaneous increase in tensions in the South and East China Seas. In doing so, however, China risked angering Arab Gulf allies that it has courted assiduously, and with whom it will need smooth relations to assure its energy security in the future.

A similar conflict is present to an even greater degree in regard to China's Iran policy. While China's Gulf Arab allies have been fervently opposed to the Assad regime in Syria, they regard Iran as the far greater threat – indeed, in their view, Assad is a mere junior partner to the Iranian regime. Yet China's closest relationship in the region is with Iran, with which it enjoys not just a commonality of interests – whether based on energy relations or a shared desire to constrain American power – but a close affinity. Chinese officials have termed the Sino-Iranian relationship a strategic partnership, rather than primarily a commercial one. The modern Sino-Iranian relationship, officially established in 1971, predates China's need for oil imports, and even predates its opening of relations with the United States; the historical relationship between China and Iran goes back even further.

This conflict has proven harder for China to dodge than that over Syria. While China used its position in the so-called P5+1 group of countries to delay and dilute UN sanctions and resolutions and international demands of Iran, it nevertheless voted in favor of those resolutions and remained more or less aligned with the United States on the issue. It also temporarily reduced its oil imports from Iran in 2011–2012, due not only to American pressure but to direct lobbying by Saudi Arabia and the UAE. It did, however, subsequently increase its oil imports from Iran to record levels as American policy toward Tehran softened and the threat of a Western military strike on Iran diminished. Beijing is well-positioned for a much stronger strategic and economic relationship with Iran in the wake of the Iran nuclear agreement; however, that may prove incompatible with its need for equally cordial relations with other major oil exporters such as Saudi Arabia and the UAE, whose own rivalry with Tehran may intensify in the deal's aftermath. The difficulty of the conundrum facing Beijing was underscored by President Xi Jinping's decision to cancel a planned trip to Iran, Saudi Arabia, and Egypt in April 2015 rather than be drawn into the debate surrounding the Arab intervention in Yemen against Iranian-backed rebels.

Future Policy Directions

Even as it pursues greater economic engagement with the Middle East to satisfy its energy needs, it is not at all clear whether China desires or is capable of greater political and security involvement there. Yet its calculus may change if events continue on their present trajectory. If the American disengagement from the region continues, instability there is unlikely to abate, and China may feel compelled to – or possibly see an opportunity to – adopt a more active approach to advancing its regional interests, especially its energy security. It may also be drawn further in by regional states, who tend to look for external support in their regional conflicts. Indeed, signs of increasing Chinese involvement in the region are already abound. These include the PLAN missions to combat piracy and evacuate Chinese citizens from Libya and Yemen, the appointment in 2002 of a Chinese special envoy for the region (matching similar positions in the US, Japan, and many European states), or the increased pace of high-level official Chinese visits to the region and vice versa.

However, deeper Chinese involvement in the Middle East is not inevitable, but will depend on a variety of factors. Foremost among these will be China's own fortunes domestically and in its neighborhood. Precisely how these factors will affect China's Middle East policy is difficult to predict, though it seems likely that the greater China's own economic difficulties, and the greater the extent to which it must devote diplomatic and security resources to Asian conflicts, the less it will seek to be involved in the Middle East. In addition, Central Asia may not only compete for China's diplomatic attention but, if it provides a reliable land route for Chinese energy imports, diminish Beijing's dependence on the Middle East's sea lanes.

China's involvement in the region will also be affected by the extent to which the apparent American disengagement from the region is temporary or permanent; a more robust American role in the region will likely "crowd out" some potential Chinese involvement. The extent to which this is true will depend also on the course of Sino-American relations, especially whether increasing tensions between the US and China in East Asia spill over to their relations in other regions, or whether cooperation in theaters such as the Middle East is seen by Washington and Beijing as a balance to their conflicts in the East and South China Seas. Already there are concerning signs that the growing Chinese partnership with Iran is driven by a desire to counter US power in the region.[49] Similarly, Chinese involvement in the region may be driven in part by the extent to which its Asian rivals – such as Japan, South Korea, and India – become more involved in regional issues.

The extent to which China becomes more involved in the political and security affairs of the region will also depend on the success of its early steps in this direction. If, for example, China pays no price in its relations with Gulf Arab states for its strong diplomatic support of the Assad regime or Iran, it may be encouraged to believe that it can successfully manage conflicts among its interests in the region. Chinese involvement in the region will also depend on events; in particular, the Iran nuclear agreement may open the door for a deeper Sino-Iranian strategic relationship. Even if China chooses to step up its involvement in the region, it will likely do so slowly, and will seek to hedge its bets rather than stake out a clear policy direction or unequivocally take sides in regional conflicts.

Despite many obstacles, constructive US-China cooperation in the Middle East in advancing mutual interests could be of benefit to both countries and to the region as a whole. Whether such cooperation can be realized depends deeply on the path each country chooses to take not only in the region but in the world: it depends on whether the United States recognizes the costs of disengagement from the Middle East and rebuilds its leadership role and the security architecture it undergirded; and whether China can shake off a zero-sum approach to foreign affairs and emerge as a responsible partner for Washington and others.

Notes

1. Pan Guang, "China's Success in the Middle East," *Middle East Quarterly* 4.4, (1997): pp. 35–40.

2. Energy Information Administration, "Countries Index," Department of Energy, http://www.eia.gov/countries/index.cfm?view=consumption.

3. "BP Energy Outlook 2035." BP, Jan. 2014. Available at: http://www.bp.com/content/dam/bp/pdf/Energy-economics/Energy-Outlook/BP_World_Energy_Outlook_booklet_2035.pdf

4. Ibid.

5. Energy Information Administration, "Countries Index," Department of Energy, http://www.eia.gov/countries/index.cfm?view=consumption

6. "BP Energy Outlook 2035." BP, Jan. 2014. Available at: http://www.bp.com/content/dam/bp/pdf/Energy-economics/Energy-Outlook/BP_World_Energy_Outlook_booklet_2035.pdf

7. Ibid.

8. Ibid.

9. Keith Bradsher, "Amid Tension, China Blocks Vital Exports to Japan," *New York Times*, September 22, 2010, Global Business Section, http://www.nytimes.com/2010/09/23/business/global/23rare.html?pagewanted=all&_r=0

10. "The China-Philippine Banana War," *Asia Sentinel*, June 6, 2012, Society Section, Available at: http://www.asiasentinel.com/society/the-china-philippine-banana-war/

11. US Library of Congress, Congressional Research Service, *US Trade and Investment in the Middle East and North Africa: Overview and Issues for Congress*, by Shayerah Ilias Akhtar, Mary Jane Bolle and Rebecca M. Nelson, CRS Report R42153 (Washington, DC: Office of Congressional Information and Publishing, March 4, 2013). Available at: http://fas.org/sgp/crs/misc/R42153.pdf

12. Marianne Stigset and Gelu Sulugiuc, "Suez Canal, Carrying 8% of Trade, Open Amid Unrest," *Bloomberg*, January 31, 2011, News Section. Available at: http://www.bloomberg.com/news/2011-01-31/egypt-s-suez-canal-carrying-8-of-world-trade-remains-open-amid-violence.html

13. Energy Information Administration, "Today in Energy," Department of Energy, September 5, 2012, Available at: http://www.eia.gov/todayinenergy/detail.cfm?id=7830

14. Elizabeth Bumiller, Eric Schmitt and Thom Shanker, "US Sends Top Iranian Leader a Warning on Strait Threat," *New York Times*, January 12, 2012, Middle East Section, Available at: http://www.nytimes.com/2012/01/13/world/middleeast/us-warns-top-iran-leader-not-to-shut-strait-of-hormuz.html?pagewanted=all

15. Ben Blanchard, "China Urges Stability in Strait of Hormuz," *Reuters*, December 29, 2011, US edition, Available at: http://www.reuters.com/article/2011/12/29/us-china-iran-idUSTRE7BS08E20111229

16. United Nations Meetings Coverage and Press Releases, "Security Council Requires Scheduled Destruction of Syria's Chemical Weapons, Unanimously Adopting Resolution 2118 (2013)," United Nations. Available at: http://www.un.org/press/en/2013/sc11135.doc.htm.

17. These have included UN Security Council resolutions 1696 (2006), 1737 (2006), 1747 (2007), 1803 (2008), 1835 (2008), 1929 (2010), and 2231 (2015).

18. "A History of Iran's Nuclear Program," Iran Watch, March 1, 2012. Available at: http://www.iranwatch.org/our-publications/weapon-program-background-report/history-irans-nuclear-program

19. John Pomfret, "US Says Chinese Businesses and Banks are Bypassing U.N. Sanctions against Iran," *Washington Post*, October 18, 2010, World Section. Available at: http://www.washingtonpost.com/wp-dyn/content/article/2010/10/17/AR2010101703364.html

20. Jacques deLisle, "9/11 and US-China Relations," *Foreign Policy Research Institute*, September 2011. Available at: http://www.fpri.org/articles/2011/09/911-and-us-china-relations

21. Zhao Huasheng, "China and Afghanistan: China's Interests, Stances and Perspectives," Center for Strategic and International Studies, March 2012. Available at: http://csis.org/files/publication/120322_Zhao_ChinaAfghan_web.pdf

22. Timothy Gardner, "US Concerned Foreign Fighters in Syria are Working with Yemenis," *Reuters*, July 13, 2014, US edition. Available at: http://www.reuters.com/article/2014/07/13/us-usa-syria-holder-idUSKBN0FI0VZ20140713

23. Ben Blanchard, "China Says May Have Citizens Fighting in Iraq," *Reuters*, July 28, 2014, US edition. Available at: http://www.reuters.com/article/2014/07/28/us-iraq-security-china-idUSKBN0FX0FV20140728

24. US Library of Congress, Congressional Research Service, *US-China Counterterrorism Cooperation: Issues for US Policy*, by Shirley A. Kan, CRS Report RL33001 (Washington, DC: Office of Congressional Information and Publishing, July 15, 2010). Available at: http://fas.org/sgp/crs/terror/RL33001.pdf

25. Michael Singh and Jacqueline Newmyer Deal, "China's Iranian Gambit," *Foreign Policy*, October 31, 2011. Available at: http://www.foreignpolicy.com/articles/2011/10/31/china_iran_nuclear_relationship

26. John J. Tkacik Jr., "The Arsenal of Iraq Insurgency," *Weekly Standard* 12.45 (2007). Available at: http://www.weeklystandard.com/Content/Public/Articles/000/000/013/956wspet.asp

27. James Brandon Gentry, "China's Role in Iran's Anti-Access / Area Denial Weapons Capability Development," *Middle East Institute*, April 16, 2013. Available at: http://www.mei.edu/content/china%E2%80%99s-role-iran%E2%80%99s-anti-access-area-denial-weapons-capability-development

28. Polling data on these trends abound. See, for example http://www.pewresearch.org/fact-tank/2014/05/28/obama-charts-a-new-foreign-policy-course-for-a-public-that-wants-the-focus-to-be-at-home/

29. "China offers $16 million in aid for Syria refugees," Associated Press, June 5, 2014. Available at: http://bigstory.ap.org/article/china-offers-16-million-aid-syria-refugees

30. Ibid.

31. These were "to promote political relations on the basis of mutual respect, to forge closer trade and economic links so as to achieve common development, to expand cultural exchanges through drawing upon each other's experience, and to strengthen cooperation in international affairs with the aim of safeguarding world peace and promoting common development." See Pan Zhenqiang, "China and the Middle East," in *China's Growing Role in the Middle East: Implications for the Region and Beyond*, (DC: Nixon Center, 2010), pp. 73–95. Available at: http://www.cftni.org/full-monograph-chinas-growing-role-in-me.pdf

32. Gabriel Wildau, "New Silk Road Raises Hopes for Increased China-Arab Trade," *Financial Times*, June 29, 2014, http://www.ft.com/cms/s/0/11190312-f874–11e3–815f-00144feabdc0.html#axzz39SYYbhSs.

33. Abdulaziz Sager, "GCC-China Relations: Looking Beyond Oil – Risks and Rewards," in *China's Growing Role in the Middle East: Implications for the Region and Beyond*, (DC: Nixon Center, 2010), pp. 1–21, http://www.cftni.org/full-monograph-chinas-growing-role-in-me.pdf.

34. *China in the Middle East: Statement before the US-China Economic and Security Review Commission*, 113th Congress (2013) (Statement by Dr. Jon B. Alterman). Available at: https://csis.org/files/attachments/ts130606_alterman.pdf

35. Pan Zhenqiang, "China and the Middle East," in *China's Growing Role in the Middle East: Implications for the Region and Beyond*, (DC: Nixon Center, 2010), pp. 73–95. Available at: http://www.cftni.org/full-monograph-chinas-growing-role-in-me.pdf

36. Dennis C. Blair, "False Trade-Off on Bahrain," *Hill*, February 12, 2013. Available at: http://thehill.com/blogs/congress-blog/foreign-policy/282337-false-trade-off-on-bahrain

37. Emile Hokayem, "They've Come a Long Way in 60 Years: and So Have We," *National*, October 4, 2009.

38. Tamsin Carlisle, "China is Right Market at Right Time for Gulf," *National*, August 18, 2009, Business section. Available at: http://www.thenational.ae/business/china-is-right-market-at-right-time-for-gulf

39. See, for example, Carlo A. Sdralevich et al, "Subsidy Reform in the Middle East and North Africa," (Washington, D.C.: International Monetary Fund, 2014).

40. Michelle FlorCruz and Jacey Fortin, "The Takeover: Stable China Looks To Volatile Middle East For Investment Opportunities As West Backs Away," *International Business Times*, May 11, 2013, Economy section, US edition Available at: http://www.ibtimes.com/takeover-stable-china-looks-volatile-middle-east-investment-opportunities-west-backs-away-1249621

41. "Dutch dredging firms win new Suez Canal mega contract," DutchNews.nl, October 20, 2014. Available at: http://www.dutchnews.nl/news/archives/2014/10/boskalis_wins_suez_canal_mega/

42. David Pierson, "Online Call for Protests in China Prompts Crackdown," *Los Angeles Times*, February 26, 2011. Available at: http://articles.latimes.com/2011/feb/26/world/la-fgw-china-crackdown-20110227

43. *China in the Middle East: Statement before the US-China Economic and Security Review Commission*, 113th Congress (2013) (Statement by Dr. Jon B. Alterman). Available at: https://csis.org/files/attachments/ts130606_alterman.pdf

44. Louis Charbonneau, "Russia U.N. Veto on Syria Aimed at Crushing West's Crusade," *Reuters*, February 8, 2012, US Edition. Available at: http://www.reuters.com/article/2012/02/08/us-un-russia-idUSTRE8170BK20120208

45. Pan Zhenqiang, "China and the Middle East," in *China's Growing Role in the Middle East: Implications for the Region and Beyond*, (DC: Nixon Center, 2010), pp. 73–95, http://www.cftni.org/full-monograph-chinas-growing-role-in-me.pdf.

46. Tova Cohen, "Israel Welcomes Tech-Hungry Chinese Investors," *Reuters*, May 22, 2014, US edition. Available at: http://www.reuters.com/article/2014/05/22/us-china-israel-investment-idUSBREA4L0Q920140522

47. Israeli Prime Minister Benjamin Netanyahu said that when he met with the Chinese Prime Minister, he was interested in "three things: Israeli technology, Israeli technology, and Israeli technology." He said the same of other

world leaders. See more, "PM Netanyahu addresses Presidential Conference," Consulate General of Israel in Toronto. Available at: http://embassies. gov.il/toronto/NewsAndEvents/Pages/PM-Netanyahu-addresses-Israeli-Presidential-Conference-2013.aspx

48. The four points can be found at "Chinese President Makes Four-Point Proposal for Settlement of Palestinian Question," *Xinhuanet*, May 6, 2013. Available at: http://news.xinhuanet.com/english/china/2013–05/06/c_132363061.htm

49. Michael Singh and Jacqueline Newmyer Deal, "China's Iranian Gambit," *Foreign Policy*, October 31, 2011. Available at: http://www.foreignpolicy.com/ articles/2011/10/31/china_iran_nuclear_relationship

11

China and Iran: Expanding Cooperation under Conditions of US Domination

John W. Garver

A rising global power views a rising regional power

Contrary to a common perception, the robust, cooperative relation that exists between China and the Islamic Republic of Iran is about far more than oil. There is an unfortunate tendency to reduce the Sino-Iranian relationship to Iran's supply and China's consumption of oil. Petroleum supply is indeed one important dimension of the Sino-Iranian relationship, but it is an egregious simplification to reduce that relationship to oil. The relation between the People's Republic of China (PRC) and the Islamic Republic of Iran (IRI) is also about two ambitious emerging powers who view each another as sharing many common interests and perspectives. They see one another as potential and important partners in what both believe will be a forthcoming era in which the US role in the world is much reduced. Broadly speaking, the Sino-Iranian relationship is about two like-minded and ambitious countries unhappy with the current state of US dominance of world affairs, who view a strong Sino-Iranian partnership as an important element of the post-US unipolar world that both aspire to create. It must immediately be stated, however, that this partnership operates in a context of an over-riding Chinese desire to maintain comity in relations with the United States for the sake of China's economic development drive, and thus to avoid confrontation with the United States in the Middle East.[1] Reconciling these opposites requires considerable subtlety, camouflage, denial, and obfuscation.

One authoritative Chinese study of the Sino-Iranian relationship refers to "twenty centuries" of cooperation between China and Persia.[2] The geopolitical realities of those two great empires during ancient and medieval times was that they were far enough apart that they never directly abutted and thus came into conflict, but close enough to find common enemies between their two realms, which sometimes seemed to offer opportunities for cooperation.[3] Cultural interaction over the Silk Roads between the two fecund societies, China and Persia, grew thick over the course of centuries, with Persian merchants and missionaries acting as key intermediaries introducing to China the knowledge and achievements of the broader Middle Eastern Islamic world. Persians also were the backbone that moved Chinese luxury goods, especially silk, westward across Central Asia to commercial emporia of the Levant. Even into the early 20th century when the two nations were in internal crisis, they found ground to cooperate. In 1920 Persia was the first country to sign treaties with China without the offensive practice of extra-territoriality.

The modern Sino-Iran relation began during the 1970s when Mao Zedong's China and the Iran of Shah Mohammad Reza Pahlavi shared a wide array of concerns about the expansion of Soviet influence in South Asia, the Middle East, the Horn of Africa, and the Indian Ocean. Iran under the Shah was driving to establish itself as the dominant power in the Persian Gulf-Arabian Sea with US support under the Nixon Doctrine of supporting regional powers to share the burden of containing the Soviet Union. A remarkably broad convergence of Chinese and Iranian policies developed swiftly: supporting Pakistan against further Soviet-supported Indian encroachment (following the dismemberment of Pakistan in the 1971 war), countering Soviet-supported rebellion in Oman's southern province and Soviet/Cuban moves in the Horn of Africa, and supporting Egypt's shift away from the Soviet Union under Anwar Sadat. So close did the Sino-Iranian partnership become that in his final testament the Shah paid "homage to the loyalty of the Chinese leaders" who "at the time when the Iranian crisis was reaching its peak" [in 1978] gave the Shah "the impression that the Chinese were alone in favor of a strong Iran." [4] The broader point to be made is that the modern Sino-Iranian relationship was about geopolitics, not oil.

The Sino-Iranian relation collapsed with Iran's 1979 Islamic Revolution, in part because of Beijing's close embrace of the Shah. But Beijing seized on Tehran's requirements for cheap and rugged arms during the Iran-Iraq war (which started in September 1980 and ended in September 1988) to rebuild the Sino-Iranian relationship. Iran was simply too important to allow ties to languish. Beijing made good money serving as Tehran's main arms supplier during that war. But again it is too narrow-sighted to view economics, the profit from arms sales, as the decisive factor. From Beijing's perspective, Tehran's pressing needs for cheap weapons was a

way of re-normalizing ties with Iran. It was a way of re-opening channels and dialogue with Iran's leaders, and of demonstrating to those new
leaders – ignorant and deeply suspicious of Communist China – that
China could give Iran very practical and effective assistance to Iran's
security problems as defined by Iran's rulers. By the last years of the
Iran-Iraq war, China had emerged as Tehran's major supporter in United
Nations (UN) Security Council actions to end that war. Again the broader
point: the revival of the Sino-Iran relation after Iran's Islamic revolution
was about questions of war and peace, not oil.

Beijing's fear of Soviet encirclement, or indeed its fear of attack against
its continental territory by any major power, is long past. Yet Beijing
still views Iran as an ambitious regional actor, one that happens, in
the Chinese view, to be locked in a contest with the United States for
supremacy in the Gulf region.

China's leaders have long historical memories and take a long view
of the future. When they look at Asia over the past century they see a
number of major powers who have come into conflict with China: Japan
for fifty years between 1895 and 1945 and then for another fifty years
in alliance with the United States; Russia with its seizure of vast tracks
of the Qing empire and then its aspirations in Manchuria, Mongolia,
and Xinjiang, and still again during the 1960s and 1970s; India with its
rivalry for status in the Afro-Asian world and throughout the Himalayan-
Tibetan region. There is, of course, China's stalwart ally Pakistan, but in
terms of national capabilities, Pakistan is in a different class than Russia,
Japan, India – or Iran. Of all the major powers in Asia, Iran offers the
best prospect of being a partner with China in the construction of a
new international order in Asia when the era of multi-polarity arrives
and the US role in Asia is much reduced. This, I believe, is the fundamental geostrategic logic of China's multi-dimensional cooperative with
Iran. China seeks to foster with Iran mutual understanding and trust,
and on cooperation on the basis of common interests, so as to forge,
over time, a strategic partnership with Iran that will serve as a major
element of Chinese influence in the post-American-dominated West
Asia. Accomplishing this goal without antagonizing the United States,
upon which China's modernization depends, is a difficult task requiring
considerable diplomatic skill.

Elite Chinese perceptions of the Iran-US conflict

Understanding China's strategy toward Iran begins with an understanding of *Chinese* views of current Iran-Iran tensions. Americans

frequently assume that China and the United States have common interests in the Persian Gulf: The US Navy keeps the sea lanes open to keep oil flowing from the Gulf to China and the world; China has as much to lose as the United States from intensified rivalry between Iran and Israel or the Gulf states; or that, as one of five legitimate nuclear weapons states under the Non Proliferation Treaty (NPT), China has as much interest as the United States in preventing the further proliferation of nuclear weapons. A reading of Chinese sources on Iran-US tensions indicates that the Chinese simply do not share these common and perhaps optimistic American views. A somewhat longish analysis of the actual Chinese views of top Chinese analysts is offered here as an antidote to this American ethnocentrism.

This consensus Chinese view laid out in China's top foreign policy journals is that the Iran is pushing vigorously to expand its influence in the Persian Gulf, confronting in the process an aggressive drive by the United States, which is seen as taking advantage of the "extremely unbalanced" international situation that developed following the demise of the USSR to bring under US domination all the oil producing countries of the Persian Gulf. The turmoil in the Gulf is, in essence, a struggle between US hegemony (although that word is usually avoided) and an ambitious rising regional power, Iran, who refuses to bow to American orders.

A 2006 article in *Xiandai guoji guanxi* (*Contemporary International Relations*), a journal with historic ties to the powerful Ministry of State Security, saw the United States pursuing an increasingly aggressive "hegemonist strategy" in the Middle East.[5] Washington had seized upon the 9–11 attacks to completely transform (*wanquan gaizao*) the balance of power in the Middle East via a classic hegemonic strategy of strategic intervention, unilateralism, and an acting as the world's policeman. Washington was using the huge power vacuum created by the demise of the USSR to establish control over Central Asia, South Asia, and West Asia. Establishing pro-U.S puppet regimes, as had recently been done in Iraq, was the jewel in the crown of this strategy. Via this move, Washington hoped to seize control of Iraq's oil and extend US influence to the former Soviet areas of Eurasia. [sic] With the US occupation of Iraq in 2003, the US had established a "strategic foothold" in the heart of the Arab world. It might use that "foothold" to accomplish "other big power objectives," although those objectives could not be made public. The second element of the new hegemonic drive of the United States was "democratic reform" via the Bush Administration's "Greater Middle East Plan Initiative" promulgated in 2004.

The main point of the article was that US strategy was destined to fail, producing the strategic decline of the United States in the process. The Middle East was exceedingly complex, too complex for any outside power to control, the article said. "The US exercise of power [in the Middle East] will exhaust (*xiao rou*) its strength and bring it to a situation of strategic decline (*shi qi xianru zhanlue shuaitui*)" US efforts in the Middle East would produce growing resistance from the region and would "backfire." US democratic reform efforts would alienate traditional US allies like Egypt and Saudi Arabia. It would encourage extremism and offer new opportunities to anti-US forces. It would further unite Iran, Syria, Hamas and Hezbollah against the United States. The United States would find itself in a 'quagmire of war." The United States had, in fact, fallen into a "complete trap" (*quanmian kunjing*). Its Middle East quagmire will "necessarily consume the national strength" of the US.

Regarding Iran, that country was a "rising regional hegemonic power" (*dichu baquanguo de jueqi*) and an "inveterate enemy" (*zui da si di*) of the United States. Things were going in Iran's favor. Previously Saddam Hussein's regime in Iraq had checked Iran. Now influence with Iraq's Shiite majority offered a great opportunity for Tehran. No power in the region was now capable of containing Iran, the article stated, so the United States was doing that itself. Mounting US "direct containment" of Iran was producing a growing sense of crisis in Tehran. One of the lessons Tehran learned from the US war with Iraq was the consequence of Iraq lacking weapons of mass destruction. Without such weapons, Iraqi attempts to conciliate with the US were of no use and the US dared to attack. Only military strength could deter the United States, and this was the reason Tehran took a hard-line position on its nuclear programs, and sought to expand its influence in the Arab world, activities that "directly threaten the US hegemonic position in the Middle East."

A 2008 article in *Guoji shiyou jingji* (*International Petroleum Economics*), authored by a professor at China's National Defense University, argued that the US was using the nuclear issue as a lever to force Iran to "come to terms."[6] Iran was the biggest obstacle to realization of a US plan to control the oil of the Middle East, which would enable the US to "control the whole global economy." Once the US had solved the "Iran problem," by regime change (*gaibian yilang yisilan zhengquan*), the oil resources of the Middle East would become the "strategic reserve" of the United States. Iran's core interest was survival of the Islamic regime. Increasing Iran's status, influence, and national pride were linked to regime survival. So too was nuclear technology. Iran was resisting US dictation and "to some extent … has become the symbol of third world anti-hegemony and upholding one's own interest" against the US. The West recognized that nuclear technology would further increase Iran's international status and influence, undermining the hegemonic position of the United States and possibly splitting Europe from the US. But US sanctions had not worked. The final US option was war. But this was very difficult because of the financial and political costs. Most serious of all, an attack on Iran would probably expand to become a general and long war between the Western and the Islamic countries. In this article, the author did not draw implications for China's interests.

A 2008 article in a journal *Xiya faizhou* (West Asia and Africa) of the West Asia Institute of the authoritative Chinese Academy of Social Sciences asserted that Washington pushed for more severe sanctions against Iran in the 1990s in order to "prevent Iran from getting nuclear weapons and becoming a big power in the Middle East."[7] For 20 years the objective of US and other Western nations had been to "weaken Iran." (*xiaorou yilang*). These policies had failed. The "rise of a big regional power in the Gulf was already increasingly apparent." US economic sanctions had caused Iran some economic injury, but those had been offset by an increase in a national sentiment of unity and struggle. The whole nation of Iran was united around its right of peaceful use of nuclear energy. Anti-US sentiments created by American policies confronted that country with "insurmountable obstacles." Alluding to a possible US military strike against Iran, the article stated:

> If the US does not change its policies, it will very possibly seriously injure Iranian national sentiment even to the extent of bringing a huge catastrophe on mankind (*renlai cainan*).

US policy of using sanctions to force Iran to submit was producing contradictions between Western countries, between developed and developing countries, and between resource-rich and resource-importing countries – all of which were "incompatible with US 'world leadership'." The result would be the decline of US power.

Another 2008 article in the same authoritative journal placed the US-Iran confrontation in a broader context.[8] Anti-US forces in the Middle East were growing rapidly, creating a new situation. The US had hoped to use the Iraq war and Israel's 2006 war against Lebanon and its 2007 war against Hamas in the Gaza Strip, to gain "control of the greater Middle East and control (*she yue*) the big countries of Asia and Europe" – apparently by controlling their oil supplies. The US was the prime mover behind Israel's 2006 and 2007 wars. But US war policies had backfired, stimulating anti-American passions while 160,000 US troops "sank deeper into the quagmire in Iraq." "New forces" were growing rapidly. The international influence of Iran was growing. Saudi Arabia was increasingly anti-US. Washington was unhappy with the direction of Saudi Arabian policy and "continually attempting to suppress it." The author's prescription was for the "Arab and Islamic [the latter including Iran] countries" to unite, increase military and economic cooperation, develop their strength, and form "a pole' (yi ji) in the global system, thus filling the vacuum being created by US decline.

A 2009 article in the same journal argued that the root cause of the dispute over Iran's nuclear programs was a US attempt to impose new security on the Gulf.[9] Following the Cold War, the US shifted its global strategic focus to the Gulf and set out to secure the energy of that region via a direct US military presence, because of the dependency of the West [sic] on that energy source and in order to guarantee the long-term continued growth of the US economy. The 1991 war against Iraq was the first move in this long-term grand strategy. So too were President Clinton's late 1990s Security Council resolutions and sanctions against Iraq and President Bush's 2003 regime change war against Iraq. With Saudi Arabia, Kuwait, and now Iraq part of the US "security system," Washington's objective was "regime change" (gai chao) in Iran. Iran felt threatened by the United States because of the long history of bad relations, military threats, and sanctions. Consequently, Tehran was seeking to organize a regional security order led by Iran as the most populous and economically advanced country in the region. The crux of this new system would be the expulsion of US forces from the Gulf and cooperation among the countries of the Gulf to ensure security and stability. Tehran said repeatedly that its nuclear programs were of purely non-military, but such reassurances were part of Tehran's efforts to reassure and court its Gulf neighbors. The article said nothing about China's interests and policy response to this situation.

Another 2009 article in a Chinese Academy of Social Sciences (CASS) journal by one of China's top Middle East experts, argued that Iran was growing its national power and its regional and even global influence under adverse conditions of the US and Europe trying to "contain and crush" (ezhi jiya) it.[10] Iran's nuclear programs were part of this effort. Iran's quest was driven by a sense that as a great, ancient civilization and nation, it should play a major role in the region and the world. Iran's nuclear push had begun before the 1979 revolution as part of this drive for national greatness. The same impulse underpinned it now, linked to a belief that in today's world, a nation could not be a great power without nuclear capability/weapons. The reality was that only nuclear weapons could deal with nuclear weapons, and therefore Iran needed that capability. The article's Chinese readers would have understood these sentiments, which underlay China's own 1954 decision to build "the bomb."[11]

According to article, Iran's minimum goal was the capacity to produce nuclear weapons. Its maximal goal was nuclear weapons themselves. It had already nearly achieved the first goal and the major factor determining whether Iran would move on to possessing actual nuclear weapons were the policies of the United States and Europe. Unless the Western powers could abandon sanctions and threats, drop their policies of regime change, and establish diplomatic relations with Iran, Tehran was likely to move ahead to produce nuclear weapons. The policies of the Western powers were the" basic cause of the evil situation" (*shi zuo yongzhe*). The United States was not willing to tolerate a big power in the Gulf that challenged US interests, and therefore sought "regime change" (*zhengquan gengdie*) in Iran. A US military strike against Iran's nuclear facilities was unlikely, the article asserted. Opposition by "the big powers," domestic opposition within the US, and the strength of Iran's own defense preparations made such an attack unlikely. Israel might strike, but then Iran would retaliate and the war would spread. The result would be a big war and an energy crisis. US and European sanctions would not force Iran to stop enrichment. The author did not predict the final outcome of the failure of US policies, but the implication was clear enough: Iran would probably emerge as the dominant power in the Gulf.

An early 2010 article in *Guoji Jingji Pinglun* (*International Economic Review*) viewed Iran as irrevocably pushing to the threshold of nuclear weapons capability. "Whether because of the need to resist (*dui kang*) the US, or in order to become a major power in the Persian Gulf, acquisition of nuclear weapons is an absolute enticement" for Iran, the article said.[12] "Iran would not have failed to notice that once North Korea got nuclear weapons, the US has not carried out military attacks, but has increased emphasis on diplomatic negotiations." Washington was pursuing a dual policy toward Iran: engaging with Iran while mobilizing international pressure against it, trying to overthrow the IRI government, and preparing a military strike against Iran's nuclear facilities. Since 2006, the article said, Washington had levied mounting political and economic sanctions against Iran via the International Atomic Energy Agency (IAEA), the UN Security Council, and via pressure on other countries to follow suit. These pressures have not caused Iran to change course. Instead Iran had replied to these "Western threats" by (using an old Chinese colloquium) "dealing a head on blow at the first encounter." Tehran had responded to mounting pressure, by pushing forward with its uranium enrichment programs. The article recognized that Tehran was playing loose with its obligations under the Non-proliferation Treaty (NPT). Iran's failure to ratify (and thus implement) the Supplemental Safeguards agreement with the IAEA signed on 18 December 2003 had rendered the IAEA unable to report on the actual state of Iran's nuclear program, while Tehran pushed steadily toward the threshold of producing 90% pure uranium necessary for atomic bombs. Iran's "words and behavior make it very difficult for the international community to believe its promises." Instead, there was "doubt and concern" about Tehran's ultimate goal, the article said.

Given the escalating confrontation and the conflicting "positions and interests" of "the US (including its European allies)" and Tehran, there was little prospect for a "fundamental settlement of the issue via diplomatic means," the article continued. Instead, the US was preparing for a "surgical strike," a "first strike," against Iran's nuclear facilities. The US was deploying anti-missile systems around the Gulf and conducting exercises with Iran as the hypothetical enemy. The US was deploying Diego Garcia ground attack missiles capable of destroying deep underground installations. Iran, for its part, was responding to the mounting threat of a US attack, by intensifying its defenses. A five-day military exercise practicing defense of Iran's nuclear facilities was conducted in November 2009, and in March Iran used a new indigenously produced rocket to launch a satellite. The author did not say, but his readers would have understood, that such a rocket could also deliver warheads on such places as Diego Garcia.

None of these articles discussed, or even mentioned, China's interests and how they were affected by US pressure and threat against Iran. Articles in these elite journals avoided, conspicuously so, drawing out implications for China's interests resulting from the US threat, subversion, sanctions, and hostility toward Iran. The systematic and conspicuous eschewing of discussion of China's interests and policies in these articles is almost certainly the result of guidance from above and a function of Beijing's difficult task of building a long-term partnership with Iran while not souring Sino-US ties.

Chinese support for the IRI against US-led international pressure

Policies of support for Iran in its struggle against US hegemony follow from the Chinese analysis laid out in the previous section, Elite Chinese perceptions of the Iran-US conflict. Beijing has rendered substantial assistance to Iran in its struggle against US hegemony. In debates in the International Atomic Energy Agency (IAEA) and the United Nations Security Council between late 2003 and late 2014, China gave the IRI a substantial degree of support against US-led international pressure. In every case China ultimately voted "yes" in support of US-endorsed proposals, testament to the primacy Beijing assigns to its vital relation with the United States. But along the way China delayed and diluted the sanctions ultimately confronting Tehran.

In IAEA and Security Council debates, Beijing frequently supported Tehran's stances. Beijing seconded Iran's claim to a "right to the peaceful use of nuclear energy" when Washington argued that any such "right" was nullified by Tehran's long record of nuclear activities unreported to the IAEA as required by the NPT, which Iran signed and ratified in 1968. Beijing insisted on taking at face value Tehran's disavowals of military intentions and insistence that Iran's nuclear programs targeted only such things as electricity generation and production of medical isotopes. Washington, of course, stressed the probable military nature of Iran's nuclear programs. Beijing also for many years rejected intelligence regarding Iranian nuclear programs derived via "national means" – mainly the US Central Intelligence Agency or Israel's Mossad – and would credit only information supplied by the IAEA. Beijing rejected all intimations of possible use of military force against Iran, such as the occasional statement by the United States that "all options remain on the table." Beijing vigilantly filtered out from various resolutions wording suggesting possible resort to military force against Iran. In short, during this more than seven years of international debate over Iran's nuclear programs, China was Iran's major international supporter. At the same time, Beijing ensured that Washington was satisfied with the level of Chinese cooperation on Iran, rendering pronouncements that supported the US position. In effect, Beijing left neither Tehran nor Washington completely happy with its stance, but neither was also not entirely angry. Table 11.1 outlines the "pro-US" and the "pro-Iranian" aspects of Beijing's IAEA and Security Council diplomacy.

China continued to maintain a balance between Washington and Tehran as the two sides began secret bilateral negotiations in Oman

Table 11.1   Balancing of "Pro-US" and "Pro-IRI" elements of China's UN position, 2003–2011

"Pro-U.S."	"Pre-IRI"
oppose IRI possession of nuclear weapons and uphold the NPT; demand IRI fulfill its commitments and obligations under NPT	support IRI "right to peaceful use" of nuclear energy accept at face value IRI professions of non-military intention
approve 4 Security Council resolutions threatening or applying sanctions Resolutions include demand that IRI suspend uranium enrichment	oppose and delay IAEA "referral" to Security Council considerably water-down sanctions
agree to "report" issue to Security Council agree to include reference to Article 7 U.N. Charter	oppose and long delay application of sanctions eliminate threatening language
press IR/I to be flexible and genuinely seek solution	insist on negotiated solution and oppose threat or use of military force Reject as illegitimate unilateral or extra-UN sanctions reject as illegitimate intelligence gathered by "national means"

in March 2013 and then moved toward more intense talks within the UN framework of the P-5 +1 at Geneva in October 2013. The election of moderate Hassan Rouhani as President in June 2013 gave additional impetus to the effort to reach an understanding regarding Iran's nuclear program. As this new negotiating effort was gaining steam in July, China's deputy UN representative Wang Min called on all parties to begin a new round of talks "as soon as possible." Wang continued:

> At present, all parties should seize the opportunity to mobilize the positive factors to start a new round of dialogue ... all parties should translate their confidence, adopt practical and flexible approach and properly take care of each other's concerns, and in active measures expand consensus so as to take forward the dialogue.[13]

As indicated in Table 11.2, Beijing "split the difference" between Washington and Tehran

Table 11.2   PRC balancing between US and IRI, 2013–2014

"Pro-IRI"	"pro-U.S."
sanctions are not "fundamental objective" dialogue and negotiation are "the only right, viable path	issue bears on the authority of NPT regime Iran should maintain and strengthen dialogue and cooperation with the IAEA to reach settlement of pending issues
Alleged violations of sanctions must "be based on facts and hard evidence opposes use or threatened use of force do not favor new sanctions and increased pressure on Iran	

Beijing extended high profile support for Tehran and the IRI-P5 + 1 as the 2013–2014 negotiations approached. When China's new President, Xi Jinping, met with Rouhani prior to a Shanghai Cooperation Organization (SCO) summit in Kyrgyzstan in September 2013 he reiterated China's support for "Iran's legitimate [nuclear] rights" and "appreciated the positive stance" of Iran's new government on the nuclear issue.[14] Xi also told Rouhani that China was willing to make constructive efforts to peacefully resolve the nuclear issue, including advancing talks between the concerned parties. The next month the speaker of Iran's parliament, Ali Larijani, visited Beijing, conveying to Xi Jinping Iran's hope that the talks would achieve positive results through China's cooperation.[15] The Secretary of Iran's Supreme National Security council, Ali Shamkhani, visited Beijing in November to call for increased "strategic" political and economic cooperation between China and Iran.[16] Iran-China cooperation was a model of cooperation between Asian countries founded on the basis of independent national will, Shamkhani said. The balance of regional and international power had already shifted in favor of "independent countries" as a result of the "will and the resistance" of the Iranian people. Shamkhani thanked China for opposing "unilateral sanctions" and called on China to play a "more effective role" in helping to resolve the nuclear issue. Comments by Rouhani, Larijani, and Shamkhani demonstrate that Iranian leaders considered Beijing a sympathetic and influential power. Shamkhani's Chinese interlocutor, Yang Jiechi, echoed the designation of Sino-Iranian ties as strategic and identified cultural affairs, counter-terrorism, and security-related issues in such areas as Afghanistan and Syria as areas for expanded cooperation.

Speaking to an Arab audience (via *al Jazeera*) early in 2014, PRC Foreign Minister Wang Yi tilted away from Tehran. China's opposition to Iranian development or possession of nuclear weapons was "clear cut and firm," Wang Yi said.[17] MFA representatives have reiterated this basic point a number of times over the years. China opposes Iranian development or possession of nuclear weapons, and calls on Tehran to find ways of reassuring the P-5 that it is not driving toward nuclear weapons. This stance identifies China as a responsible member of the P-5, cooperating with other P-5 powers to uphold the Nuclear Nonproliferation Regime. But at the same time China respects Iran's right to non-military, civilian research, development and use of nuclear power. China also opposes forceful economic sanctions and completely rules out the use of force. If Iran and the West can reach a settlement precluding Iranian nuclear weapons, China will have protected its relations with both and earned the reputation of peace-maker. If someday Iran fabricates nuclear weapons in undetected nuclear facilities, China can point to its formal opposition to Iran's efforts and hope that the US and other Western powers will believe it did its best to prevent this unfortunate outcome. Tehran, on the other hand, will look on China as a sympathetic and cunning power worth having as a friend.

Beijing *also* diluted and delayed the four sets of sanctions issued from Security Council deliberations. The IAEA determined in November 2003 that Iran had violated its obligations under the NPT, for example. According to IAEA rules, that organization should have swiftly referred that situation to the Security Council. In fact this was not done until February 2006. China's reluctance was a major factor creating this 26-month delay. Or, to cite another example, Washington began its push for a fourth round of Security Council sanctions in December 2009. China agreed to open discussions on that topic only in March 2010, after a delay of two and a half months. Another nine weeks were then required to reach agreement on incrementally more severe sanctions. Altogether, over the 2004–2010 period China's leisurely approach must have gained Tehran perhaps two years' time.

China also worked to weaken Security Council sanctions targeting Iran. During the negotiation of what became Resolution 1747, passed in March 2007, for example, the United States pushed for a ban on government loans for business operations in Iran. China rejected this and agreed only to sanctions targeting specific Iranian firms identified as involved in Iran's nuclear or missile programs.[18] The Resolution that eventually

resulted called on states not to grant "financial assistance and conces-
sional loans" to the government of Iran.[19] Once again Beijing balanced
with the US and ultimately reached agreement with Washington on,
and then voted for, successive sets of Security Council sanctions.

Beijing also stood by Iran by refusing to go along with unilateral US
sanctions against Iran. Between 2002 and 2009, nearly 40 Chinese entities were sanctioned 74 times by the United Status under US legislation
and Executive Orders. The annual incidence of these US sanctions is
shown in Table 11.3. Many of these Chinese entities were large, politically well-connected state-owned enterprises. Interestingly, however,
none of China's oil major oil companies were among the Chinese firms
sanctioned,[20] despite those firms' vigorous entry into Iran's energy
sector in the late 2000s the apparent applicability of US sanction laws
to those firms' investment in Iran's energy sector. In discussions with
Senate Foreign Relations Committee staffer Frank Januzzi in March 2008,
the Director General of the MFA's Arms Control Department, Cheng
Jingye, said that China's energy cooperation with Iran was unrelated
to the Iran nuclear issue. Beijing had made clear to the United States
that China's need for energy resources and China's cooperation with
Iran on energy had nothing to do with the Iran nuclear issue, Cheng
said. The US Congress needed to understand this point. Specifically,
the threat of sanctions against Sinopec was a very serious issue, Cheng
emphasized. Sinopec is very important to China, Cheng said, and he

Table 11.3   Chinese entities sanctioned
by the United States, 2002–2009

year	# entities sanctioned
2002	20
2003	8
2004	17
2005	13
2006	4
2007	6
2008	3
2009	3
total	74

Author's creation. Source: Mark Dubowitz,
Laura Grossman, Iran's Chinese Energy
Partners; Companies Eligible for Investigation
Under U.S. Sanctions Law, September 2010,
Foundation for Defense of Democracy. http://
www.defenddemocracy.org.

"can't imagine" the consequences if the company were sanctioned by the United States.[21] Beijing was willing to tolerate US sanctions against Chinese equipment and technology suppliers, but not against China's oil majors. Beijing apparently succeeded in deterring US sanctions against its oil firms. Yet as the fall off in US sanctions of Chinese firms in the latter 2000s suggests, Chinese firms operating on the basis of commercial principles may have withdrawn from Iranian operations in order to avoid US sanctions.

One can infer two decisions by China from Table 11.3. First, not complying with US lobbying for Chinese compliance with US legislation and instead allowing Chinese firms to continue normal commerce with Iran, even while those firms encounter occasional US sanctions (if and when their commercial transactions came to US attention). Second, drawing the line at Chinese investments in Iran's energy sector and threatening that US sanctions in that area would cause serious damage to PRC-US relations.

From Beijing's perspective, unilateral, national decisions cannot bind third parties; the United States cannot regulate China-Iran relations, even if other states – allies of the United States – followed the US lead with unilateral laws or regulations of their own. To argue otherwise, as the United States did, was a manifestation of arrogant, hegemonic mentality. The application of US law beyond the sovereign territory of the United States is a modern day variant of the extra-territoriality that humiliated China in the hundred years after the Opium War. As a sovereign state, China alone has the rightful power to regulate its ties with other countries. US law and Executive Orders do not over-ride China's sovereignty. If China's government agrees to regulate China's ties with Iran, perhaps via agreement with Security Council resolutions or bilateral agreements with the US government, China will scrupulously abide by those regulations and restrictions. In lieu of agreement voluntarily assumed by China's government, China's ties with Iran are unfettered.

Stress on China's sovereignty dovetailed with recognition of energy imports as a potential bottleneck for China's development. Cramping China's machinery and technology exports would not fundamentally threaten China's continued growth. Undermining China's efforts to secure the imported energy it needed might.

Beijing probably lobbied hard in Washington over this point, and the pattern of non-sanctioning of Chinese oil majors suggests an understanding has been reached in this regard.

Through its dilution of Security Council sanctions and rejection of unilateral US sanctions, Beijing provided its most important support for

Iran: keeping the door open for Chinese investment in Iran's energy sector. Several sources have tracked foreign investment in Iran's energy sector between 1999 and 2009.[22] Organizing data from these sources into a simple bar graph yields Figure 11.1. This figure makes clear that West European and Canadian oil firms were Iran's major foreign energy partners in the early 2000s. As international concern grew over Iran's nuclear programs, Western companies became wary of the political risk involved in further operations in Iran and hesitated to undertake new obligations. Chinese firms first tested the waters in exploitation of Iranian oil and gas in 2006, and then in 2007 and 2009 undertook to invest approximately US$ 48 billion in Iranian energy projects, far overshadowing all other foreign investors and making China Iran's leading energy partner by a large margin.

By helping Iran extract more oil, Beijing strengthened the revenues of Iran's government, revenues that supported Tehran's various policies. China did this, of course, not in order to help Iran, but because

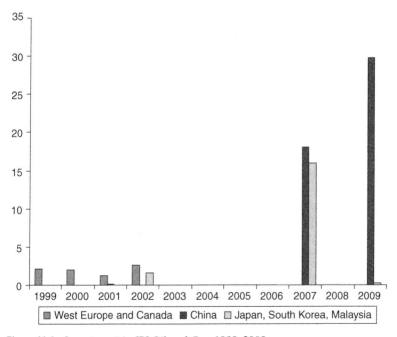

Figure 11.1 Investment in IRI Oil and Gas, 1999–2009

Author's creation. **Source:** *The Iran Sanctions Act,* CRS Report for Congress, RS20871, Kenneth Katzman, 12 October 2007. Global Business in Iran Database, Iran Tracker, American Enterprise Institute. http://www.irantracker.org

China needed ever larger quantities of imported oil and gas, and Iran was one of only a few places in the world where there remained large and unexploited energy reserves not yet staked-out by international energy majors. But there were nonetheless several links to the Iran nuclear issue. Beijing's support for Iran in IAEA and Security Council debates was one reason why Iran deemed China a reliable partner for Iran's energy development efforts. Wrapping an energy supply relation in layers of political cooperation is also part of China's energy security strategy.[23] According to Erica Downs, Beijing's calculation is that such political encapsulation will reduce chances of disruption in China's international energy imports in the event of various shocks. One not very probable shock, which China's security planners ponder, is how China would meet its energy needs in the event of a US-PRC clash that escalated to cut off China's energy imports by the United States Navy.[24] In that remote but plausible event, China, as noted earlier, would need a friendly energy-rich country in the Middle East ready to cooperate with China's emergency oil import efforts despite of American pressure and threats. From this perspective, standing by Iran in its efforts at national defense helps create a partnership in which Iran might be willing to stand by China in its own efforts at national defense in times of need. China would accrue in Southwest Asia a second all-weather friend, dovetailing nicely with China's solid entente with Pakistan. US attempts to encircle China via its pivot or rebalancing to Asia, would be outflanked and the US position in East Asia and South Asia would be counter-encircled in Southwest Asia.

China's strengthening of Iran's military capabilities

Throughout the 2000s, China assisted Iran's military development efforts. The context of this assistance was an escalating confrontation between Iran and the United States and Israel over Iran's nuclear programs, with Washington warning periodically that time was running out for a diplomatic solution and that all options remain on the table. As noted earlier, in Security Council debates over resolutions targeting Iran, Beijing vetoed verbiage insinuating military threat from documents requiring its assent. It also insisted that the Iran nuclear issue be settled exclusively by diplomatic means – via patient talks, consultations, dialogue, and negotiation – and explicitly ruled out force. Analysis in Chinese elite foreign policy journals, such as reviewed earlier in this chapter, asserted that a military strike was the ultimate goal of the US push for sanctions and condemnation of Iran. On a less public track, Beijing quietly assisted Tehran to strengthen its national defense capabilities.

According to data published by the Stockholm International Peace Research Institute Project (SIPRI) and displayed in Figure 11.4, between 2001 and 2012 China sold Iran US $ 808 million in arms, making China Iran's second-largest arms supplier after Russia, and well ahead of Iran's number three supplier North Korea. Notably, Russian sales to Iran declined markedly after 2007, from $267 million to $15 million or less thereafter, while Chinese sales remained steady. Between 2008 and 2012 China was Iran's largest arms supplier.

In terms of the content of Sino-Iranian munitions trade, China's sales included 899 anti-ship missiles targeting various classes of hostile warships, according to SIPRI. These included missiles to arm Fast Attack Craft sold by China to Iran in the 1990s and Italian-designed anti-ship missiles fired from attack helicopters.[25] Many of these missiles had been developed by Russia and/or Russia and China together specifically to target US warships and planes.[26] Several had gone into production only in the mid-2000s and included advanced target acquisition technology. Chinese sales also included 1,000 shoulder-fired anti-aircraft missiles. It must be noted that if the IRI navy ever uses these missiles against US warships, the PLA will gain extremely valuable knowledge about the effectiveness of these weapons, knowledge that would presumably enhance China's own military capabilities Table 11.5 shows Chinese transfers of anti-ship missiles to Iran.

Cooperation via the Asia Pacific Space Cooperation Organization (APSCO) was another aspect of Chinese support for Iran's military development. Sino-Iranian space cooperation traces back to 1991 when Premier Li Peng visited Iran to mark the launch of Iran's satellite for radio and television transmission.[27] The next year a workshop involving China, Pakistan, and Thailand convened in Beijing to discuss possible multilateral space cooperation. Iran joined the group in 1994 when six countries agreed to cooperate in the development of small multi-mission satellites. APSCO was established in Beijing in 2005 with the intent of developing ballistic missiles capable of launching satellites.[28] Pakistan, Iran, Bangladesh, Thailand, Mongolia, Peru, and, of course, China made up its membership. APSCO had ten joint projects as of 2010: designing, building, and *launching* light and medium class satellites of 500–600 kilograms, and research in satellites, remote sensing, and telecommunications.[29] (emphasis added by author.) The capabilities that can launch satellites into precise earth orbit are essentially the same that are used to aim warheads precisely to distant targets on earth. Reports by the US intelligence community stated that Chinese entities had provided continuous assistance to Iran's ballistic missile programs.[30]

Table 11.4 International Supply of Arms to Iran ($US million)

	2001	2002	2003	2004	2005	2006	2007	2008	2009	2010	2011	2012	total
Russia	302	95	87	15	15	353	267	15	15	11	33	15	1223
China	77	78	81	84	50	69	62	62	62	77	62	44	808
Ukraine	142	130	0	0	0	0	0	0	0	0	0	0	272
North Korea	0	116	114	27	0	0	0	0	0	0	0	0	257
Belarus	15	16	0	0	0	0	0	0	0	0	33	0	64
Germany	1	1	1	1	1	1	1	1	1	1	0	0	10

Author's creation. Source: SIPRI Arms Transfers Database, www.sipri.org

Table 11.5 Chinese transfers of anti-ship missiles to Iran*

weapon designation	description	years of delivery	number delivered/ produced
C-802/ CSS-N-8	for fast attack craft may include air-launched version	1994–2012	380
FL-6	developed on Italian missile supplied by Iran to China helicopter fired	1999–2012	265
TL-10/FL-8	developed to attack small craft	2004–2010	160
C-704	developed for Iran advanced radar seeker	2010–2011	50
C-801/CSS-N-4	includes submarine launched version	2006–2012	35

*According to SIPRI data bank, transfer of all since 2010 uncertain due to UN arms embargo.

Author's creation. Source: SIPRI Transfers of Major conventional weapons database, www.sipri.org

In 2009 Iran launched its first satellite (a small one) into space. The US Presidential spokesman, the State Department, and the Defense Department expressed "acute concern" and "grave concern." [31] The *New York Times* listed Russia, China, India, Italy, and North Korea as countries that had assisted Iran's ballistic missile and satellite programs.[32]

China also seems to have facilitated missile cooperation between Iran and North Korea. In May 2011 a group of seven international experts commissioned by the Security Council to monitor compliance with sanctions levied against North Korea following its 2006 and 2009 nuclear tests reported to the Security Council that there appeared to be regular exchanges of ballistic missile technology between Iran and North Korea, in violation of UN sanctions and conducted via chartered flights of the national airlines of North Korea and Iran. Proscribed missile components were reported to be trans-shipped through "a neighboring third country."[33] Multiple but unidentified diplomats said the third country was China. The Chinese expert on the panel refused to sign the report, and shortly after the leaking of its content, China's Assistant Foreign Minister "totally den [ied] such reports."[34] Whatever the veracity of the UN expert panel report turns out to be, it comports with a larger pattern of Chinese assistance to Iran's missile development efforts.

The pattern of China's support for the IRI's military development suggests that China's leaders have concluded that *a militarily strong Iran serves China's interests*. Purely commercial interests in China certainly help drive such trade. But it is likely that those commercial interests operate within a permissive environment created by a high level Chinese decision to allow this arms trade to continue in spite of strong American objections and injury to China's international reputation as a responsible stake holder. The exact nature of China's interests can be inferred from the elite journal analysis of Iran-US relations reviewed earlier in this chapter. Iran is a country of considerable relative capability that is resisting a US drive to dominate the Persian Gulf and its oil. Success of that putative US effort would strengthen US global hegemony to China's disadvantage, while failure of US efforts would significantly diminish US influence and move the world in the direction of multi-polarity. Iran's leaders, as sovereign rulers of a sovereign state, have decided that they need missile capabilities to strengthen their country against US military threats, subversion, sanctions ,and efforts at regime change, and have asked China to assist in that effort. Granting those requests for assistance not only serves China's short term strategic interests of expanding China's exports and importing oil, but also serves longer term strategic needs as well. Assisting Iran fend off US pressure functions as an investment in an all-weather partnership over the longer term.

An omen of the future Sino-Iranian relation may have come in October 2010 when the IRI opened its airports for the first time to foreign aircraft and allowed a squadron of four Su-27 warplanes of the PLA-Air Force to refuel in route to military exercises with Turkey in central Anatolia.[35] A further deepening of the military relation came in September 2014 when a PLA-N missile destroyer and missile frigate entered the Persian Gulf to conduct a five-day joint exercise with the IRI navy. According to the *Times of Israel* this was the first time PLA-N warships had entered the Persian Gulf. It was also the first time PLA-N ships visited Iranian ports, breaking a pattern tracing back to 1985 when Chinese warships began making friendship port calls to Indian Ocean ports. Until the 2014 visit, PLA-N warships conspicuously avoided Iranian ports. Apparently by 2014 China's leaders deemed the times propitious for closer naval ties. Shortly after the joint exercise, IRI navy commander Habibollah Sayyari visited Beijing. PRC Defense Minister Cheng Wanquan welcomed the Iranian leader and lauded the "good cooperation on mutual visits, personnel training and other fields in recent years."[36]

The Strategic logic of China's Iran policies

Movement of the world toward multi-polarity has long been a high-ranking objective of Chinese diplomacy. China's 2008 White Paper on national defense, for example, said that "Economic globalization and world multi-polarization are gaining momentum. It continued:

> The rise and decline of international strategic forces is quickening, major powers are stepping up their efforts to cooperate with each other and draw on each other's strengths. They continue to compete with and hold each other in check...Therefore, a profound readjustment is brewing in the international system....Meanwhile, hegemonism and power politics still exist...[37]

Multi-polarity is a condition in which the position of the United States (and formerly the USSR, too, which Beijing long deemed one of two "superpowers") would be much reduced and China's position correspondingly much enhanced. The United States would merely be one of a half-dozen or so powers of roughly equal strength, rendering China much less vulnerable to US pressure. Chinese analysts recognize many factors contributing to the global movement toward multi-polarity, most fundamentally perhaps the economic and technological trajectories of China and the United States themselves. But the emergence of new regional powers independent of the United States, such as Iran in the Persian Gulf, contributes to multi-polarity. The success of US efforts to bring the oil riches of the Middle East under Washington's control via aggression, intimidation, and coercion against Iran would run counter to multi-polarity. Control of Iran's oil riches by a country quite independent of the United States and friendly toward China, would move the world toward multi-polarity. Of course, all of this cannot be openly stated, less it convince Washington that China is, after all, a peer competitor with the United States.

There is a second moral, or perhaps ideological, level of Chinese sympathy for Iran's struggle against US hegemony. There is considerable resentment in China at what is perceived to be US policies hostile to China. In the Chinese view, out of ignorance and arrogance the United States – certainly the media, Congress, and public opinion if not the President and his top foreign policy advisors – is hostile to China's Communist-led political system. The US connives to foster anti-China sentiments among China's neighbors – Japan, India, Vietnam, Australia, etc. – and to encourage those countries to link up to contain China. Washington interferes in China's internal affairs and occasionally conspires to destroy China's territorial unity by arming Taiwan. Washington demands that China comply with US unilateral decisions – sanctions against Iran – even though China's leaders do not consider those decisions to be in accord with China's own interests nor have they been approved by any United Nations body. The management of these complaints is, of course, the mainstay of diplomacy between the PRC and the US One of the offshoots of this litany of Chinese grievances against the US is a distinct lack of Chinese sympathy for US efforts to secure Chinese cooperation with what are perceived, as the articles quoted in this chapter illustrate, as American efforts to bludgeon Iran into submission.

There is a third level to China's sympathy for Iran's anti-US struggles: succession politics among the top Chinese Communist Party (CCP) elite. Membership on the Standing Committee of the Political Bureau of the CCP and designation as the first ranked member of that Standing Committee is determined by maneuvering among several hundred of the leaders of the bureaucratic organizations running China. In that competition, the People's Liberation Army (PLA) has a significant voice and is unlikely to approve anyone it deems too willing to go along with US schemes injurious to China's interests. The PLA also tends to take a

hard realist view of China's security situation, which leads it to value the
US being bogged down in wars and open-ended confrontations in the
Middle East, far from the center of gravity of China's interests. China's
"new nationalism" which dwells on the anti-US grievances outlined
above also creates a climate in which ambitious CCP leaders need to
demonstrate toughness on handling the United States. There are divergent voices in China; a mediation by China's foreign ministry in 2009
demonstrates a Chinese effort to end the Iranian-US confrontation.
But as I will be show, the dominant Chinese policy seems to be one of
sustaining Iran in its struggle with the United States.

The core element of China's foreign policy is maintaining a cordial
relation with the United States, which traces to China's "opening and
reform" decision of 1978 in which it decided to draw on the multiple
inputs of the global capitalist economy to modernize and develop
socialist China. Deng Xiaoping and his comrades understood that
avoiding confrontation with the United States (unless over China's core
interests) was vital for success of that long term development drive. This
thinking remains a premise of China's foreign policies. Determination
to maintain cordial ties with the United States does not mean, however,
that China does not support Iran's struggle against US hegemony. It
means, rather, that such support must be rendered in ways that do not
undermine Sino-US comity.

The evidence does not suggest that China's support for the IRI between
2003 and 2011 has seriously injured Sino-American cooperation. Some
analysts, commentators, politicians, and officials have grumbled about
China's support for the IRI, but there is no doubt that a quest for cooperation remains the overwhelmingly dominant, mainstream US approach
to China. Sino-American dialogues at multiple levels have expanded
as China supported Tehran against Washington. Sino-American cooperation, tacit and explicit, on various issues has grown exponentially.
This includes cooperation in the Middle East, as exemplified by Beijing's
participation in crafting and endorsing four sets of ever more severe
(even if only incrementally more so) Security Council sanctions against
Iran.[38] The reality is that the PRC is simply too strong and has too much
influence in too many areas for most thoughtful Americans to contem-
plate abandonment of cooperation with China. The economic benefits
of the rapidly deepening economic partnership are simply too great to
endanger. Unless Beijing challenges US core interests, the same caveat
that abides in China's calculations toward the United States applies.

China's balancing of its cooperation with Washington against Tehran
and its cooperation with Tehran against Washington seems to have

worked well in advancing China's interests in both capitals. Subtle tactics have facilitated Beijing's balancing act. Missile cooperation was housed in the innocuous seeming APSCO. A blind eye was turned to third-party activity with which China could plausibly deny association. Beijing's efforts to delay and dilute Security Council sanctions were cast in terms of high principle: insistence on dialogue and negotiation, upholding the authority of the United Nations, achieving a consensus among the Permanent Five. The purely commercial nature of China's oil investments was insisted upon. Public military interactions with Iran were minimized. After visits in 2004 and 2005 by the deputy director of China's committee on Science, Technology and Industry for National Defense and the commander of China's Nanjing Military Region, respectively, the annual almanac of China's foreign ministry reported no more military interactions between the two countries.[39] PLA Navy warships also conspicuously avoided Iranian ports. Between 1985 and 2006, PLA warships called 20 times at Indian Ocean ports of Pakistan, Sri Lanka, Bangladesh, Thailand, India, Malaysia, Tanzania, and South Africa.[40] PLA warships showed China's flag all around the Indian Ocean littoral, but not in Iran. The formation of "strategic partnerships" is an important element of Beijing's current diplomacy; China has formed strategic partnerships with many countries – Russia, India, Pakistan, Myanmar, France, Brazil, Egypt, the European Union, the Association of South East Asian Nations, many African countries –but not with Iran. And in repeated joint statements issuing from summit level Sino-American interactions, China's leaders declared China willing to cooperate with the United States on the Iran nuclear issue. Most important of all, the increment of Chinese cooperation with Washington on Iran has been adequate to satisfy US leaders and keep them coming back for more. Beijing's skillful diplomacy has, in fact, effectively balanced between Tehran and Washington.

During the Maoist era, Chinese leaders used to speak openly of managing the contradictions between other states to China's advantage. That nomenclature is no longer favored, but the practice still remains. By giving the US a certain level of cooperation in managing the "Iran nuclear issue," while simultaneously giving Tehran a certain level of support in the face of US pressure on Iran, Beijing has effectively pursued two seemingly contradictory goals. It has maintained the Sino-American comity upon which its long-term development drive is premised. At the same time it has moved the world in the direction of multi-polarity by undermining the American scheme for hegemonic control of Persian Gulf oil. It remains to be seen whether this dual approach will prove short-sighted and undermine a more deeply founded partnership with the United States well into the 21st century.

Notes

1. China's determination to "not confront the United States in the Middle East" was one of the major findings presented in Jon Alterman, John Garver, The *Vital Triangle: China, the United States, and the Middle East*, Washington: Center for Strategic and International Studies, 2008.
2. Zhu Jiejin, *Zhongguo he yilang guanxi shigao* (Draft history of China-Iran relations), Urumqi: Xinjiang renmin chubanshe, 1998.
3. The epic clash in 751 CE between a Tang Chinese army and an Umayyad army at Talis in today's Kyrgyzstan was a clash between China and an Arab, not Persian, empire.
4. Mohammad Reza Pahlavi, *The Shah's Story*, London: Michael Joseph, 1980, p. 147.
5. Tian Wenlin "Meiguo de zhongdong zhanlue jiqi lishi mingyun" (America's middle east strategy and its historic destiny," *Xiandai guoiji guanix*, 2006, No. 8, p. 1–7.
6. Li Daguang, "Meiguo de shiyou liyi yu ylang he wenti,"(US oil interests and the Iran nuclear issue," *Guoji shiyou jingji* (International petroleum economics), 2008, no. 1, p. 56–59.
7. Wu Cheng, "Meiguo dui yilang zhizai xiaoguo fenxi," (Analysis of the effectiveness of US sanctions against Iran," *Xi ya feizhou* (West Asia Africa), 2008, no. 1, p. 74–7.
8. Wan guang," "Dangjin zhongdong de xin liliang he xin gezhu," (new forces and the new situation in the contemporary Middle East), *Xi ya feizhou* " (West Asia and Africa), 2008, no. 1, p. 5–9.
9. Wang Bo, "Meiguo yu yilang gouxiangde haiwan anquan zhixu zhi zheng:" (The conflict between the US and Iran in Designing the Gulf Security Order, *Xi ya ieizhou* (West Asia and Africa), 2009, No. 9, p. 5–9.
10. Wang Jinglie, "Yilang he wenti yu zhongdong diyuan zhengchi" (The Iran nuclear issue and milddle eastern geopolitics), *Ahlabo shijie yanjiu*, (Arab World studies), July 2009, no. 4, p. 3–9.
11. John W. Lewis, Xue Litai, *China Builds the Bomb*, Stanford University Press, 1988.
12. Chu Jin, "Yilang he wenti de 'jie' you 'bujie'" (Resolution or non-resolution of the Iran nuclear issue), *Guoji jingji pinglun*, 2010, # 3, p. 138–148.
13. China calls for new talks on Iran nuclear issue, Xinhua wang, 16 July 2013. http://news.xinhuanet.com/english/world/2013-07/16/c_125012583.htm
14. "Xi Jinping: China willing to play constructive role on Iran nuclear issue," and ""Xi Jinping meets presidents of Iran, Mongolia, Tajikistan," both in, Xinhua wang, 13 September 2013.
15. "Beijing ready to expand ties with Tehran, Chinese leader." *Tehran Times*, 30 October 2013. www/tehrantimes.com
16. "Iran, China seek to increase strategic political and economic cooperation," *Tehran Times*, 8 December 2013.

17. "China FM calls for full implementation of Geneva nuclear agreement," 9 January 2014. www;news.xinhuanet.com
18. Key nations split over Iran sanctions," China Daily, 12 March 2007. World News Connection. Http://wncldialog.com.Hereafter cited as WNC.
19. Resolution 1747 (2007), United Nations Security Council. S/RES/1747 (2007)
20. The study sourced for Figure 11.2 identifies the specific Chinese firms targeted.
21. Wikileak documents. 08BEIJING1141, 26 March 2008. http://cablegate. wikileaks.org/tag/CH-0.html
22. *The Iran Sanctions Act*, CRS Report for Congress, RS20871, Kenneth Katzman, 12 October 2007. Global Business in Iran Database, Iran Tracker, American Enterprise Institute. http://www.irantracker.org
23. Erica Downs, *China's Quest for Energy Security*, Rand Corporation, 2000.
24. Regarding the possible escalation of a Sino-US clash over Taiwan see, Richard C. Bush, Michael O'Hanlan, *A War Like No Others: The Truth About China's Challenge to America*, John Wiley, 2007.
25. "Transfer of Major Conventional Weapons, Sorted by Supplier, China to Iran, 1995–2009." SIPRI.
26. Richard Fisher, Jr., "China's Alliance with Iran Grows Contrary to US Hopes," International Assessment and Strategy Center, 20 May 2006. http://www. strategycenter.net
27. John Garver, *China and Iran: Ancient Partners in a Post-Imperial World*, Seattle: University of Washington Press, 2006, p. 107.
28. "Aerospace official Says Iran Building Satellite-Carrying Missiles," Iranian Student News Agency, 15 March 2005. WNC.
29. The APSCO website is: http://www.aspsco.in/
30. *Ibid.*
31. Pentagon: Iran's Domestic Satellite Launch is Grace Cause for Concern, " Fox News, 3 February 2009.
32. Nazila Fathi, William Broad, "Iran Launches Satellite in a Challenge for Obama," *New York Times*, 4 Feburary 2009.
33. Louis CharBonneau, Reuters, "North Korea, Iran trade missile technology: UN," *The Globe and Mail*, 14 May 2011. http://www.theglobeandmail.com
34. Agence France-Presse:"China dismisses UN missile report on North Korea, Iran," 18 May 2011.
35. "Iran opens airspace to China warplanes," Press TV, 3 October 2010. http:// www.presstv.ir. "Chinese warplanes refueled in Iran enroute to NATO exercise in Turkey," World Tribune, 12 October 2010. http://www.worldtribune.com
36. Justin Jalil, "China seeks stronger military ties with Iran," *Times of Israel*, 23 October 2014. www.timesofisrael.com
37. China's National Defense in 2008, Information Office of the State Council of the People's Republic of China, January 2009. Beijing. http://english.gov.cn
38. China has also cooperated with and minimized tension with Washington on Iraq-related issues. See Alterman and Garver, *Vital Triangle, China, the United States, and the Middle East,*Washington, D.C.: Center for Strategic and International Studies, 2008.
39. This was through 2008 as reported in the 2009 almanac.
40. Christopher D. Yung, et al., *China's Out of Area Naval Operations; Case Studies, Trajectories, Obstacles and Practical Solutions*, China Strategic Perspectives No. 3, December 2010. Center for Strategic Research, National Institute of Strategic Studies, National Defense University. P. 12–13.

12
The Future of Sino-Iran Relations
Manochehr Dorraj

Introduction

Iran and China's expanding economic and political relations have a significant regional and global impact that as of yet has not received much scholarly scrutiny. This chapter examines the historical roots, evolution, and development of the Sino-Iranian relationship with a special emphasis on post 1979 period. Many bilateral economic and political issues bind the two nations, such as trade in arms, energy, manufactured goods, and technology. But this relationship also has a political and strategic dimension that serves both nations well. Based on the analysis of the present dynamics, I speculate on possible future trends.

As two historic and self-conscious civilizations with great imperial pasts that were colonized by Western powers, Iran and China share a psychological basis of identification. This sense of a common historical experience is buttressed by a long history of trade and mutual ties that go back more than 2,000 years through the Silk Road that tied China to Iran, Central Asia, and Arabia. This long history of mutually beneficial relations is complemented by a lack of any war or major conflict between the two countries in the past. This background stands in sharp contrast to a long history of war and conflict both nations experienced in their bilateral relations with the West. Lacking the baggage of colonialism and neo-colonialism and having no history of war and conflict in the Middle East lends China a clean slate and acts as a political asset that facilitates the expansion of its relations with Iran.

Iran and China have also a mutual history of cultural ties and influences that go back to the reign of Hans and Parthians in the 6th and 7th centuries. This history includes the impact of Zoroastrianism,

Manichaeism and Nestorian Christianity – all three pre-Islamic religions of ancient Persia – on the development of Buddhism in China as well as and influencing Chinese astronomy and the development of printing, and paper money and the popularity of Chinese porcelain in Persia. Persian poetry, cooking, and the game of Polo also became very popular in China during the Tang dynasty.[1]

This historical backdrop of mutually a beneficial relationship served as a solid foundation for the future expansion of relations between the two nations. Due to the limited scope of this study and the limitation of space; however, we cannot delve into the historical nuances of this relationship. The evolution of the relationship in the 20th century was highlighted by Muhammad Reza Shah's aversion to normalization of its relationship with Communist China due to Iran's close alliance with the United States (US) during the Cold War. The ascendance of the Sino-Soviet conflict in the 1960s and the ensuing normalization of relations between the US and China in 1971 served as catalysts for the normalization of relations between Tehran and Beijing. The substantial expansion of relations, however, occurred only after the Islamic revolution of 1979.

The Ties that bind: the Islamic Republic and China

Immediately after the Iranian revolution of 1979, China recognized the Islamic Republic, affirming its support for the new government and its anti-imperialist policies. Chinese officials also expressed their interest in the expansion of the bilateral relationship. However, the onset of the Iraq-Iran war in 1980 posed a dilemma for Beijing, which aspired to maintaining good relations with both countries. During the war (1980–1988), China's balancing act involved selling weapons to both countries. In the aftermath of the Iran hostage crisis of 1980, while China condemned the taking of US embassy personnel as hostages, it refused to join the US and its Western allies in imposing sanctions on Iran and severing relations with the Islamic Republic. Quite to the contrary, Beijing saw the frayed relations between Iran and the West as a golden opportunity to expand ties with arguably one of the most strategically significant countries in the region. Tehran, for its turn, feeling the pressure of Western allies to isolate it internationally, welcomed China's offer of expanding bilateral economic and political ties.[2]

Unable to buy weapons on the global market and facing Saddam Husain's invasion, Tehran particularly welcomed China's willingness to provide it with armaments. Thus, the expanding Iran-China relations since 1979 have moved forward on several fronts, including trade, energy, and military cooperation. With the passing of Ayatollah Khomeini in 1989 and the ascendance of President Rafsanjani to power, Tehran abandoned the policy of "neither East nor West." Facing the escalating Western economic pressure and attempt to isolate it internationally, Tehran opted for an "Eastern Strategy," forging closer alliances with both China and Russia.

Trade relations

In the aftermath of the Iraq-Iran war, when the Islamic Republic undertook its war reconstruction policy, trade relation between Iran and China expanded considerably, doubling the trade volume between the two countries compared with the pre-war period. In the 1990s, due to inauguration of Iran's "Eastern Strategy" and the subsequent quest for closer relations with China and Russia in order to offset the pressure of Western sanctions, the bilateral trade between the two countries increased exponentially. During the 1990–2001period, the annual bilateral trace expanded by 55%. In 2003, China was responsible for 9.5% of Iran's imports. By 2006, China overtook Japan as Iran's major trade partner in Asia. In 2007, the bilateral trade between China and Iran increased by 27% and reached $15 billion, making China Iran's number one trade partner in the world.[3] In 2012, the leadership of both countries pledged to expand their annual bilateral trade of $45–$50 billion to $100 billion by 2016.[4]

Whereas three fourths of China's primary imports from Iran are oil and gas, base materials and petrochemicals, Iran's imports from China in contrast are more varied, including manufactured and high technology goods, capital goods, broad band, and engineering services. China has also played an active role in building Iranian infrastructure. The Chinese have built subway systems and railroads in several large Iranian cities, including Tehran and Mashhad. They have built roads, dams, tunnels, bridges, fisheries, ports, automobile and cement factories and other infrastructure throughout the country[5]. By doing so, they have imbedded themselves deeply in the Iranian economy and play a significant role in providing social services.

Energy relations

Since the implementation of China's open-door economic policies in 1978, that country has experienced an impressive rate of growth of 7%–10%. As a result, Beijing sought to expand its trade and economic ties globally. To sustain its mercurial economic rise on the global stage, China had to provide the fuel needed for its economic take off. Until 1993, domestic production was sufficient and could respond to the growing demand. However, with the expansion of its middle class, additional demand for automobiles, electricity, and a rapidly growing industrial infrastructure, China had to import large amount of its domestic energy needs. As the levels of pollution in major Chinese cities has become chronic in the last three decades, China has also sought to diversify its energy mix away from coal, which historically has been responsible for 75% to 60% of China's energy supply. A combination of these factors compelled Beijing to take a closer look at the region of the world with the largest energy reserves, the Middle East.

Possessing the fourth largest oil reserves (157 billion barrels, roughly 10% of global reserves) and the largest gas reserves in the world (33.8 trillion cubic meters, roughly 18.2%, followed by Russia and Qatar), Iran is an energy giant. China's oil and gas reserves, in contrast, are 2% and 1% of global reserves, respectively.[6] In addition, due to the damages incurred to the Iranian energy infrastructure during the Iraq-Iran war and the deleterious impact of the sanctions imposed on Iran in the last 30 years, particularly the June 2012 sanctions that included the energy and the banking sectors, Iran currently produces only about 1 million barrels a day (vs. Saudi Arabia's 11.5 million barrels per day). Prior to 2008, Iran produced 4.2 million barrels a day and during the Shah's regime it produced as much as 6 million barrels a day. This combination of low rate of extraction and massive reserves indicates that much of Iran's energy sources are untapped. With the proper investment and the modernization of Iran's energy infrastructure, the upside for its massive yet unexplored resources are substantial, and it can be a major source of long-term energy supply to China. Thus, China's rapidly rising energy demand and Iran's potential as a major supplier (only second after Saudi Arabia in the Middle East region) have made the energy connection as one of the most pivotal links in the relations between the two countries.

Currently, 80% of China's imports from Iran is oil., Whereas in 1977, China imported only 300,000 tons of Iranian oil, by 2002 Iran was responsible for more than 15%of China's total oil imports. In 2003, China imported 12,393,834 metric tons of oil from Iran.[7] The imposition of the Iran-Libya Act in 1996 by the Clinton Administration, which barred international energy companies from investing more than $20 million in Iran's oil and gas sector, presented China with a dilemma: how to continue its investment in Iran's energy sector without violating the US sanctions and risking damage to its more significant ties with the United States. By the early 2000s, in part, due to US pressure, many European companies had exited the Iranian energy market. Thus, Beijing saw a golden opportunity to expand its energy ties with the Islamic Republic, displaying a willingness to assert itself against the US on matters it regards as the key issues of its national security, with energy security being at the top of its list.

In 2002, when Hu Jintao ascended to power and initiated the "going out" policy, major Chinese state-owned energy companies were given a mandate to sign long term energy contracts and to secure China's energy supply for the long haul. Thus, by 2005, the two countries had drafted a memorandum of understanding and signed a contract worth $70 billion that would export 250 million tons of Iranian natural gas to China for the next 30 years.[8] As the US-led sanctions in 2006, 2007, 2008 forced many Western energy companies to cut back on their investment in Iran's energy sector, China saw this void as a great opportunity to expand its investment in Iran's energy sector.

During the 2006–2008 period, China's investments in Iran reached $18 billion. In 2009, this was followed by Tehran granting Beijing the right to explore the large Azadegan and Yadavaran oil fields and to explore Iran's Caspian Sea oil and gas reserves as well. Thus, the volume of energy trade between the two countries for the 2000–2009 period tripled, making China the largest consumer of Iranian oil and gas in the world. However, in 2010, under the pressure by US, China's imports of Iranian oil declined by 31%; in 2011, it recovered and reached 559,000 barrels per day. But in 2012, with the imposition of new sanctions that included Iran's energy sector and the banking system, Tehran's ability to export its energy diminished 22%, reaching 434,000 barrel per day. In May 2013, China managed to get a waiver from the US government and to a large extent became exempt from sanctions. This exemption increased China's imports of Iranian oil by 50%. China's imports expanded from 371,500 barrels per day in April 2013 to 555,557 barrels per day a month later.[9]

The fourth set of sanctions and Iran's urgent need to sell its oil proved to be a boon to Beijing as it was able to buy Iranian oil at a discount and pay for it in yen. Chinese leaders also stipulated that Tehran should buy goods and commodities from Beijing with the oil income that China kept in its banks. Should Iran and the Western allies resolve the nuclear standoff and the sanctions be lifted in future; this situation could change, as Iran would have a larger choice of customers for its energy sources.

Arms trade and nuclear cooperation

With the onset of Iraq-Iran war, due to imposition of sanctions on Iran, China and North Korea were among a few countries in the world that were willing to sell armaments to the Islamic Republic. China also provided Iran with assistance to develop its anti-ship missiles as well as short- and long-range missiles. Through transfer of technology, China also helped to modernize the Iranian military infrastructure. The total value of China's arms transfer to Iran between 1980 and 2010 is estimated to be between $4–$10 billion.[10] China has also helped Iran to build a missile factory near the city of Isfahan, transferred dual technology to Iran, and provided technology to Iranian scientists. Thus, Iran became capable of developing its own home-made missiles.

Throughout early1990s, Iran remained the largest recipient of Chinese armaments in the Middle East. However, due to US government pressure on Beijing, it reduced its arms and military technology transfer to Islamic Republic between 1995–2005. Since then, Russia has emerged as the number one provider of armaments to Iran in the world and currently China ranks number two. However, between 2005- 2009, Iran was the second largest recipient of Chinese missiles after Pakistan, including many ballistic, anti-ship and anti-aircraft missiles. In 2005, Iran became a member of Asia -Pacific Space Cooperation Organization (APSCO). This organization focuses on space and satellite technologies and serves as an instrument for China-Iran missile cooperation.[11] Because Iran does not have a strong air force, missile technology is considered to be its strategic weapons, which allow it to destroy distant targets and defend its air space and shipping lanes. As such, the Chinese have played a significant role in building Iran's defense capabilities and contribute to its national security.

China has also played an instrumental role in development of Iran's nuclear program and capability. China trained Iranian nuclear scientists in uranium enrichment and nuclear-related technology. In 1985, it provided the nuclear facilities built before the revolution by the French near the city of Isfahan, with four teaching and research reactors. China also provided Iran with laser technology, zirconium tube production to hold uranium, and the Tokamak nuclear fusion reactor.[12] In 1991, China secretly transferred nuclear isotopes to Iran that enabled it to master the basic chemistry of atomic power. A few years later, Beijing transferred to Tehran the design for a uranium conversion facility.[13] In the early 1990s, China also helped the Iranian government to build a uranium conversion facility near Isfahan. Later, China also transferred to Iran dual use centrifuges, electromagnetic isotope separation devices named calutron, and provided assistance with uranium mining and conversion, all essential components in the development of Iran's nuclear program.[14] By 1997, during the US-China Summit, the United States pressured China to substantially diminish its assistance to Iran's nuclear program. Given the significance of bilateral China-US relations in political calculus of Beijing, China relented. Since then, Russia has assumed the more significant position in transfer of nuclear technology to Iran, including building the nuclear plant in Bushehr and the heavy water plant in Arak.

Nuclear diplomacy and the bilateral ties

In the last three decades, China has attempted a delicate balancing act between Iran and the United States, trying to maintain bilateral ties with the two antagonists. This balancing act was tested when Iran's nuclear standoff heated up in the last 15 years and culminated in imposition of four sets of sanctions. With each occasion, after initially dragging its feet, and not immediately voting for sanctions, China relented and voted for the sanctions – after receiving some political concessions from Washington. China's balancing act involved deployment of a dual strategy: While China did not want to see crippling sanctions on Iran, given the large amount of bilateral trade between the two countries, China also saw the sanctions against Iran as an opportunity to squeeze out the competitors from the lucrative Iranian market and solidify its position as its number one trade partner.

China voting for Iranian sanctions while Iran continued to maintain its strong ties with China is indicative of an uneven relationship in which China holds more cards than Iran. What began as a cooperative relationship of supposedly equals evolved into a dependency, which, given the context of Tehran's international isolation and imposition of sanctions, has led Iran to become much more dependent on Beijing than China is on Iran. Beijing can always buy more oil from Saudi Arabia or Angola, but Iran does not have as many alternatives.[15] At times China has even functioned as a life raft for Iran amidst a stormy sea filled with hostile warships. It remains to be seen if this type of dependency would end should the nuclear standoff between Iran and the West be resolved.

The future trends in Sino-Iran relations

Future Sino-Iran relations will likely be influenced by two predominant factors. The first one is linked to China's grand global strategy and its implications for the Middle East. The second one is linked to Iran's prerogatives in a post-sanctions world and the possibility of a détente with the United States that would expand its choice of trade and energy partners and spin possible new political alliances.

Xi Jinping, the Chinese president, in his articulation of Beijing's new global strategy called "one belt, one road "has called for creation of a "New Economic Silk Road " and a "Maritime Silk Road," intended to expand China's investment, trade, and influence in Eurasia, and West and South Asia, among other parts of the world. This new reincarnation of the Silk Road, which dates back more than 2,100 years, is indicative of the Chinese leadership's intent to deepen its relationship with the energy-rich Middle Eastern nations in whose ranks Iran figures prominently. China also believes Asia and Asian affairs should be governed by Asians rather than a non-Asian hegemonic power like the United States. In the view of Chinese leaders, the United States' pivot to Asia initiative and its attempt to forge closer relations with India, as exemplified by the Bush and Obama administrations' policies, are both designed to contain China's expanding influence in East Asia. China's expanding relations with West Asia are seen as an attempt to push back against US containment policy. In addition, Chinese analysts argue that in the last two decades, the United States and Japan used to be the largest economic partners for China, but the new thinking behind the "one belt, one road" strategy is based on the realization that the New Silk Road Economic Belt and the New Maritime Silk Road "contains 4.4 billion people (63% of the world's population) with an aggregate GDP of $2.1 trillion (29% of the world's aggregate wealth)." But for this region to realize its development potential, it is imperative that China invest in its infrastructure and build high-speed train lines, ports, highways, as well as Internet and broadband infrastructure to further connect China to this region and facilitate trade and commerce.

Seen in this larger context of China's global strategy, Iran with its vast energy resources and population of 80 million can play a crucial role as the centerpiece in the realization of China's new vision for gaining influence over a larger region. Iran's geography offers a gateway to Central Asia and the Caspian Sea to its North as well as a gateway to the Persian Gulf to its south., Should the nuclear standoff between Iran and the P5+1 nations be resolved in the near future, unencumbered by the possible negative political cost of a relationship with an isolated and shunned Islamic Republic, China may welcome the lifting of sanctions on Iran as an opportunity to seek more expansive relations with Tehran.

On the Iranian side, there are two possibilities. Should the nuclear standoff end and sanctions be lifted, Iran's international isolation would end, thus diminishing the necessity for its "Eastern Strategy." If this possibility materializes, the future of Sino-Iran relations would have a slower pace and may be more limited in its scope, as Iran would have a larger choice of trade partners. Another possibility is that Iran could expand its relationship with China, which would serve both sides well. Given the history of mistrust between Iran and the United States, Tehran may want to utilize its bilateral relations with China to hedge against the perceived vulnerabilities that any close dependence on the US and its allies may bring.

Conclusion

Despite their ideological adherence to two divergent visions, one informed by Marxism-Leninism that regards religion as the opiate of the masses, and the other guided by a Shi'ite Islamic religion that serves as a foundation for a theocracy, Iran and China have found common ground.. The ties that bind Iran and China are historic, economic, military, and political. The two countries have had a history of mutually beneficial economic, political, and cultural ties that go back to the 7th century and the Silk Road that connected the two empires. Since the onset of Iranian revolution of 1979, the two nations have used their common history of conflict with Western colonial powers, their support of non-alignment and Third World solidarity and aspiration to create a multi-polar world as a political back drop for expanding economic and military ties. So far the relationship has been for the most part transactional rather than strategic, whereby the primacy of mutual economic interests trumps any long-term politically costly alliances. This is evident in China's willingness to vote for the four sets of US-/UN-led sanctions against Iran in order to be in the good graces of the US and its allies. It is also evident in China's treatment of Iran's application for membership in the Shanghai Cooperation Organization (SCO). To prevent the likelihood that China might have to support Iran in case of a US or Israeli military attack against it, Beijing granted Tehran an observer status as opposed to a full membership.

Should the nuclear standoff be resolved and an Iran -US rapprochement occur, the pace and the scope of Sino-Iran relations may slow in the short term. For the reasons chronicled in this chapter, barring a fundamental change of political systems in Tehran and Beijing, and in light of a history of recent political conflict both nations have experienced with the West, this mutually beneficial relationship, which has served both sides well so far, is likely to continue in future. Not only as an insurance policy against possible future conflicts with US and its allies, but also because of the fundamental changes taking place in the realignment of political power globally and in the West Asia region. Chinese aspirations for a deeper relationship with the West Asia region in order to push back against US attempts to contain the rise of China would also play a significant role in China taking new initiatives in order to maintain and strengthen the bilateral ties that has served it and Iran well so far.

Notes

1. John W. Garver (a), *China and Iran: Ancient Partners in a Post-Imperial World* (Seattle, WA: University of Washington Press, 2006), 14.
2. Anoushirvan Ehteshami, "The Foreign Policy of Iran" In Raymond Hinnebusc and Anoushirvan Ehteshami (eds), *The Foreign Policies of the Middle East states* (Boulder and London: Lynne Rienner, (2002), 283–309.
3. Garver, op. cit., 76.
4. Scott Harold and Alireza Nader, "China and Iran: Economic, Political and Military Relations" *Rand Corporation, Occasional Paper Series* (2012), 10.
5. Garver, op.cit., 249–252.
6. British Petroleum Statistical Review of World Energy 2014. See also http://www.bp.com/en/global/coporate/about/bp/energy-economics/statistical-review-of-world-energy/2013-in-review/oil.html
7. Manochehr Dorraj and Carrie L. Currier, "Lubricated With Oil: Iran-Chain Relations in a Changing World", *Middle East Policy*, Volume XV, Number2, 2008. 71–72.
8. Garver (a), op.cit. 271.
9. Reuters, 21 June 2013.
10. Harold and Nader, op.cit. 7.
11. John Garver (b), "China-Iran Relations: Cautious Friendship With America's Nemesis," *China Report*, Vol.49, No.1 (Summer 2013), 48–85.
12. Carrie Liu Currier and Manochehr Dorraj, "In Arms We Trust: The Economic and Strategic Factors Motivating China-Iran Relations," *Journal of Chinese Political Science*, Vol.15, no.1 (March 2010), 58.
13. John Garver (b), "China-Iran Relations: Cautious Friendship with America's Nemesis" *China Report*, Vol. 9, no.1 (Summer 2013), 75.
14. *Ibid.*
15. John Calabrese, "China and Iran: Mismatched Partners," *The Jamestown Foundation Occasional Papers*, (August 2006), 1–18.

Conclusion: China's Growing Presence in the Middle East

Niv Horesh and Ruike Xu

The last two decades have witnessed China's expanding economic footprint in the Middle East. China is currently the foremost trading partner and largest oil importer of several Middle Eastern countries. With the implementation of Xi Jinping's "One Belt, One Road" in 2015,[1] China looks set to further strengthen its economic and diplomatic influence in this region.

Yet, for China, a smooth relationship with the United States (US) is of paramount importance in its foreign policy towards the Middle East, given that the US "has been the unparalleled power in the region since the British withdrawal from the Persian Gulf more than three decades ago".[2] It is therefore imperative to analyse China's presence in the Middle East primarily through the lens of Sino-American relations.

China's Policy towards the Middle East

Since the People's Republic of China (PRC) was established in 1949, China's foreign policy towards the Middle East has undergone several significant changes. The first 30 years of the PRC's Middle Eastern policy bore the imprint of Mao Zedong's legacy. During the Mao era, China viewed its relations with Middle Eastern countries via the prism of ideology. With the influence of Mao's intermediate zone theory,[3] China criticized leaders of several Middle Eastern countries (with the exception of Israel) as "anti-revolutionary rulers" and "feudal dictators" while supporting anti-colonial efforts in the region.[4] China was more sympathetic to the Arab world after the US started to provide substantial military and economic assistance to Israel in 1967.

Aside from its traditional criticism of American imperialism in the Middle East, China's Middle Eastern diplomacy was also based on

anti-Soviet goals after the split of the Sino-Soviet alliance in 1960. Due
to its ideological stand (unremittingly revolutionary, secular, and anti-
imperialist), China's diplomatic relations with most Middle Eastern
countries became paralyzed.[5]

China supported Arab national liberation movements. Nonetheless,
its impact on such liberation movements was mostly symbolic, with
only token assistance provided to revolutionary forces in the region.[6]
In Chapter 5, Mohammed Shareef pointed out that the Kurdish liberation movement in Iraq was, for example, partly inspired by Maoism.
Some political parties in Iraq's Kurdistan region, such as the KDP and
the PUK, were once advocates of Maoism. But today Maoism has faded
into insignificance in the Middle East. What appeals to most Middle
Easterners about China is the success of its economic modernization.
Culturally, though, China and the Middle East remain distant despite
fast expanding people-to-people contacts.

Under Deng Xiaoping, China's Middle Eastern policy became more
pragmatic, and it sought to forge good relations with as many Middle
Eastern countries as possible. Arms sales, which aimed to fund economic
modernization, dominated China's economic relations with the Middle
Eastern countries in the 1980s and early 1990s. And since China became
a net oil importer in 1993, oil has occupied an increasingly prominent
place in Sino-Middle Eastern relations.

China's relationship with countries in the region at present is "one
of calculation rather than emotion".[7] In order to secure access to oil
and gas, China aims to befriend all, but avoids formal alliance with
any country in the Middle East. For example, as Mohammed Shareef
noted in Chapter 5, for the sake of guaranteeing its optimal gains in
Iraq's oil industry, China plays a double game in Iraq, seeking to develop
good relationships with both Arab Iraq and the Kurdish region at the
same time. As a consequence, since 2013 China has become the largest
investor in Iraq's oil sector, making it the largest beneficiary of the post-
Saddam oil boom in Iraq.[8]

China's efforts to cultivate amicable relations with the Kurdish region
in Iraq are also a balancing act in its relationship with Turkey. At the
same time, however, the Uyghur issue in Xinjiang has long been a sensitive node in Sino-Turkish relations. As Robert R. Bianchi illustrated
in Chapter 4, Turkey made the sharpest criticism of China's suppression of the Ürümqi protests in 2009. A friendly relationship with the
Kurds in Iraq can be leveraged by China in forcing Turkey to keep a
low-profile towards the Xinjiang problem, as Turkey would be threatened by a broader Chinese-Kurd alliance. As Christina Lin argued in

Chapter 3, China seeks Turkey's cooperation over Xinjiang in exchange for supporting Turkey's stance vis-a-vis the Kurdish minority within Turkey proper.

In retrospect, China's Middle Eastern policy has been extremely successful over the past decades, as evidenced by China's friendly relationships with all countries in the region, including both the close allies and strategic foes of the US in the Middle East. In addition, China's cultural aloofness prevents it from being bogged down in the turmoil in the region. Unlike the US, China "has no allies anywhere whose economic or other interests it must defend on the battlefield or in the international fora."[9]

Middle Eastern peoples (with the exception of Israelis) largely take a less sanguine view of the US role than that of China's role in the region, "seeing the United States inheriting the role of imperial Britain and shaping its policies in such a way as to advance imperial power at the expense of subject peoples."[10] Nevertheless, while some leaders may be inclined to develop a closer relationship with China so as to alleviate their overdependence on the US, there is no indication yet that China would be preferred as security arbiter over the US or Russia. And while China's "peaceful rise" narrative is framed as an alternative to what is cast as Euro-American war-prone neo-imperialism, a more powerful China is not yet unanimously welcomed across the Islamic world, particularly in view of its rejection of the Arab Spring, its pro-Assad position, and its image problem over treatment of Xinjiang's Uyghurs.

Egypt, the second largest recipient of US aid after Israel, has arguably moved closer to China. As Yasser M. Gadallah has mentioned in Chapter 6, Egypt is one of only five countries in the African continent that have been chosen by China to host a special economic zone. Egypt and China updated their bilateral relations to a "comprehensive strategic partnership" after the visit of Egyptian President al-Sisi to China in December 2014.[11] Similarly, Saudi Arabia has sought to develop a more intimate political relationship with China after the 9/11 terror attack in part due to its uneasiness about "the U.S. effort to democratize the Middle East by means of the Broader Middle East and North Africa Initiative."[12] Even Turkey seeks to develop a closer political relationship with China, as Zan Tao argued in Chapter 2, because it feels frustrated with the West, in particular the US and the European Union (EU).

However, China's omnidirectional friendship policy has become more tenuous since the Arab Spring started to spread through the Middle East in early 2011. China played a double game during NATO's intervention in Libya, supporting Qadhafi while opening a door to the opposition groups.[13] Due to China's secret support of Qadhafi and belated and milder support of the opposition groups, China suffered economic pains in the post- Qadhafi Libya.[14] Moreover, Chinese flags were set alight in some Arab cities following China's veto of the UN Security Council Resolution on Syria in February 2012.[15] According to Muhamad S. Olimat, due to China and Russia's veto, they "earned the displeasure of Arab public opinion. For the first time, Chinese and Russian flags were burnt to substitute for the traditional burning of Israeli and American flags."[16] Worse still, mutual distrust between China and the US deepened due to China's backing of Russia in the UN over the Syrian crisis.

American hypersensitivity to the China-initiated Asian Infrastructure Investment Bank (AIIB), which aims to fund the afore-mentioned "One Belt, One Road" projects, epitomizes its distrust of China.[17] The fact that the US suffered a diplomatic failure in trying to dissuade its allies from joining the AIIB arguably demonstrates an emerging systemic shift on the world stage. The US's long-standing allies in the Middle East, such as the Gulf Co-operation Council (GCC) states (with the exception of Bahrain), Israel, Jordan, and Turkey, have joined the AIIB in the face of American opposition. Even Iran, traditionally the US's enemy in the Middle East, became a founding member of the AIIB. In the Sino-American show-down with respect to the AIIB, China has clearly won the hearts and minds of regional power-brokers, even if it is not yet popularly held as an antidote to the US inasmuch as Putin's Russia does. Concomitantly, it would be naïve to assume that the participation of American allies in the Middle East in the AIIB signals that they are willing to abandon their alliance with the US in pursuit of a potential alliance with China.

The US is and will remain an indispensable military ally for these countries in the Middle East. Its role as the security protector of its Middle Eastern allies is unlikely to be replaced by China in the fore-seeable future. Since the GCC's security framework is an extension of the North Atlantic Treaty Organization (NATO), the GCC states are still reluctant to embrace a security partnership with China at the cost of their alliance with the US.[18] Neil Quilliam argued in Chapter 9 that China will not replace the US (Western) alliance with the GCC states at least in the medium term. Israel and Jordan will also have to stay under the security umbrella of the US. The fact that Israel bent to American pressure to curb its arms sales to China, as Niv Horesh pointed out in Chapter 8, demonstrates Israel's proclivity to side with the US when having to make a choice between the US and China. Strategically, Israel's "Look East" option remains rather limited as compared with its long-term "Look West" option. Given that the Turkey-US alliance has been anchored in NATO for more than six decades, as Zan Tao argued, it is unlikely for Turkey to build a wholesale substitute strategic partnership with China in the near future.

In other ways, though, it is all but certain that China will play a larger role in Middle Eastern affairs in the coming decades.[19] Even though China does not intend to displace the US primacy in the Middle East, the natural result of its economic expansion and increasing influence is the relative shrinkage of American dominance in this region. Therefore, it is understandable that the US holds deep apprehensions about China's expansion of influence in the Middle East. In spite of this, the US would be ill-advised to overplay its distrust of China in the Middle East. China's expansion is largely commercial. As Gawdat Bahgat argued in Chapter 7, China will not challenge the US's position as the predominant military power in the Middle East unless seriously challenged in other regions. As a matter of fact, it has at present neither the capability nor willingness to engage in open confrontation with the US in this region. China still deliberately punches below its weight in diplomatic and security terms.[20]

Religious cleavages: implications for Sino-American relations

Twelve years have passed since the US spearheaded the invasion of Iraq in March 2003. Yet, the situation in the Middle East seems as volatile as ever. The Middle East is still rife with conflicts and religious cleavages. In fact, this region is experiencing a new 'mini-Cold War' in which Iran and Saudi Arabia are the two principal protagonists.[21] As Henry Kissinger acutely observes in his book titled *World Order*:

> The conflict now unfolding is both religious and geopolitical. A Sunni bloc consisting of Saudi Arabia, the Gulf states, and to some extent Egypt and Turkey confronts a bloc led by Shia Iran, which backs Bashar al-Assad's portion of Syria, Nuri al-Maliki's central and southern Iraq, the Militias of Hezbollah in Lebanon and Hamas in Gaza. The Sunni bloc supports uprisings in Syria against Assad and in Iraq against Maliki; Iran aims for regional dominance by employing non-state actors tied to Tehran ideologically in order to undermine the domestic legitimacy of its regional rivals.[22]

The latest theatre for the bitter rivalry between the Saudi Arabia-led Sunni block and the Iran-led Shia block is Yemen where the Saudi

Arabia-led coalition has sought to quash the rebellion of the Houthis, a Shia minority backed by Iran.[23] The US has provided logistical support, intelligence, and weapons to the Saudi Arabia-led coalition. In the meantime, it accused Iran of providing military aid to the Houthis.[24]

To be sure, the Sunni block is not an ironclad alliance. On the contrary, there have been internal competition and even conflicts within the Sunni block. According to F. Gregory Gause III, "The Saudis, the Muslim Brotherhood and its regional allies like the Justice and Development Party (AKP) government in Turkey, the Salafi Jihadists of al-Qaeda, its affiliates, and its ideological counterparts like the Islamic State, and other Sunni groups are locked in a conflict over what the proper political role of Islam should be in the Sunni world."[25]

Apart from Saudi Arabia, Turkey is the other heavyweight in the Sunni block. It has competed with Saudi Arabia for Sunni leadership over the past decades, in a manner "...reminiscent of past relations between the Saudi Kingdom and the Ottoman Empire."[26] With the memory of the past glory of the Ottoman Empire, Turkey has aspired to be a regional superpower since the end of the Cold War. As Christina Lin has mentioned in Chapter 3, the demise of the Soviet Union offered Turkey an opportunity to play a role of regional superpower with the advocacy of pan-Turkism in the early 1990s. Turkey sought to build a "Turkish-speaking community of states stretching from the Adriatic to the Great Wall of China" by developing good relations with the Turkic states in Central Asia.[27] In the first Turkic summit in Ankara, then Turkish President Özal announced that "if we can exploit this historic opportunity in the best possible way, if we do not make any mistake, the 21st century will be the century of the Turks."[28] However, the cause of Pan-Turkism soon lost its momentum in Ankara due to the unwillingness of the Turkic states in Central Asia to develop a privileged partnership with Turkey. The establishment of the Shanghai Cooperation Organization (SCO) in 2001 demonstrated that the Turkic states in Central Asia attach more weight to their relations with China and Russia than with Turkey. It is equally noteworthy that Turkey became a dialogue partner of the SCO in 2012 and is currently seeking to upgrade its status to "observer state" in the SCO. By also taking into account Turkey's participation in the AIIB, it is clear that Turkey has tried to pivot to the East in recent years.

Since the AKP took power in 2002, Turkish foreign policy has reoriented toward neo-Ottomanism, aiming to make Turkey the leader in the Islamist world. As a result, the AKP has placed more emphasis on the Middle East.[29] Ahmet Davutoğlu, who currently serves as Turkish Prime Minister, is the main architect of Turkey's pan-Islamist foreign policy.[30]

His policy of "zero problems with neighbours" was partly designed to increase Turkey's influence in the Arab Middle East at the expense of Turkey's three decades-old military pact with Israel. Concomitantly, Turkey has become an active player in the new mini-Cold War in the Middle East. Since Turkey and Saudi Arabia diverge starkly over the pursuit of political order in the Middle East, they can only forge a partial partnership in containing Iran's influence in the Middle East. Turkey's sympathies with a moderate, electoral Islamism have been a stumbling block to greater Turkish-Saudi coordination.[31]

Israel, the only non-Muslim country in the Middle East, occupies a unique place in the struggle between the Sunni bloc and Shia bloc. Its tilt to the right under Benjamin Netanyahu remains a main obstacle to normalization of its relations with the Sunni bloc led by Saudi Arabia. To make matters worse, as the former US Ambassador to Saudi Arabia Charles W. Freeman points out, "In many ways, acceptance of Israel's legitimacy [in the West] is receding, not advancing, under the impact of the racial and religious bigotry its policies are seen to exemplify."[32] In spite of this, Arab countries in the Sunni bloc form a tacit and unusual partnership with Israel so as to deter Iran, which has attempted to secure regional hegemony in recent decades. For instance, according to Henry Kissinger, "Saudi Arabia and Israel share the same general objective with respect to Iran: to prevent the emergence of an Iranian military nuclear capability and to contain it if it becomes unavoidable."[33]

In addition to state actors, the non-state actors, such as Al Qaeda affiliates and ISIS compound the security situation in the Middle East. In particular, the sudden rise of ISIS in Iraq and Syria, which had merely been an offshoot of Al Qaeda before February 2014, demonstrates the continuing threat of Islamist terrorism in the region. ISIS has since proven an escalating threat to all countries in the Middle East. The US Middle Eastern allies joined the American-led coalition in fighting ISIS. Iran did not participate in the American-led coalition, but helped Iraq to fight the ISIS militants in its own way.[34] In spite of international efforts in curbing its threat, ISIS remains an alarming challenge to the stability of the Middle East.

This new Middle East mini-Cold War surrounding ISIS has profound implications for Sino-American relations. The US, Russia, and China are the three biggest outside powers heavily involved in the region. The tensions, turmoil, and violence wracking the Middle East "...have put the three countries' interests at stake."[35] Yet, China's interests are narrower than that those of Russia or the US in the Middle East. China has no ally to protect, and no vital economic or ideological assets in the region save free access to oil. By contrast, Russia and the US have made serious commitments to safeguard the security of their allies, especially Assad's Syria, Israel, and Saudi Arabia.

Furthermore, China remains heavily reliant on America's Fifth Fleet in securing oil supplies through the Strait of Hormuz. Given the inadequate capability of its navy in projecting power to the Middle East, China will continue to "free ride" on the American oil sea-lane security architecture for the years to come.[36] Therefore, China expects that the US will continue to maintain its naval presence in the Persian Gulf. China's limited attempts to diversify oil transportation routes – by investing in pipelines, for example – would "...not be enough to compensate for potential losses from a breakdown in sea lane security."[37]

For the US too, success in the Middle East increasingly depends on China's cooperation, for example in applying pressure on Iran to abandon its nuclear programme. As Yitzhak Shichor rightly argued in Chapter 1, Sino-American moves are complementary on a variety of Middle Eastern issues. There remains no near-term substitute for Middle Eastern oil for China just as there is no near-term effective alternative in sight to the American security umbrella in the region.[38] Similarly, Gawdat Bahgat argued in Chapter 7, the US and China are likely to work together to promote and ensure economic and political stability in the Middle East. China can be an increasingly important partner to the US in the region. Both China and the US should avoid seeing their relations through a zero-sum lens. China and the US's interests are aligned in dealing with at least three thorny security issues in the Middle East, including the terrorism of ISIS, the Iranian nuclear crisis, and the longstanding Israel-Palestine conflict.

In the long-run, as Michael Singh observed in Chapter 10, the shale revolution may ease the US dependence on Middle Eastern oil, thereby demotivating it somewhat from engaging more deeply in Middle Eastern affairs. Nevertheless, the Middle East will remain an important source for US oil imports in the near future. Therefore, instead of openly criticizing China as a global "free rider," as President Obama did in August 2014,[39] the US should arguably make overtures to China so as to encourage it to take "a more responsible posture toward the Middle East."[40] Ultimately, however, Chinese intentions will be rightly tested by Washington *not* in the Middle East *per se*, but in the Pacific. Will Sino-American convergence of interests in the Middle East, especially as regards free access to oil, translate into greater Chinese willingness to accommodate US allies' views as regards East and South China Sea territorial disputes?

ISIS as a common threat

China has of late shown more concern over the spread of ISIS, which potentially threatens not only China's economic interests in the Middle East, in particular in Iraq, but also China's core security interests in Xinjiang province. First, China has more at stake than any other foreign country in Iraq with regard to oil, given its status as the new largest investor in Iraq's oil industry. If the advance of ISIS had not been stalled by the US-led coalition airstrikes,[41] ISIS would have seized Baghdad and thus put Chinese oil interests in Southern Iraq at risk.[42] Secondly, ISIS poses a serious threat to stability in Xinjiang province. The ISIS leader Abu Bakr Al-Baghdadi named China *first* in a string of 20 countries mooted as battlegrounds in which to wage jihad; he also threatened to occupy Xinjiang as part of establishing an aspirant caliphate.[43] What makes matters worse in Chinese eyes are unconfirmed reports of increasing home-grown radicalization of Uyghurs in Xinjiang. There may be currently about 300 Chinese nationals fighting alongside ISIS in Iraq and Syria, and there are more Chinese Muslims trying to flee Xinjiang to join ISIS.[44] It is highly likely that "radicalized Uyghurs traveling abroad to train and fight will return with skills that could bolster China's domestic insurgency."[45] Furthermore, if ISIS gains a foothold in Central Asia and the Middle East, it will jeopardize China's development of the New Silk Road economic initiative ("One Belt, One Road").[46]

Faced with the growing threat of radicalization, China has tacitly shown more willingness to help the US combat ISIS in the Middle East, thereby upping the ante for a new type Sino-American partnership. Indeed, in December 2014, Iraqi Foreign Minister Ibrahim Jafari revealed that China had offered to help Iraq fight ISIS with support for air strikes.[47]

The Israel-Palestine conflict

Peace in the Middle East will be elusive if the long-lasting Israel-Palestine hotspot issue is not adequately and enduringly resolved.[48] nearly seven decades have elapsed since the creation of Israel, but prospects for successfully resolving the Israel-Palestine conflict remain remote. In fact, there are signs that the conflict between Israel and Palestine is set to escalate, as evidenced by Israeli Prime Minister Benjamin Netanyahu's recent disavowal of a two-state solution to the Israel-Palestine conflict,[49] as well as by Hamas's current scheme to build a separate Islamic state of Palestine in the Gaza Strip.[50] There are currently 135 UN member states recognizing the state of Palestine, and it is likely more countries will be recognizing it in the years to come.[51]

The US is more than likely to remain the most crucial player in helping resolve the Israel-Palestine conflict. Its efforts in dealing with this tough challenge over the past decades, however, have been largely unsuccessful.[52]

In the eyes of most Arabs, the US failure in the Israeli-Palestinian peace process stems to a large extent from its inability to serve as an "honest broker."[53] Nevertheless, there is not yet a great appetite building up across the Arab world for China or Russia to challenge the US as the leading broker, and the EU is perceived as weaker than ever before. Both Russia and China have seen relations with Israel improve over the past few years despite turmoil elsewhere in the region. Neither is the Chinese position here antagonistic toward the US. In fact, Wu Sike, the former Chinese envoy to the Middle East, had suggested that since the US could not resolve the Israel-Palestine conflict singlehandedly, it should encourage countries like China to join mediation efforts.[54]

In May 2013, both Palestinian President Mahmoud Abbas and Israeli Prime Minister Benjamin Netanyahu paid a visit to China. In his meetings with both leaders, Chinese President Xi Jinping put forward a four-point proposal for resolving the Israel-Palestine conflict. Shortly after that, China hosted a Middle East peace forum titled "UN International Meeting in Support of Israeli-Palestinian Peace," which brought together "UN officials, diplomats, academics, and present and former members of the Palestinian and Israeli parliaments."[55] In January 2014, the Chinese Foreign Minister signaled China's willingness to join the Quartet, a mechanism including the US, Russia, the EU and the UN, so as to promote peace talks between the Palestinians and Israelis.[56]

The Iranian nuclear crisis

For China, its most challenging relationship in the Middle East is with Iran. Its broad and close partnership with Iran over the past decades has been largely a marriage of convenience and expediency rather than affection. Zachary Keck argues that "Should Iran avoid a conflict with the US in the next few years, it's likely to find China to be its most menacing threat in the future."[57]

To some extent, the strong partnership between China and Iran has been underpinned by their shared distrust of the US in the Middle East. Iran regards China as a potential ally against the US. It has become dependent on China as its "chief diplomatic protector in the face of internal and external pressures."[58] But China is reluctant to hug Iran too closely for fear of antagonizing the US. Iran's pursuit of nuclear weapons is in part attributable to its deep insecurity in the face of the US military presence in the Gulf. A nuclear Iran, however, contravenes the interests of both the US and China.[59] According to Henry Kissinger, the Iran nuclear issue is "at heart about international order – about the ability of the international community to enforce its demands against sophisticated forms of rejection, the permeability of the global non-proliferation regime, and the prospects for a nuclear arms race in the world's most volatile region."[60]

Neither the US nor China believe the Iranian claim that its nuclear programme is for peaceful purposes.[61] If Iran's nuclear ambition is not thwarted, it would put both the US and China's interests at risk. A nuclear Iran would worsen the security situation and further antagonize Israel and Sunni Arab countries, which have been regarding Iran's nuclear weapon as their greatest nightmare, thereby bringing the Middle East into greater upheaval. In this scenario, both the US and China's energy security in the region would be gravely threatened.

If Iran's nuclear programme succeeds, it may provoke nuclear proliferation across the Middle East. Some Arab countries, such as Saudi Arabia and Egypt, may also pursue the nuclear option.[62] In addition, having already emerged as the largest strategic beneficiary in geopolitical terms from the American misadventures in Iraq, and having gained the upper hand in its competition with Saudi Arabia, Iran's nuclear weapons would enable it to become the almost unstoppable regional hegemon, posing serious challenges to Sino-American interests in the Middle East in the long run.[63] It is in the interests of both the US and China to prevent Iran from dominating the Middle East.

Until not long ago, China was held partly culpable for Iran's development of nuclear weapons. In fact, China had provided direct nuclear support to Iran prior to 1997. According to Scott Harold and Alireza Nader, "From 1985 to 1996, China provided Iran with various types of critical nuclear technology and machinery and helped to acquire others, assisted Iran in uranium exploration and mining, and helped Iran master the uses of lasers for uranium enrichment."[64]

China and the US have been at loggerheads over the efficacy of harsh economic sanctions on Iran. As a result, as John W. Garver argued in Chapter 11, China delayed and diluted the US-supported UN sanctions against Iran and thus helped to buy Iran two years' time to advance its development of nuclear weapon between 2004 and 2010. China's undisrupted investment in Iran's oil industry in defiance of American-led sanctions has made China Iran's largest oil importer and largest foreign investor; it hardened Iran's determination not to accede to Western restrictions on nuclear development.[65]

Notwithstanding China's balancing act between Iran and the US, Chinese tacit intervention has on occasion been instrumental over the past few years in *thwarting* Iran's efforts in pursuit of nuclear weapons.[66] China has voted "yes" on all the UN Security Council (UNSC)-authorized sanctions on Iran between 2006 and 2012, even though it sided with Russia to water down the UNSC Resolutions, thus making sanctions less stringent than the US and its Western allies had proposed. Moreover, China has been a participant of P5+1 and worked with France, Russia, the UK, and the US plus Germany to negotiate with Iran with the purpose of resolving Iran nuclear crisis diplomatically. China, according to Erica Downs and Suzanne Maloney, is "the linchpin of the international sanction regime against Iran and, by extension, of the effort to forestall Iran from acquiring a nuclear capability."[67]

On account of China's long-standing amicable relationship with Iran, China has more leverage than any other member of P5+1 with Iran, which enables it to play a constructive role as broker in the nuclear talks. According to the former Chinese ambassador to Iran, Hua Liming, "[w]hen the two parties came across irresolvable problems, they would come to China, which would 'lubricate' the negotiation and put things back on track."[68]

It was not a coincidence that China accepted Iran's application for entry into the AIIB as a founding member on 3 April 2015, only one day after the historic Iran nuclear deal framework was agreed between the P5+1 and Iran.[69] Iran's willingness to sign the nuclear deal framework facilitated its entry into the AIIB. This is a critical point to make in conclusion: the AIIB initiative is usually depicted as the fulcrum of the all-encompassing, global Sino-American contest; however, at least in the Iranian context, and as improbable as this may sound at first, Iran's accession to the AIIB may actually betoken much broader Sino-American complementarity.

Notes

1. The "one belt and one road" initiative refers to the Silk Road Economic Belt and the 21st Century Maritime Silk Road. It aims to strengthen China's economic ties with Central Asia, the Middle East, Africa and Europe by building new railroads, highways, pipelines, power plants, dams, mines, and industrial zones. See Lucio Blanco Pitlo III, "China's 'One Belt, One Road' to Where," *The Diplomat*, 17 February 2015, http://thediplomat.com/2015/02/chinas-one-belt-one-road-to-where/; Robert Bianchi, "China, Islam, and New

Visions of the Old World," Middle East Institute, 3 March 2015, http://www.mei.edu/content/map/china-islam-and-new-visions-old-world.

2. Jon B. Alterman, "China's Soft Power in the Middle East," in Carola McGiffert (ed.) Chinese Soft Power and Its Implications for the United States, A Report of the CSIS Smart Power Initiative, March 2009, p. 63, http://csis.org/files/media/csis/pubs/090403_mcgiffert_chinesesoftpower_web.pdf.

3. Muhamad S. Olimat, *China and the Middle East: From Silk Road to Arab Spring* (London: Routledge), 2013, p. 18.

4. Guang Pan, "China's Success in the Middle East," *Middle East Quarterly*, Vol.4, No.4, 1997, http://www.meforum.org/373/chinas-success-in-the-middle-east.

5. Steve A. Yetiv and Chunlong Lu, "China, Global Energy, and the Middle East," *The Middle East Journal*, Vol.61, No. 2, 2007, p. 201.

6. Jon B. Alterman, "China in the Middle East," Statement before the U.S.-China Economic and Security Review Commission, 6 June 2013, p. 2, https://csis.org/files/attachments/ts130606_alterman.pdf.

7. Jon B. Alterman, John W. Garver, The Vital Triangle: China, The United States, and the Middle East (Washington: Centre for Strategic and International Studies), 2008, p. 4.

8. Kristin Deasy, "China the Biggest Investor in Iraq's Emerging Oil Sector," *Global Post*, 5 June 2013, http://www.globalpost.com/dispatch/news/regions/middle-east/iraq/130605/china-quick-pounce-emerging-iraqi-oil-industry.

9. Chas W. Freeman, "The Middle East and China", Middle East Policy Council, 17 February 2015, http://www.mepc.org/articles-commentary/speeches/middle-east-and-china.

10. Jon B. Alterman, "*China's soft power in the Middle East*, in Carola McGiffert (ed.) Chinese Soft Power and Its Implications for the United States, A Report of the CSIS Smart Power Initiative, March 2009, p. 70, http://csis.org/files/media/csis/pubs/090403_mcgiffert_chinesesoftpower_web.pdf.

11. Shannon Tiezzi, "China's Egypt Opportunity," *The Diplomat*, 24 December 2014, http://thediplomat.com/2014/12/chinas-egypt-opportunity/.

12. Jon B. Alterman, John W. Garver, The Vital Triangle: China, The United States, and the Middle East (Washington: Centre for Strategic and International Studies), 2008, pp. 34–35.

13. Jon B. Alterman, "China in the Middle East," Statement before the U.S.-China Economic and Security Review Commission, 6 June 2013, p. 9, https://csis.org/files/attachments/ts130606_alterman.pdf.

14. Steven Sotloff, "China's Libya Problem," *The Diplomat*, 14 March 2012, http://thediplomat.com/2012/03/chinas-libya-problem/.

15. Gabriel Domínguez and Ju Juan, "Soft Power-China's Expanding Role in the Middle East," 2 April 2015, http://www.dw.de/soft-power-chinas-expanding-role-in-the-middle-east/a-18233271.

16. Muhamad S. Olimat, *China and the Middle East: From Silk Road to Arab Spring* (London: Routledge), 2012, p. 3.

17. Shannon Tiezzi, "America's AIIB Disaster: Are There Lessons to be Learned," *The Diplomat*, 18 March 2015, http://thediplomat.com/2015/03/americas-aiib-disaster-are-there-lessons-to-be-learned/.

18. Imad Mansour, "The GCC States and the Viability of a Strategic Military Partnership with China," Middle East Institute, http://www.mei.edu/content/map/gcc-states-and-viability-strategic-military-partnership-china#_ftn11.

19. Jon B. Alterman, "China in the Middle East," Statement before the U.S.-China Economic and Security Review Commission, 6 June 2013, p. 1, https://csis.org/files/attachments/ts130606_alterman.pdf.
20. Gabriel Domínguez and Ju Juan, "Soft Power-China's Expanding Role in the Middle East," 2 April 2015, http://www.dw.de/soft-power-chinas-expanding-role-in-the-middle-east/a-18233271.
21. F. Gregory Gause III, "Beyond Sectarianism: The New Middle East Cold War", Brookings Doha Centre Analysis Paper, July 2014. http://www.brookings.edu/~/media/research/files/papers/2014/07/22-beyond-sectarianism-cold-war-gause/english-pdf.pdf.
22. Henry Kissinger, *World Order* (London: Allen Lane), 2014, p. 144.
23. Martin Reardon, "Saudi Arabia, Iran and the 'Great Game' in Yemen," *Al Jazeera*, 26 March 2015, http://www.aljazeera.com/indepth/opinion/2014/09/saudi-arabia-iran-great-game-ye-201492984846324440.html.
24. David D. Kirkpatrick, "Tensions between Iran and Saudi Arabia Deepen over Conflict in Yemen", The New York Times, 9 April 2015, http://www.nytimes.com/2015/04/10/world/middleeast/yemen-fighting.html?_r=0.
25. F. Gregory Gause III, "Beyond Sectarianism: The New Middle East Cold War," Brookings Doha Centre Analysis Paper, July 2014, p. 16, http://www.brookings.edu/~/media/research/files/papers/2014/07/22-beyond-sectarianism-cold-war-gause/english-pdf.pdf.
26. Abdulmajeed al-Buluwi, "The Saudi-Turkey Cold War for Sunni Hegemony," 1 April 2014, http://www.al-monitor.com/pulse/originals/2014/04/saudi-arabia-turkey-muslim-brotherhood-sunni-middle-east.html.
27. Nozar Alaolmolki, *Life after the Soviet Union: The Newly Independent Republics of Transcaucus and Central Asia* (New York: State University of New York Press), 2001, p. 67.
28. Dietrich Jung and Wolfango Piccoli, *Turkey at the Crossroads: Ottoman Legacies and a Greater Middle East* (London: Zed Books), 2001, p. 180.
29. Zeyno Baran, *Torn Country: Turkey between Secularism and Islamism* (Stanford: Hoover Institution Press Publication), 2010, p. 117.
30. Behlül Özkan, "Turkey, Davutoglu and the Idea of Pan-Islamism," *Survival*, Vol.56, No.4, 2014, pp. 119–140.
31. F. Gregory Gause III, "Beyond Sectarianism: The New Middle East Cold War", Brookings Doha Centre Analysis Paper, July 2014, p. 16, http://www.brookings.edu/~/media/research/files/papers/2014/07/22-beyond-sectarianism-cold-war-gause/english-pdf.pdf.
32. Chas W. Freeman, "The United States, the Middle East, and China," Middle East Policy Council, 5 June 2013, http://www.mepc.org/articles-commentary/speeches/united-states-middle-east-and-china.
33. Henry Kissinger, *World Order* (London: Allen Lane), 2014, p. 133.
34. Babak Dehghaneh, "Insight – Iran's elite Guards fighting in Iraq to push back Islamic State," Reuters, 3 August 2014, http://uk.reuters.com/article/2014/08/03/uk-iraq-security-iran-insight-idUKKBN0G30GG20140803.
35. Henry Kissinger, *World Order* (London: Allen Lane), 2014, p. 141.
36. David Schenker, "China's Middle East Footprint," The Washington Institute, 26 April 2013, http://www.washingtoninstitute.org/policy-analysis/view/chinas-middle-east-footprint.

37. Jon B. Alterman and Christopher K. Johnson, "Gulf Roundtable: China and the Gulf," CSIS, 26 April 2013, http://csis.org/files/attachments/130426_Summary_JohnsonAlterman.pdf.
38. Steve A. Yetiv and Chunlong Lu, "China, Global Energy, and the Middle East," *The Middle East Journal*, Vol.61, No.2, 2007, p. 199.
39. Bree Feng, "Obama's 'Free Rider' Comment Draws Chinese Criticism," New York Times, 13 August 2014, http://sinosphere.blogs.nytimes.com/2014/08/13/obamas-free-rider-comment-draws-chinese-criticism/.
40. Flynt Leverett and Jeffrey Bader, "Managing China-U.S. Energy Competition in the Middle East", *The Washington Quarterly*, Vol.29, No.1, Winter 2005–2006, p. 199.
41. Erin Banco and Hanna Sender, "Six Months after The Fall of Mosul, ISIS is Stalled, Unable to Seize Baghdad", *International Business Times*, 10 December 2014, http://www.ibtimes.com/six-months-after-fall-mosul-isis-stalled-unable-seize-baghdad-1746408.
42. Christina Lin, "Al Qaeda and ISIS Have Declared War on China–Will Beijing Now Arm the Kurds," ISPSW, October 2014, http://www.isn.ethz.ch/Digital-Library/Publications/Detail/?id=185086.
43. Christina Lin, "Al Qaeda and ISIS Have Declared War on China–Will Beijing Now Arm the Kurds," ISPSW, October 2014, http://www.isn.ethz.ch/Digital-Library/Publications/Detail/?id=185086.
44. Christina Lin, "ISIS Caliphate Meets China's Silk Road Economic Belt", Rubin Centre Research in International Affairs, 22 February 2015, http://www.rubin-center.org/2015/02/isis-caliphate-meets-chinas-silk-road-economic-belt/.
45. Kyle Mizokami, "China Has an ISIS Problem", The Week magazine, 2 March 2015, http://theweek.com/articles/541531/china-isis-problem.
46. Cristina Silva, "ISIS Caliphate News: Islamic State Sending Militants to Central Asia, India, China and Europe, Iran Warns," International Business Times, 16 April 2015, http://www.ibtimes.com/isis-caliphate-news-islamic-state-sending-militants-central-asia-india-china-europe-1884677.
47. Najmeh Bozorgmehr and Lucy Hornby, "China offers to help Iraq defeat Sunni extremists", http://www.ft.com/cms/s/0/3f4dc794–8141–11e4-b956-00144feabdc0.html#axzz3bElaTgN7. *Financial Times*, 12 December 2014.
48. Wang Yi, "Wang Yi Gave an Interview to Al Jazeera", 9 January 2014, http://www.fmprc.gov.cn/mfa_Eng/wjb_663304/wjbz_663308/2461_663310/t1116509.shtml.
49. Aron Heller, "Israel's Netanyahu Says Palestinian State Will Not Be Established on His Watch", *The World Post*, 16 March 2015, http://www.huffingtonpost.com/2015/03/16/israel-election-2015_n_6876964.html.
50. *Khaled Abu Toameh, "Hamas's Plan: A Hamas State of Palestine in Gaza (For Now)", Gatestone Institute, 17 April 2015*, http://www.gatestoneinstitute.org/5576/hamas-state-palestine.
51. Ishaan Tharoor, "Map: The Countries that Recognize Palestine as a State," *The Washington Post*, 7 November 2015, http://www.washingtonpost.com/blogs/worldviews/wp/2014/11/07/map-the-countries-that-recognize-palestine-as-a-state/.
52. Manochehr Dorraj, "China's Evolving Policy toward the Palestinian-Israeli Conflict", China Policy Institute Blog at the University of Nottingham, 20 March

2015, https://blogs.nottingham.ac.uk/chinapolicyinstitute/2015/03/20/
chinas-evolving-policy-toward-palestinian-israeli-conflict/.

53. Guy Burton, "Firm for Now: China's Support for the Oslo Accords", China
Policy Institute Blog at the University of Nottingham, 24 February 2015,
https://blogs.nottingham.ac.uk/chinapolicyinstitute/2015/02/24/firm-for-
now-chinas-support-for-the-oslo-accords/.

54. Wu Sike, "Leave Room for China in the Middle East Peace Process", *China
and US Focus*, 14 May 2013, http://www.chinausfocus.com/foreign-policy/
leave-room-for-china-in-the-middle-east-peace-process/.

55. Gabriel Dominguez, "China: The new Mideast power broker", *DW*, 18 June
2013, http://www.dw.de/china-the-new-mideast-power-broker/a-16889585.

56. Wang Yi, "Wang Yi Gave an Interview to Al Jazeera", 9 January 2014, http://
www.fmprc.gov.cn/mfa_Eng/wjb_663304/wjbz_663308/2461_663310/
t1116509.shtml.

57. Zachary Keck, "China and Iran: Destined to Clash", *The Diplomat*, 17 October
2013, http://thediplomat.com/2013/10/china-and-iran-destined-to-clash/.

58. Scott Harold and Alireza Nader, "China and Iran: Economic, Political, and
Military Relations", Occasional Paper at Centre for Middle East Public Policy
of Rand, 2012, p. 5.

59. Jon B. Alterman, "China's Hard Choices on Iran", *CSIS*, 14 October 2009,
http://csis.org/files/publication/1009_MENC.pdf.

60. Henry Kissinger, *World Order* (London: Allen Lane), 2014, p. 159.

61. Muhamad S. Olimat, *China and the Middle East: From Silk Road to Arab Spring*
(London: Routledge), 2012, p. 80.

62. Muhamad S. Olimat, *China and the Middle East: From Silk Road to Arab Spring*
(London: Routledge), 2012, p. 72.

63. Max Tholl and Stephen M. Walt, "Iran is the Main Beneficiary of the Iraq
War," *The European*, 20 March 2013, http://www.theeuropean-magazine.
com/stephen-walt–3/6617-ten-years-after-the-iraq-invasion.

64. Scott Harold and Alireza Nader, "China and Iran: Economic, Political, and
Military Relations," Occasional Paper at Centre for Middle East Public Policy
of Rand, 2012, p. 8.

65. Shannon Tiezzi, "How China Complicates the Iranian Nuclear Talks," *The
Diplomat*, 25 November 2015, http://thediplomat.com/2014/11/how-china-
complicates-the-iranian-nuclear-talks/.

66. Geoffrey Kemp, *The East Moves West: India, China, and Asia's Growing Presence
in the Middle East* (Washington: Brookings Institution Press), 2012, p. 78.

67. Erica Downs and Suzanne Maloney, "Getting China to Sanction Iran," *Foreign
Affairs* March/April 2011, http://www.foreignaffairs.com/articles/67465/
erica-downs-and-suzanne-maloney/getting-china-to-sanction-iran.

68. Peter Ford, "Iran nuclear talks: Can China Keep Negotiations on Track," *The
Christian Science Monitor*, 30 March 2015.

69. Julian Borger and Paul Lewis, "Iran Nuclear Deal: Negotiators Announce
'Framework' Agreement", *The Guardian*, 3 April 2015, http://www.
theguardian.com/world/2015/apr/02/iran-nuclear-deal-negotiators-
announce-framework-agreement.

Index

233

CPSIA information can be obtained at www.ICGtesting.com
Printed in the USA
BVOW06*0943200516

448885BV00018B/27/P